Christianity and 'the World'

Christianity and 'the World'
Secularization Narratives through the Lens of English Poetry A.D. 800 to the Present

David Martin

The Lutterworth Press

The Lutterworth Press
P.O. Box 60
Cambridge
CB1 2NT
United Kingdom

www.lutterworth.com
publishing@lutterworth.com

Paperback ISBN: 978 0 7188 9578 5
PDF ISBN: 978 0 7188 4840 8

British Library Cataloguing in Publication Data
A record is available from the British Library

First published by The Lutterworth Press, 2021

Copyright © David Martin, 2020

Published by arrangement
with Cascade Books

All rights reserved. No part of this edition may be reproduced, stored electronically or in any retrieval system, or transmitted in any form or by any means, electronic, mechanical, photocopying, recording, or otherwise, without prior written permission from the Publisher (permissions@lutterworth.com).

I have never separated the writing of poetry from prayer. I have grown up believing it is a vocation, a religious vocation.

—Derek Walcott, "The Art of Poetry"

A cultured society that has fallen away from its religious tradition expects more than the aesthetic can deliver. The Romantic desire for a new mythology gives the artist . . . the consciousness of a new consecration. He is something like a "secular saviour" for his creations are expected to achieve on a small scale the propitiation of disaster for which an unsaved world hopes.

—Hans-Georg Gadamer, *Truth and Method*

Contents

The Rationale of This Book | ix
Acknowledgments | xvii

Introduction | 1
Chapter 1—An Overview of the Problem | 14
Chapter 2—Ninth to Sixteenth Centuries | 21
Chapter 3—Seventeenth and Eighteenth Centuries | 30
Chapter 4—The Nineteenth Century: The Early Romantics | 43
Chapter 5—The Mid-Victorians | 51
Chapter 6—The Early Twentieth Century | 83
Chapter 7—War Poets; Pacifists and Marxists;
    Poets of Wars Post-1945 | 91
Chapter 8—Eliot and Auden | 108
Chapter 9—Faith and Place | 118
Chapter 10—Larkin to Hughes; Plath to Duffy | 129
Chapter 11—Donald Davie, Charles Sisson, and Geoffrey Hill;
    Denise Levertov, Andrew Motion,
    and Michael Symmonds Roberts | 137
Chapter 12—Conclusion | 147
Chapter 13—Afterword | 158

Appendix—Hymnody | 166

Bibliography | 183
Index | 191

The Rationale of This Book

This book is not an exercise in literary criticism though I have had recourse to literary criticism in order to write it. Rather it brings together themes I have pursued as a sociologist for over half a century concerning the relation of Christianity to the profane dynamics of the social order or what the New Testament saw as the lure of "the world": "What does it profit a man if he gain the whole world and lose his own soul?" The "world" in this sense does not refer to God's creation, but rather to man's creation. This is the corrupt realm of principalities and powers governed by what anthropology calls "negative reciprocity" or tit-for-tat, but also referred to in characteristically extreme terms by Simone Weil as the "Social Beast." This corrupt realm with its endemic struggle over scarce resources is the universal default position of human society and one that resists the positive reciprocity taught by the Gospels. It is the reality with which we have to deal, not just in politics, where the dynamics of power and wealth are particularly obvious, but in personal life.

I was brought up in an evangelical home in Mortlake, South-West London. My preacher father, who was, like my mother, "in service," expected the coming of the Lord. I was early exposed to papers like *The Herald of His Coming* and *The Christian Herald*, as well as to *Foxe's Book of Martyrs*, *The Pilgrim's Progress*, lurid accounts of our future state, and a peripatetic search for the real "hot" Gospel. Apart from that background rumble of eschatology, we were quite normal and respectable, not to say modestly aspiring. When I won a scholarship to the local grammar school in 1940 the background rumble dissolved into thin air, though I still assiduously attended the local and quite conventional Methodist church. My mother approved of this, in spite of the calls it made on my time at the expense of schoolwork, because she thought it a morally safe haven during the dangers of adolescence. This was, as it happened, a serious mistake. Eventually I translated Christianity into a pacifist understanding of the Gospels informed by the radicalism of William Blake. So far as my parents were concerned the outward form sounded familiar and reassuring, whatever the change of content implied by (for example) Blake's "The Everlasting Gospel." I still used language like my father's, religious language, and avoided the terrible wound I would otherwise have inflicted on him. Nor was this a simple case of double talk on my part. That would have been intolerable. It was in part because I responded intensely to poetry and music, and regarded both as ancillary to faith. That was true even when I read Thomas Hardy, because I had formed a passionate attachment to my mother's part of south Dorset, with its parish churches and chapels, and a pleasing melancholia of the omnipresent dead induced by its Roman and Iron Age monuments. Poetry was for me very much related to place, say to poets in the Orkneys or the Lake District or Cornwall. Remoteness meant separation from corruption and that was true even of Hardy's Dorset, even though he was really half a Londoner.

Very much later I recognized clear parallels with the affections cherished by the poet-engraver David Jones. He lived in Brockley in South-East London, and his preacher father was actively involved with *The Christian Herald*. He shared my revivalist background and had just my saturation in the traditional Bible, but he was passionately attached to Wales as "the land of his fathers." For Jones, as for me, poetry was a celebration of place.

Most people imagine that a fundamentalist background constricts as well as setting you apart. Certainly it creates a sense of difference but it also confers many advantages. A fundamentalist background fosters creative tensions and seriousness and the skills of persuasive rhetoric, and it introduces you to music through constant singing. Hymns were my first poetry and I played them on the piano for my father to sing, stretching out his arms while probably imagining his listeners in Hyde Park. Without this background I might not have taken so naturally to poetry, to the pleasures of speaking, or to Bach, Handel, and Mendelssohn. You can start singing evangelical choruses and Wesley hymns and easily end up in the Bach choir, sensing religious meaning by proxy, or in my case a serious commitment to the piano and the classical repertoire. My father imagined me going far beyond his little coteries in Hyde Park and preaching to a vast audience in the Albert Hall, like his hero, the illiterate but eloquent evangelist Gypsy Smith. For my part I imagined moving a vast audience in the Albert Hall, like the popular pianist Eileen Joyce, with the Grieg piano concerto. You can start off with sermons and the Bible and end up wanting to speak and write, as well as intuitively attuned to the metaphysical poets. I might have been useless at the periodic table, but, once I encountered Donne and Ruskin, I knew what they were about, in a way most of my fellow students did not. That way I became an effective speaker as Liberal candidate in the school's "mock election" in 1945. Liberals were a minority, but we did surprisingly well. Preaching is close cousin to arguing and debating.

Confused aims and diversions ensured that I ended up in neither university nor music academy, but a Methodist teacher training college. There I mistakenly tried to treat it as a university. I read a great deal of Wordsworth off the syllabus, including "The Prelude," and rejected the set book of Georgian verse to write (with enthusiastic permission) on Hopkins, Masefield, Hardy, and Eliot. I became saturated in Hopkins and Eliot, and this reinforced my sense that poetry was closely aligned with religion. I also wrote (with puzzled permission) a long essay on plainsong and Byzantine hymnody. These two exercises confirmed my assumption that music and poetry agreed with each other, and that both were closely aligned with religion. Other literary excursions might suggest the rivalry of the arts with religion over similar territory, but as long as I absorbed Hopkins, read avidly about the wonders of the Romanesque, and listened to the Mass in B Minor the alignment was more obvious than the rivalry. I could listen to Bach and Handel and know God was in his heaven. Doubt has no place when the trumpets and drums enter in "Dona nobis pacem" and "Worthy is the Lamb."

But by now I was skirting increasingly intrusive questions. The first question turned on the standard supposition of everyday secular thinking that something irreversible had happened to religious belief with the massive changes of the "secular" Enlightenment, as well as with the religious ambiguities of Romanticism, where poets and musicians took on themselves the task of redemption. The second question pointed in a rather different direction: if that were so, then why was Eliot—for me at the time *the* modernist poet, though I lacked that vocabulary—saturated in religion? The same was true of Rilke, if in a very different key. At the time of reading them as a young person, I didn't pose the question theoretically, but once I did, it seemed that there was no unilinear secularization narrative. Instead there were secular shifts and there were oscillations. Modernity did not straightforwardly deliver the secular goods as expected. The lens of poetry revealed *both* a secular shift as required by the linear secularization narrative, especially with the onset of Enlightened reason and empirical science, *and* also an oscillation not confined to people like Eliot and Rilke. How to understand Poulenc, Messiaen, and Stravinsky in the most aggressively secular countries in Europe, or Britten in England, or MacMillan in a Scotland that has replaced faith by nationalism? At the same time Eliot himself thought something had happened in modernity that "had never happened before": the worship of false gods like the nation or the dialectic, and indifference to all gods. I found this in Eliot's play *The Rock* and thoroughly absorbed everything he said there about the current crisis of civilization: about the heart of man "swinging between hell gate and heaven gate," and "the gates of hell shall not prevail." When I read David Jones much later I would have observed the same paradox: a passionate Christian who recognized that a singular "break" (his term) had occurred in his own time in the cultural position and status of Christianity. I might have asked another question and one that recurs in my book: why were so many of the major poets and musicians who embraced faith specifically attracted to Catholicism, in its Roman, Anglican, and Orthodox variants? Matthew Arnold, the poet-prophet of the future and one who notoriously reduced Christianity to "morality tinged with emotion," was conspicuously wrong about the kind of faith that would engage the intelligence in the future. He could not have imagined, for example, the kind of faith which came to animate composers, for example, Schnittke and Gubadalaina, under the impact of the secularist tyranny of Soviet Russia.

I am now jumping forward a long way autobiographically, but I became intrigued by the different secularization stories in poetry, music, and architecture, each having elements of linearity, but differently, and each subject to oscillation, especially in modernity, but, again, differently. What was it about poetry and music that they were both potently allied to faith and potent rivals? What was it that distinguished the solid, corporate, and internally consistent poetry of liturgy as a protected space where acknowledgement of ruin can be followed by restoration, acceptance, and peace, from the fragmented intuitions of individuals? Such questions pervade this book. And my interim answer about the potent affinities of faith, poetry, and music, vaguely derived from Coleridge, has been that all three exhibit the peculiar logic of the pictogram not the diagram and do so through pulsation. Even where poets present arguments, in Milton, for example, they do not pursue a linear logic.

In poetry I also became aware that it could exhibit secular and religious tendencies in contrary motion, as in the nineteenth century, and also that it could admix non-Christian religious elements: both Germanic and classical paganism in earlier centuries, of course, but, increasingly in the last two centuries mysticism and spirituality—what Robert Schumann called "religion without religion." This was crucial. Christianity was not a simple entity that governed minds in the past and then dissolved under the acids of modernity. It was several kinds of composite, and its core proclamation entered subversively into the mainstream by half capitulating to systems very differently based, just as it did at the very beginning of Christian "establishment" in England around 900 AD. "The Dream of the Rood" partly subverted and partly capitulated to the Germanic/Anglo-Saxon paganism of *Beowulf*. It challenged "the world" and the universal default position of "negative reciprocity" while infiltrating alternative possibilities. Moreover, the establishment of Christianity was not simply its capitulation to "the world" understood as blameworthy but a process that was inevitable once something as strange and counter-cultural as Christianity had emerged. A poem that brought home to me the unique dialectic introduced by Christianity into the social order was Longfellow's "The Sicilian's Tale: King Robert of Sicily." King Robert was a representative of the negative reciprocity and the relentless pursuit of wealth and power of Norman civilization and growled furiously when the meaning was explained to him of "Deposuit potentes de sede et exaltavit humiles" which he heard monks singing.

That is only half the story lying behind this book, though it might seem to provide quite enough explanatory clues to be going on with. For a fuller picture I have to return to autobiography. In 1950 I read Albert Schweitzer on the eschatology informing the Gospels and felt my world quiver fundamentally on its axis. Nothing in my background had prepared me for this. If I had read Browning through different eyes I would have seen what was at stake and not rested simply on what seemed to me the affirmations of "Abt Vogler" or "Saul." The result of this inner turmoil was that, while teaching in primary schools from 1952 onwards, I entered by a kind of inner necessity into a program of extra-mural self education in order to deal with problems that ultimately went back to my father's revivalism. Schweitzer was devastating because he suggested in the course of a survey of mainly German Biblical criticism that the Gospels reflected contradictory emphases. They did so within precisely the eschatological perspective my father as someone who left school at eleven believed literally. I had thought my pacifist reading of the Gospels a straightforward exercise whereby Jesus enunciated progressive principles for all time, but I now saw it could be vulnerable to a mode of understanding for which the love-teaching of Paul as well as Jesus was an "interim ethic" bound up with what could be seen as eschatological delusion. To steady my wobbling axis I had to read a great deal of serious theology, first a large segment of the corpus of biblical criticism to get Schweitzer in perspective, but also theology more generally, including systematics. It was in the latter pursuit that I eventually encountered Reinhold Niebuhr and a Christian realism about violence that first challenged and ultimately destroyed my pacifism. Niebuhr did something else in a book I cannot now identify. I was a confirmed progressive who knew what was right for the world and also knew we were bound to reach the world's preordained goal, however bumpy the ride en route. But Niebuhr in this forgotten book wrote about the different costs and benefits associated with conservatism, liberalism, and socialism, and that meant I had permission to (say) read Burke sympathetically.

That is one trajectory. I now have to indicate another intersecting trajectory. In the middle of class warfare in primary schools in the mid-nineteen fifties, and after excoriating domestic warfare leading to divorce, I pursued sociology by private study through correspondence. Initially I did so to acquire a scientific validation of my progressive views on violence, notably my objection to capital punishment, but also on warfare generally. (I recollect a sociologist writing to *The Times* to say that sociology was a left-wing subject because it was true.) But I started to have doubts, not about capital punishment, where I thought morality and evidence reasonably concordant, but about warfare. The deliverances of sociology struck me as very ambiguous but pointing towards a realist understanding of politics. After all, these deliverances concern issues that are matters of perspective as well as evidence, so not straightforwardly susceptible to the arbitration of science as right or wrong. I tussled with the implicit Marxist underpinning of sociology, and also with the positivism with which the Marxism was often incongruously allied, to the point where one tutor on my correspondence course refused to tussle further. I effectively abandoned the course, particularly as it virtually ignored the sociology of religion as so much epiphenomenal froth on the surface of the really real. I encountered Troeltsch and even Durkheim and Weber by trawling off the course and finding what I wanted in the university library or in my own extremely restricted resources. These included a collection of essays by Max Weber (to be discussed below, because they were so life changing.)

The doubts about pacifism generated by sociology meshed with my reading of Niebuhr on political realism. After winning a scholarship for post-graduate study at the LSE in 1959, I wrote a doctoral thesis on pacifism, especially between the two World Wars, which left my pacifism on the road to ruin, though not yet specifically rejected. I had not yet grasped that rejecting the logic of pacifism would commit me to a very different logic. All the same, one sign of my changing beliefs was that I left the Campaign for Nuclear Disarmament (CND). I was on the cusp of supporting what I now saw as the realistic and responsible exercise of power (as played out in a famous debate between the Labour party leader, Hugh Gaitskell, and Bertrand Russell, a leader of CND). I was also on the cusp of accepting the constrictions of tradition and custom and what was politically viable. The mixture of pacifism and violence, anarchism and dissident Marxism in the student movement only a little later confirmed me in the view that this was secular millenarianism laced with antinomian sexuality, and that it replicated aspects of Christianity from its very beginnings: bringing in the kingdom by violence or refusing to do so, as at the most profound moment in the confrontation of Jesus with Pilate. "My kingdom is not from hence *else* would my servants fight." And all this was happening under my eyes in the most distinguished school of the social sciences dedicated to reason and fact, as its motto, *Rerum cognoscere causas*, proudly proclaimed.

Here I must abbreviate. Once free of the correspondence course, I started some particularly intensive reading in the autumn of 1958 that brought me close to breakdown, given that I was also teaching primary classes of 42. First, on the train from Paddington to Newport, I read Popper on *The Poverty of Historicism*. I took from this book the idea that the world was not marching to a predestined end according to a version of secularized providence to which I must conform. This was the faith of so much sociology, and I was now *free* to disbelieve it. Historical necessity did not have me in its grip. I was even free to suspect the "masters of suspicion." Everything was open.

At roughly the same time, I read Max Weber with even more profound consequences. There was his essay on "Politics as a Vocation," which distinguished between the politics of righteousness and the politics of responsibility. Here then was a realist politics that still retained a moral perspective. Then there were two essays whose titles and contents made very little initial sense to me: one on the social psychology of the world religions and the other on "religious rejections of the world and their direction." I did not see religion, or rather Christianity in particular, as world-rejecting. At least I did not see it that way until I realized that Christianity rejected a world profoundly resistant to love, peace, and forgiveness. In short it was profoundly athwart any possibility of incorporation in the structures of established power and *must* retune itself to those structures if it were to infiltrate them with an alternative vision. That way it would generate a double entendre whereby the sword of the Spirit was in constant tension with the sword of state, or whereby the spiritual temple of the universal Israel of God's people was in tension with the real sacred centers, physical territories, and borders of any number of national Israels. This understanding complemented what I said earlier about the secular spirit of wealth and power in the person of King Robert of Sicily overhearing the monks singing the Magnificat with hostile unease. Christians might move between setting up God's kingdom by violence or by rejecting violence, but in power they might infiltrate alternatives within the world as it is.

Why, then, at the age of eighty-seven did I decide to write a book about the oscillations and contradictions of the secularization stories to be read in English poetry? I have already hinted at the reason: unlike music and painting, though poetry employs images, metaphors, and ambiguity, it does so in words and can be discussed in words. It also cannot avoid the entanglement of faith and "world" as part of its subject matter or hinterland. In my own biography I found sustenance in poetry as my anchor as against the dubieties of purely propositional belief. Propositions did not provide answers to what Eliot called "the life questions." The relevance of poetry as a source and testing ground for my arguments about secularization narratives seems to me clear enough. I am not engaged with the issues of form and style at the heart of literary criticism as a technical discipline, but with the significance of poetry as evidence of the state of Christianity in England at any particular period, and of influential states of mind and opinion among educated and uneducated alike. I examine how that evidence reinforces or contradicts other secularization narratives which draw on empirical social data about decline from a putative "religious" condition to a seemingly self-evident "secular" condition. I contend that Christianity's resistance to "the world" and its profane dynamic is an important strand in English poetry as is the opposite: the necessary compromises that established Christianity has to make to infiltrate that world. Understanding this enables one to see what counts culturally in terms of meaning as much as the rather different process of counting the distribution of practices and beliefs, though that, too, has its secular shifts and oscillations. Any convincing secularization narrative needs to take both modes of analysis into full account.

Acknowledgments

I emphasize that those who made comments are not responsible for my efforts. They are Stephen Prickett (who thought the ideas important but queried the method); my daughter, Jessica Martin, sometime college lecturer in English and Fellow at Trinity, Cambridge and a priest-theologian now Canon Residentiary at Ely Cathedral; my son Jonathan Martin, who test-read the MS from a "lay" perspective; and my wife, Bernice Martin, who commented astutely during the evenings when I read aloud poetry from *Beowulf* and *Pearl* to Geoffrey Hill, and also commented on my manuscript. I am very grateful to Simon Jarvis for formatting the manuscript for me.

The author and publisher gratefully acknowledge permission to quote from the following poems in this book:

Carol Ann Duffy, "Prayer," from *Mean Time*, published by Anvil Press Poetry, 1993; copyright Carol Ann Duffy; quoted by kind permission of the author, c/o Rogers, Coleridge and White Ltd.

Robert Graves, "Babylon," from *Fairies and Fusiliers*, published by Hubbard Press, 2008; quoted by kind permission of the Estate of Robert Graves, c/o Carcanet Press.

Alfred E. Housman, "An Easter Hymn," from *More Poems*, published by Jonathan Cape, 1936; quoted by kind permission of the Estate of the author, c/o Henry Holt.

Norman Nicholson, "The Bloody Cranesbill" and "On the Dismantling of Millom Ironworks," from *Collected Poems*, published by Faber and Faber, 2009; quoted by kind permission of the Estate of the author, c/o Peters Fraser and Dunlop.

Siegfried Sassoon, "Counter-attack" and "Alone," from *Collected Poems 1908–1956* published by Faber and Faber; copyright Siegfried Sassoon; quoted by kind permission of the Estate of George Sassoon, c/o Barbara Levy Literary Agency.

Charles H. Sisson, "The Usk" and "What a Piece of Work is Man," from *In the Trojan Ditch*, published by Carcanet, 1974; quoted by kind permission of the Estate of the author, c/o Carcanet.

Edith Sitwell, "Still Falls the Rain" and "The Shadow of Cain," from *Collected Poems* by Edith Sitwell, reprinted by permission of Peters Fraser and Dunlop (www.petersfraserdunlop.com) on behalf of the Estate of Edith Sitwell.

Introduction

Over the years I have been interested in how the secularization narrative plays out differently in the different arts, and I have looked, in particular, at the visual and plastic arts, classical music and architecture.[1] In this book, I consider how the secularization narrative plays out in English poetry. I believe that English poetry, over the whole span of its history from (say) the ninth century to the present, provides an extraordinarily sensitive lens for thinking about the changing nature of the Christian presence, as well as about its absences and the presence of other elements admixed with and sometimes alien to it.

There are various foci of my interest. One quite central focus turns on the ways in which a faith which, in its primary scriptures, has such strong reservations about the worldly institutions of wealth, violence, and power, interacts with, and adjusts to, very different ways of understanding. These might be pagan codes of honor, or classical humanism, or "the" Enlightenment. I ask how far "unworldly" Christianity, once established, adapts to "the world" (or secularizes) to meet very different and opposed construals of proper action and motive. Two obvious examples concern the markedly antagonistic construals of proper action and motive both in the Dark Ages (so-called) and in the Middle Ages, emanating from the aggression of the male warrior and associated codes of honor. One way and another, this tension remains active in Christianity throughout its established history.

The actions of Norman knights all over Europe and the East Mediterranean littoral illustrate the chasm between the Christianity of its normative scriptures in the Gospels and what the Normans took for granted. Just how deep this chasm ran was nicely caught by Longfellow in a poem where King

---

1. "Secularization in the Arts: the case of music," in Martin, *The Religious and the Secular*, 79–99; "Music and Religion: Ambivalence Towards the Aesthetic," in Martin, *Christian Language and Its Mutations*, 41–68; "Fifth Commentary: on the Return of the Liturgical in Modernist Music and Poetry and the Reconciliation Achieved by Liturgical Poetry and Music," in Martin, *Ruin and Restoration*, 81–98.

Robert of Sicily comments on the impertinence of monks chanting the radical sentiments of the Magnificat, "*Deposuit potentes*"—"He hath cast down the mighty from their seat and exalted them of low degree." In conventional understanding, the brutality of the knightly honor code, especially of the crusaders, is construed in a standard trope as Christians (as usual) behaving badly, but this is quite superficial. We are dealing with the inevitable partial secularization of a primitive Christianity radically opposed to the primacy of aggressive violence and wealth. (That the crusaders may have helped prevent the Islamicization of Europe is another and very complex question, as is the question of the splendors of their civilization from Monreale in Sicily to Durham.)

This understanding of secularization is quite distinct from the conventional understanding based on the fluctuations of belief and practice, though the two understandings are bound to be connected, because, where Christianity is politically established, there are extraneous motives for religious conformity. We are rather rarely, if ever, straightforwardly charting the lineaments of a purely personal faith. I am pointing to something that ought to be very obvious. Christianity is conspicuously unsuitable as a basis for political order, and is subject to radical modification (or secularization) once installed in that role. The resulting tension and interaction is precisely what gives "Christian" civilization its peculiar character. Indeed, Christian civilization is distinguished by the tension between limit and transformation, between what ineluctably is and a grand "what if?," and the secret seeds of the Gospel operate both within the walls of the church and extramurally. They take root wherever they fall. And the "impossible possibility" of Christianity mandates monasticism: high dedication, often with others of like mind, to sacrificial living.

Another focus of interest is the admixture within Christianity of (say) alchemy and astrology, and, indeed, of elements of obsolete and obsolescent science. Obviously a key aspect of secularization narratives concerns the erosions associated with science, including the "science" of biblical criticism. I am also very interested in the group of crucial changes associated with Romanticism. These include the subjectivization of faith, the historicization of experience, and the revolutionary and progressive rejection of faith (or at any rate of the politically established church) as integrally implicated in injustice. They also include the emergence of personalized spiritualities and alternative religions—and, along with all that, the surprising resilience of Christianity in modernity at precisely the juncture where it is ceasing straightforwardly to be implicated in the dynamics of political action and cultural establishment. What that resilience might mean is explored in the text, and is a central theme. Following the logic of my more than five decades of work on secularization, I am, throughout, critical of secularization, understood as unilinear movement from the religious to the secular. I hope it will be clear how that critique meshes with my considerably longer if more intermittent engagement with peace and violence.

My critique does not mean that the nexus of changes given conventional expression" by the secularization narrative has no substance, nor that secularization theory can be dismissed as merely mythological. It contains mythological and ideological prescriptions as well as empirical descriptions, but that does not deprive it of explanatory power, once the prescriptive ideology of secularism is separated from secularization as a process. Indeed, I indicate various secularizations at different junctures in this book. There is, for example, the point at which the state becomes semi-secularized, and religion no longer provides the primary legitimation of political order. Religious institutions become differentiated, no longer built comprehensively into the key structures of state power. I also consider what David Jones called "the Break," which I interpret as the point when Christianity became culturally disestablished. Poets might be explicitly Christian, or have some engagement with Christianity, negative or positive; or they might be merely unengaged and indifferent.

I assume that English poetry represents an extraordinary peak of human achievement, and that it is, with music, one of the activities most closely related to religion, both as providing a support for faith and as providing alternatives to it. My epigraph from Derek Walcott, taken from a piece where he also speaks of gratitude, benediction, and silence, witnesses to the sheer complexity of the relationship. I believe that the relation of poetry to religion, either in its role as support or supplementation or in its role as an alternative, lies in its resistance to abstraction. Just as religion is an orientation to "the world" that resists reduction to ratiocination or abstract propositions, so poetry resists reductive paraphrase as a form of argument. Questions about conceptualization and abstraction, about paraphrase and argument, in poetry, and in poetics more generally, provide a major focus of my intellectual enterprise.

I have already implied a critical distinction between religion as a political phenomenon and religion *sui generis*. That needs careful unpacking, because I am not talking about religion as such. Contemporary comment on what religion *as such* does or does not do is endemic, but from a sociological viewpoint it is a complete waste of breath. For me, as a sociologist, generic "religion" is an illusory entity, a particular located construction, about which no generalizations are possible. Rather than discussing religion, I am talking specifically about *Christianity* as a very distinctive faith, especially so in its relation to power. Judaism and Islam are amenable to the dynamics of politics in a way primitive Christianity is not. That throws into doubt the politically useful construct "Judaeo-Christianity," because in the critical matter of "rejecting the world" (as sociologists in the Weberian tradition formulate the matter) Christianity is very different from Judaism, however much it depends on it for its thematic repertoire.

I am saying that Judaism, like Islam, is not in need of secularization to be politically viable. In principle, it is already viable, even though it lacks a detailed theory of the political, such as is to be found in Machiavelli. Of course, until recently, Judaism has had scant opportunity to provide the legitimation of the state, but there is no inherent problem about its doing so. Judaism grows out of, and is nourished by, political aspirations related to release from slavery either in Egypt or Babylon. That conspicuous realism, making it the template for all manner of liberation movements, whether they are universal political ideologies like Marxism or particular forms of nationalism, also of necessity renders it morally ambiguous, in the way all political action is ambiguous. Moral ambiguity inheres in all political action. After all, in its normative scriptures Judaism replicates the violence it suffers in actual or anticipated violence on others. It participates in the negative reciprocity of the political, as the inevitable consequence of positive solidarity and demarcations of "the other," in a way that makes it simultaneously a paradigmatic narrative of *release* from oppression and a paradigmatic narrative of the *exercise* of oppression, either recollected in its account of the occupation of the Promised Land, or anticipated prophetically in the reversal of the humiliation of the Jewish people. The Hebrew Scriptures tell it how it is, both as regards liberation and oppression, so that we who inherit its scriptures may celebrate and lament accordingly. I may, as a Christian inheriting the Hebrew Scriptures, emphasize the potentials for liberation, in the way that African-Americans have, for the most part, focused on celebration, rather than lament. But that the narrative is bound to be double-edged, insofar as it is political, is also clear. "Blessed is he that taketh thy little ones and dasheth them against the stones" (Ps 137:9) is a beatitude consonant with the treatment of the Amalekites and the first-born of Egypt, whether by supposed divine command or divine intervention.

But then, within the prophetic tradition, there emerges another hermeneutic possibility that sidelines political salvation, through a redemptive suffering which takes upon the group or upon the "elect remnant" the appalling cost of the violence written into human affairs. This conception of receiving violence (conveyed in the image of the dumb lamb) without the normal correlative of negative reciprocity and retribution is not a straightforward possibility of ordinary politics. But it is the seedbed of Christianity: the teachings of the Gospels and the narrative of the crucifixion are based on the rejection of negative reciprocity by an individual identified as the dumb lamb of prophecy. The Lamb is in his own person the divine victim of unjust violence, even though reversion to elements of negative reciprocity can be traced in oscillations within that primary redemptive narrative and throughout subsequent Christian history. Those oscillations between the workings of the invisible kingdom "not of this world" and making the kingdom come by violence, are associated with other oscillations. These move between antinomianism and perfectionism, between the elevation of the erotic and the setting aside of the erotic, and between internecine anarchy and total control. They are characteristic of what we might call the whole revolutionary Christian scenario. Exemplary withdrawal and exemplary violent revolution are mutually implicated.

This is by no means a diversion into the history of religions. It is an attempt to show how the issue of secularization, understood as Christianity's partial acceptance of political necessity, is bound up with the issue of violence. It includes the acceptance of violence as an expression of the solidarity of Us as against the solidarity of Them in the Darwinian struggle for inherently scarce "goods." As I said earlier, my preoccupation with the issue of violence over the last sixty years is integrally bound up with my preoccupation with secularization. The connection is made by Christ himself: "My kingdom is not of this world, else would my servants fight" (John 18:36). Penitence and forgiveness are not political virtues, and politicians who forgive their enemies are on their way out of politics. To embrace the primacy of the child and the outsider, to make the first last, to reject the anxieties of "the morrow," to reward equally those who work for the last few minutes and those who work all day, to recommend unlimited forgiveness, and to set aside family and even a place to live—"the Son of man hath not where to lay his head" (Matt 8:20)—is to imagine a world without power, for good or for ill. Such ideas can only work by infiltration, not implementation. (This is not to say, of course, that a broad political ethic compatible with Christianity is all that difficult, based on the status of the human, covenantal relations, neighborliness, the rejection of exploitation, and of the divinization of the political order or wealth. The real difficulty comes with balancing different principles in concrete cases, especially where all available choices are between degrees of evil. The belief in "a" Christian political solution is illusory.)

One understands the contrast between a politically viable Judaism and Christianity by contrasting the approach of the two faiths to the motifs of exile, return, Promised Land, temple, and Jerusalem. In Judaism we are talking about real exiles, and real returns to the Promised Land, or to Jerusalem and its temple, all of which is part of the ongoing struggle for identity (my people) and identifiable space (our place and its borders). In Christianity we see a comprehensive switch of exile, temple, and peaceful city to the universal realm of metaphor. The most obvious switch to metaphor occurs in the reading in the liturgy for Easter Eve of the story of Noah, to be understood as code for humanity's entering the ark of salvation, prior to the sign of peace brought by the dove. The same metaphorical transformation occurs in the treatment of the crossing of the Red Sea as the Easter crossing from death to life. Once again, it is important to notice the role of oscillation in the governing narrative whereby exiles and returns, temples and cities, wildernesses and mountains, move backwards and forwards between universal and heavenly metaphors and particular and earthly promises.[2] The oscillation is sufficiently evident in the Gospels themselves for fundamentalists (not to mention some of the radical reformers of early modernity) to imagine the inauguration of a real kingdom on the Davidic model.

Here I anticipate an analysis below by Daniel Chua that fits my overall argument perfectly. According to Scripture, the heavenly imagery, for example, the city of peace, Jerusalem, is located "above" (Gal 4:26) and it comes on earth "as in heaven" by the secret working of potent seeds. The kingdom lies in wait. But then, roughly in the years 1790–1820, human action finally tries to bring the kingdom on earth by exemplary violence. It fully realizes in a secular mode the premonitory sacred violence of the English revolution. It defies the scriptural warning that the "kingdom cometh not by violence," and that means that God becomes otiose, as divine powers are harnessed to work in history, not secretly but openly. And this is the more plausible because institutional religion has been, to a large extent, absorbed by the politics of reaction, in a way that completely compromises its revolutionary message, except as discerned by a poetic prophet like William Blake. Indeed, it is even absorbed by the revolution itself, as established revolution reverts to religious legitimation, as in Napoleon's coronation. Universalism of all kinds has a coercive potential when faced by obstinate particularity. Napoleon provides an instructive instance of the coercive universalism of Enlightenment by seeking to eliminate the obstinate particularity of Israel: forced marriages would convert Jews into Frenchmen. If one wanted another instance it might be provided by Beethoven, whose sublime and forceful musical rhetoric set about bringing about the kingdom on earth, only to find Napoleon a Messiah false to the cause in proclaiming himself an earthly emperor. Thereafter the role of the perpetually postponed earthly revolution was transferred to art and poetry as its only possible carrier. As

---

2. Seligman and Weller, *How Things Count as the Same*.

in the epigraph from Gadamer, art takes on a consecrated role and burden as secular savior.

But this burden cannot be carried by poetry even though a great deal of poetry now acts as substitute religion and as a politics of frustrated yearning. This is where the rhetoric of poetry mimics the rhetoric of religious transformation, aided by the reinforcements of verbal music shared by both, and falsely projects transformation as a potential available in the here and now. Poetry is powered by the seductive devices of rhythm, alliteration, rhyme, assonance, and resonance. It is no more propositional and argumentative than is Christianity, but the illumination of the quotidian world it shares with Christianity is purely personal and not hedged about by an understanding of limits created by Christianity's prolonged collective encounter with historical realities. That means that its illuminations are not guided by the exercise of responsibility: that is, by the fusion of principle with chronic exigency that the political vocation properly requires.

Poetic rhetoric can be the vehicle for this evasion of political responsibility. It uses the invocative and the evocative derived from religious sources and imagery to say, "Just look at that," confident that its persuasive power will be self-evident. It bypasses argument and the constraints of analysis and causal historical narrative, exactly as Yeats explicitly proposed in his attack on philosophy. Prose can do the same, of course, and rhetoric is a major resource of political polemicists, but prose lacks the element of numinous surprise, even as it retains the capacity for tight empirical and causal analysis.

What, however, poetry does draw from Christianity, especially after the dire and minatory events of the twentieth century, are two suspicions set loose from their theological root. They are a suspicion of wealth and a suspicion of power, not based on a principled rejection of the world but on a preference for being nice and for exhibiting approved attitudes that take little account of costs further down the line or of the unavoidable paradoxes of political action. This is a major source of unanchored righteousness and the taproot of free-floating moral indignation. No wonder moralistic versions of Christianity, either on grounds of dubious biblical criticism or a sentimental preference for good endings, seek to excise the terrible conclusion of the proclamation of kingdom on Golgotha. If only the injunction to love or to imagine an alternative order of things could be the solution. I want to be clear. Liberal aspiration to amelioration is one thing, and admirable; I identify my own values as liberal in the tradition of L. T. Hobhouse and T. H. Green. Liberal refusal to face the frustrations built into the reality principle is another. This refusal, rooted in a secularized providence, is the source of chronic expressions of frustration with a world that will not conform to the liberal script and bring history to an end as imagined by liberal triumphalists like Fukuyama.

As argued earlier in relation to the emphases of the Gospels, radical Christianity, in its proclamation of the kingdom "not of the world," nourishes elements that belong quite clearly to the narrative of redemption but cannot be realized on the political plane. These emphases are also the "elements" literally embodied in the Eucharist, which celebrates a gift not dependent, like political gifts, on a cycle of reciprocity. It is simply available to be received with praise and thanksgiving, and rests on the achievement of peace, forgiveness, and reconciliation through penitence and confession. As the political revolution bears its bloody fruit in the elimination of opponents, and then mutates into the aesthetic, the return of initial hope and aspiration for another world, proclaimed and enacted in the protected enclave of the liturgy, becomes possible.

That long excursus attempts to explain why I am especially interested in the extent to which the supportive version of the link between poetry and religion is maintained in modernity, and even reinforced. I label that reinforcement as the "return of the liturgical," and I canvass the reasons for it, for example, the impact of the horrors of the twentieth century, especially on the more optimistic versions of progressive liberalism, or, indeed, on all expressions of human perfectibility which have no need of salvation. Liturgy, as I have already suggested, begins in brokenness and passes from penitence to thankfulness, from praise to the exchange of gifts in love, from a sense of the presence to reconciliation and peace. A reinforcement of religion in modernity is precisely not what conventional secularization theory would anticipate, although it is not as if poetry has figured much, if at all, in sociological accounts of secularization. My critique is throughout embedded quite precisely in a rejection of secular providence and teleology, and of the associated remodeling of man to fit the falsely predicted future that has among its ideological roots everything covered by Karl Popper's *The Poverty of Historicism* (1957).

I see the return of the liturgical as expressing a renewed sense, in a peak of human creativity, of the Christian narrative of ruin and restoration, corruption and redemption. As just explained, I relate that to the transfer of the Christian *telos* and *kairos* to history, and thus to all the bloodstained attempts to realize God's kingdom on earth, especially from the end of the eighteenth century to the end of the twentieth. Here I can let Daniel Chua speak for himself by way of some suggestive arguments in his *Absolute Music and the Construction of Meaning* (1999). There he writes of the demand to act, rather than to wait, in fin-de-siècle crises where revolution or terror or messianic tyrants try to force the apocalypse to manifest itself here and now and break finally with the past and with the yoke of man's "self-incurred tutelage."[3] Truth is to be disclosed by history, as humankind shapes the perfect future from its own resources. Kant even muttered the words of the *nunc dimittis*, "for mine eyes have seen thy salvation," as he heard of the French revolution. But there is, of course, no *parousia*, only the ordeal of its prolongation. "The revenge of God on mankind for stealing his *kairos* was aesthetic theory," the solving of the problem of politics through the aesthetic, as it spun out the end and yearned for an unattainable future.[4] Art became the language of the revolution in person.

I am not for a moment suggesting that some modern poets are straightforwardly engaging in the writing of liturgy. That would convert a remarkable proximity into an inappropriate identity. It may well have been the case, as Christopher Isherwood observed of Auden, that even in his secular years he had a tendency to combine grand opera with high mass, but he was not writing liturgy. What he eventually did was to write something with liturgical characteristics in his "Horae Canonicae." In the same way, Eliot's "Ash Wednesday" and Geoffrey Hill's *Tenebrae* are para-liturgical works, rather than liturgy proper. Liturgy has its own proper autonomy as the concrete embodiment and reenactment of the Christian narrative in the company of other Christians.

It will be obvious that I have had recourse to the vast amount of material now available through the internet. I have read and often read aloud a vast amount of English poetry from *Beowulf* to the present, but I have also had to rely on critical guides to a vast terrain, and on competent summaries. Before writing this book, I was a reader of poetry, but not well-versed in criticism and schools of criticism. I have had to acquire and absorb much critical literature in the course of writing, and, in doing that, I have stumbled on kinds of literary analysis that might have stayed permanently out of my sight. I am, after all, a sociologist, and the "subtle schools" have not detained me overmuch. For a sociologist, I may be unusually well acquainted with poetry, as I am also unusually well acquainted with theology, but that is not much of a claim, given the preoccupations of most of my sociological colleagues. It happens to be a consequence of my peculiar formation as someone who failed to enter university to read English (not to mention failing a scholarship to the Royal Academy of Music) and who read literature and theology almost entirely as a project of self-education. As a result of this idiosyncratic formation, I have scant expertise in literary criticism, beyond some shadowy ideas about close reading, deconstruction, and historicism.

3. Chua, *Absolute Music*, 129.
4. Chua, *Absolute Music*, 246.

Reluctantly, I have used potted biographies to locate poets before making comments, usually quite brief, about poetic placement and achievement. That makes decent prose quite difficult. At the same time, my treatment has become more extended the closer I have come to the special problems of the modern period. That applies in particular to the situation which Eliot characterized in *The Rock* as never having happened before: people either turning to no gods and or to false gods like the dialectic.[5] And I have chosen my numerous secular poets, for example Thom Gunn and Carol Ann Duffy, mainly as presenting *types* of perspective.

I am interested in the different ways in which poets negotiate the axes of human life existentially, emotionally, and intellectually. I want to explore what meaning, purpose, and hope, or lack of meaning, purpose, and hope, they discern in the human predicament. That includes the irresolvable paradoxes (or *aporias*) that afflict and bedevil all the schemes we devise to shape experience and organize our perspectives. In what different ways, for example, do two Christian poets, Robert and Elizabeth Barrett Browning, approach the great questions of their shared faith? In what different ways do two Christian poets, Eliot and Auden, parse the great questions, the former in a Catholic manner and the latter in a Protestant manner? Sometimes these questions are embedded in much larger cultural and theological contexts that I can do no more than gesture towards. And it must be obvious that I cannot hope to present a representative sample of so many secular poets contrasted with so many religious ones. This is a qualitative, almost a phenomenological study, and it selects signal features of broad literary landscapes. It maps without counting.

There is a broad argument undergirding my approach, and it relates to the particular form of secularity present in the latter years of the eighteenth century, compared with the religious preoccupations of the seventeenth century up to the 1670s and the religious preoccupations of the nineteenth century after the 1830s. There is a debate among literary critics of the Victorian period explicitly focused on secularization, and on whether we discern harbingers of modern secularity in the poets of the nineteenth century. This is an instance of literary and sociological interests overlapping, and it means that in reading the literary critics I find myself on familiar ground. For example, I find myself running into references to the work of Charles Taylor on secularization over the last half millennium. Naturally, from my own critical position, I sympathize with those who do not want to subsume the literary study of late nineteenth-century poetry within the problematic of the secularization thesis. But the issue is plainly very complicated and I

---

5. Eliot, *The Rock*, section 7, in *Collected Poems, 1909–1962*, 177–78.

have spent some time on those like Arnold, Clough, Swinburne, Hardy, and Housman whom I call avatars of secularity.

In every sphere of discussion and with respect to every period, I have become aware of alternative and contradictory approaches. There is a lack of consensus with regard to many of the issues central to the present enquiry. For example, there are various views about the religious sublime in the eighteenth century, bearing directly on whether we may characterize that century as secular. Some observers argue that the supposedly secular century was simply religious in a different way. That kind of argument is just as endemic in sociology as it is in literature. As in sociology, so in literary criticism: arguments turn on the definitions you deploy and the conceptual boundaries you draw. I know there are those who see Wordsworth as more straightforwardly Christian than I take him to be. Without anything approaching consensus, I am forced to make my own judgments. As St. Joan said to the inquisitor in Shaw's famous play, "With what other judgment can I judge but my own?"

Several important issues arise here. One relates to subjective meaning, rather than objective counting. In standard discussions of secularization from a sociological perspective, most of the evidence is quantitative, and concerns religious belief and practice and the role of religious institutions. If you are a historian or sociologist, you can count bodies in church in the Victorian period over a given time scale to determine a statistical trend. But you cannot count changes in meaning. At most you may chart changes in vocabulary, and in the import of specific terms as indices of changes in meaning and ethos, a process of particular significance in any study of secularization in poetry. For example, "faith," in the vocabulary of Tennyson, has a much more attenuated meaning than it would have had for Donne. Such changes count crucially, but they cannot be counted. At best they can be identified as more or less indicative or influential.

Another issue relates to how you understand the essence of a faith and what you believe to be its constitutive characteristics, however much these may shift according to context. This looks like essentialism, and essentialism counts as an intellectual crime, but enquiries about the changing travails of faith and doubt presuppose that you know in what precisely you have believed or doubted. When the political scientist Mark A. Smith argues that Christians today share more with secular coevals than with Christians in the past, you are forced to ask what is essential and what expendable about Christianity.[6] Without some presupposition about what properly constitutes Christianity, you could not even ask when and how the Christian faith

---

6. Smith, *Secular Faith*.

has been so subject to revision that another faith has taken its place. *The Triumph of the Therapeutic: Uses of Faith after Freud* (1965) by Philip Rieff maps the way the releases of culture have undermined the controls and created the autonomous self-regarding individual who questions all notions of good and evil, purpose and authority.[7] That assumes that you know what it is that has been replaced

As I have already indicated, one major focus for me over the years has been to see how alternative secularization narratives play out in relation to the different arts: for example, the contrast between a narrative based on the visual arts and one based on "classical" music or, in this case, English poetry. In that enterprise we are dealing with questions of meaning that sociologists have always found difficult to integrate with analyses based on structural processes such as functional differentiation and privatization. The difficulty is so great that it is rarely even attempted. There are accounts of changes in intellectual orientation, for example, studies of the cultures of doubt in the late nineteenth century, and there are studies of religious practice in the decades up to and following the 1851 census, but it is not easy to integrate them. Owen Chadwick's *The Secularisation of the European Mind in the Nineteenth Century* (1976) is one important attempt to do so.[8] Charles Taylor's writings, especially *A Secular Age* (2007), are remarkable essays in integration, though there is always a tendency in any analysis to slip either towards sociology or the history of ideas.[9] In the second half of the nineteenth century, it really is difficult to know by what criteria anyone might validate Matthew Arnold's claim to be "wandering between two worlds, one dead, the other powerless to be born," or his suggestion that what we once took for religion and philosophy will be replaced by poetry. These assertions are very germane, indeed crucial, to this present enquiry, but the criteria of verification are not obvious. Matthew Arnold thought deference to scientific criteria important, but his own gnomic statements do not conform to them any more than his statements about the receding sea of faith conformed to the actual state of religion in the mid-nineteenth century.

A major problem concerns the way secularization narratives are based on different time scales. One narrative is based on a historical tripod based in the high Middle Ages or in high Victorianism, seen as high points of religion. Once accept a baseline located at a high point, and decline inevitably follows. Other narratives are based on the changes initiated by the scientific revolution from the late seventeenth century on, or else on

---

7. Rieff, *Triumph of the Therapeutic*.
8. Chadwick, *Secularisation of the European Mind*.
9. Taylor, *A Secular Age*.

the changes initiated by the French Revolution. A third relevant narrative, considerably more complex, is organized over three millennia and involves the emergence of Christianity itself as part of the Axial Revolution, which exhibited a reserve towards "the world," in the light of a transcendent possibility or eschatological promise. In this text, all these time scales are in play, but it is worth emphasizing that the very idea of Christian challenge to, and compromise with, the imperatives of the secular world, belongs to the perspective derived from the Axial Revolution.

What I attempt here is affiliated with the extended secularization narrative based on three millennia, rather than with narratives based on the half a millennium since 1500, or on the period since 1870 or since 1960. It takes off from the ninth century, when Christianity was first fully established in England, and, in the course of taking root, incorporated paganism and adapted to it. I find it difficult to assess to what extent that incorporation extended to the pagan mode of enchantment, but it seems clear that the incorporation extended to the pagan honor code. The pagan honor code provides the default position of human society, and has fundamental implications for the conduct of the political realm. It was the ethos adopted by those whom Nietzsche called the "blond beasts of prey." Against this profoundly embedded code, Christianity made very partial headway, and, in the twentieth century, the beasts of prey posed a direct challenge, and helped push forward "the Break" noted by David Jones.

That apart, it is clear that in one form or another, paganism is constantly resurgent, not just in the Renaissance, but by way of the education of elites in Greek and Latin culture over many centuries. That in itself trails complexities, because Renaissance humanists not only practiced a common rhetoric that in reality prevailed from Chaucer until the late eighteenth century, as Brian Vickers has argued, but treated the classics as para-scriptures, susceptible to Christian interpretation. That authorizes how Milton, or indeed Samuel Johnson, used the Bible and the classics as part of the same frame of reference.

Chapter 1

An Overview of the Problem

This overview focuses on the problem posed by the sixteenth century, considered as simultaneously the century of the Reformation and of Renaissance humanism. If you take a major anthology of the poetry of the century compiled in 1991 by Emrys Jones, you will find remarkably little specifically Christian poetry, and much of what you do find is written by Roman Catholics or by people who became Roman Catholics. That is to say, it is written by people already endangered to the point where they had nothing to lose by poetic self-disclosure.[1] The preeminent case is that of Robert Southwell, but he is not alone and one immediately asks the old question concerning a Protestant aversion to the arts associated with the embrace of iconoclasm. As we shall see, the issue of the dominance of the secular in sixteenth-century poetry is very complicated, but the pervasive presence of a secular Renaissance humanism in the person of a poet like Thomas Wyatt is initially very striking.

Wyatt was to some extent Italianized, and so became the channel whereby the Petrarchan sonnet was introduced into English, and, with it, a reinforcement of such conventional themes as the cruel mistress. At the same time there is another side, also of Italian inspiration, that has to do with his *Penitential Psalms*, discussed later. When it came to religious and political loyalty, Wyatt adapted to whatever the exigent occasions of the Henrician court demanded of him. But then we have to weigh Wyatt at the Henrician court against Spenser writing about the moral quest after the Reformation in the time of Elizabeth. We have to think about Shakespeare, a generation later, as a Renaissance humanist pursuing the immortality of

1. Jones, *New Oxford Book of Sixteenth Century Verse*.

fame, but also pursuing such Christian themes as reconciliation and resurrection. I am in a preliminary way indicating difficulties relating to chronology, and also problems relating to a very dangerous political context when characterizing a "secular" sixteenth century.

Suppose there is a good case for characterizing the sixteenth century as, at least, relatively secular, in spite of, or (more likely) because of, the rise of Puritan enthusiasm. After all, the Reformation pursuit of a purer faith carried potent secularizations and desacralizations in its sense of the universal vocation open to every "even Christian" rather than the virtuoso callings of the professed religious, in its truncation of priestly mediations, and in the robust republicanism latent in its account of authority or *Obrigkeit*.[2] There is an endemic problem of categorization here, because we can either treat the Reformation as trailing crucial secularizations, or as a relocation of the sacred. Nor is that the end of the matter, because it may be that the Protestant impact on education is not obviously either a secularization or a relocation of the sacred. Milton's tract of 1644, *On Education*, is radical in undermining the old system of logical disputation and metaphysics to substitute a focus on "sensible things," but I am not sure where it lies in the problematic of secularization or a relocated sacred. Milton wanted an education for the requirements of personal and public virtue, and serving as a discipline of the active life which suggests a relocated sacred. Another problem underlies the question of secularization or a relocated sacred, and it is that from the perspective of godly Protestants, and, for that matter, of reforming Catholics, England in the sixteenth century veered between superstition and indifference. The "parish Anglicanism" of the time was Laodicean and lukewarm from the godly standpoint. This vexed question is all of a piece with approaches for which the supposed "sea of faith" in the Middle Ages was an optical delusion. The upper surface of the mid-sixteenth century lay over another lower world which was quite worldly, just as the upper surface of the mid-nineteenth century lay over another quotidian world which was quite religious.[3] The optic shapes the viewpoint.

However we assess the social and artistic consequences of initial Lutheran, and then Calvinist, influence in England, this "secular" period is followed in the seventeenth century by an extraordinary efflorescence of Christian poetry, in the persons of Donne, Herbert, Vaughan, Crashaw, Traherne—and Milton. But we are again plunged in the questions of the dubious category of the Metaphysicals, to which I return later, given that Donne and Herbert are a crucial generation earlier than Vaughan, Crashaw,

---

2. Howard and Noll, *Protestantism after 500 Years*.
3. Duffy, *Reformation Divided*, 347–75.

and Traherne. Once again, we are dealing with problems of political context, and a very partial fit between chronology and periodicity. Donne lived from 1573 to 1631, whereas Vaughan lived from 1621 to 1695, though his main contribution, *Silex Scintillans*, dates from 1650 and 1655. To put Milton (1608–1674) in that particular list of great religious poets is obviously problematic: in so many ways he is a conspicuous outlier. Marvell also has to be discussed as an outlier, so far as the Metaphysicals are concerned. What does seem clear is that by the 1660s or a little later the efflorescence of Christian poetry is over, and a major poem like Dryden's "Religio Laici" (1682) is a poem about religion rather than a religious poem in a sense that would apply to the poetry of Donne or Herbert. *My underlying contention is that, however you configure the history of poetry, the intermittent presence and absence of major Christian poetic voices does not conform to a narrative of linear secularization.*

The eighteenth century presents a complex problem as a key period conventionally characterized as the Age of Reason. It will become clear, in the course of the analysis below, that the conventional characterization trails serious contradictions and paradoxes. Nevertheless, I identify a "secular" highpoint in the late eighteenth century that, like the secular highpoint in the sixteenth century, precedes the splendors of the mid-nineteenth century. I aim to trace the incidence of Christian poetry *from* a low point in 1775 and *up to* a high point in the mid-Victorian period, even though there is a well-established narrative treating the mid-Victorian period as one of conspicuous questioning and doubt. I take it for granted that this established narrative has been under severe strain for some time, for reasons that should become increasingly clear. Once I have surveyed the Victorians, both with regard to religious revival up to 1850 and incipient secularization (maybe) after that date, I look at a surprising presence of Christianity in the twentieth century, indicated by poets like Eliot, Auden, and David Jones. I shall say more about this in the "Programmatic Anticipation" that opens the chapter on the Victorians. Of course, I shall have to show in the course of the main analysis below in what ways 1775 was a genuinely low point. It is not my objective to focus all that much on the extensive sociological and historical evidence, but it is now generally accepted that the late eighteenth century was a low point in religious practice and belief in England (and incidentally in the sister society of the United States), so that, by 1806, two thirds of parishes had no resident priest, and Easter attracted very few communicants. The rise in the incidence of religious poetry was accompanied by the astonishing rise in religion under the impact of Evangelicalism and the Oxford Movement. What is interesting about the 1851 census is not so much that it signaled the future rise of indifference but it documented the antecedent rise of religion.[4] Of course, I do not assume a high congruence between elite and popular religion, nor that in matters of secularization popular opinion haltingly follows elite opinion, as the concept of the avant-garde would lead us to expect.[5] Disjunctions between elite perceptions and quotidian realities are not only possible but likely. At this juncture in the argument I merely note that Christopher Smart, a major Christian poet, died in 1771. I also observe that, while Samuel Johnson lived until 1784, his great religious poem, *The Vanity of Human Wishes*, dates back to 1749. His devotional poems thereafter are comparatively minor. Treating 1775 as a major historical baseline enables me to explore a period when poetry and what you might call the immediate literary surrounds were markedly non-Christian and even pagan.

OTHER TYPES OF PROBLEM

I now introduce a rather different type of problem, but one of singular importance. Christianity is not only intermittent in its presence and absences, but intermixed with and inflected by very different materials, often antithetical to it. Throughout the centuries under scrutiny here, Christianity provides the formal frame of accepted belief. It is installed in the seats of power, and provides an accepted medium of argument and debate, so that when dissent emerges, established Christianity is bound to be its target. That is obvious: Milton railed against the monarchical and prelatical "deformations" of Christianity. But one needs to understand just how Christianity in power is inflected in a fundamental way by the very fact of its establishment. Without ceasing to maintain some kind of recognizable identity as "Christian," it becomes admixed with very different religious and quasi-scientific materials, so that in the sixteenth century it is a compound of "itself" and Renaissance humanism of different varieties, alchemical and neo-platonic. Dr. Dee of Mortlake, whom Queen Elizabeth herself consulted, mixed magic, science, and hermetical philosophy with beliefs eclectically garnered from Christianity. The separate realms and disciplines we take for granted today were then partially fused. In a similar way, in the eighteenth century, Christianity, at least in the persons of its established representatives, often conformed to enlightened perspectives, in particular to natural religion, and even yielded up its character to the point where the church was an organizational shell

---

4. Some idea of the state of religion may be acquired from two books by Jenny Uglow, *The Pinecone* and *In These Times*.

5. Weightman, *Concept of the Avant-Garde*.

only partially occupied by a Christian spirit. This shell is understandably the target of Blake, Keats, Byron, and Shelley.

The historical inflection of Christianity takes so many forms, and generates so many different secularization stories, that I need briefly to canvass some of the most important. One influential early modern story focuses on optics, gravity, cosmology, and the new world opened up by exploration, while another story is located in the nineteenth century and is based on the corrosive effects on faith of scientific advances in geology and biology. But there are different, though connected, stories that are quite differently focused—for example, on the effects of urbanization and industrialization, or on changing forms of political legitimation, or on the demotion of the church as a key political player, or on the major cultural break associated with Romanticism and subjectivization. There is a near-contemporary story dealing with a major break in the twentieth century as the church becomes to a serious degree culturally disestablished, and partially deprived of its territorial base. We are back to the question of "the Break" posed earlier and to a whole nexus of questions turning on what T. S. Eliot meant by the arrival of something that "has never happened before." Has Christianity faced a new antagonistic culture of progress and of self-realization? If so, this could be counted a singularly important secularization. It seems to me that this debate has taken a particularly radical form in Germany. Karl Löwith, for example, contended that we have moved away both from pagan historical cycles and Christian anticipation of the kingdom to a position that may be derived from Christianity but is opposed to it. Such a revolution in consciousness is only indirectly linked to counting how many people account themselves "Christian." Christians could themselves be suborned by this silent revolution, just as at different times they have been suborned by Mammon and power, and coped too easily with "the embarrassment of riches."[6] If such a revolution is in train, it forces the institutional church to question its identity and to ask how it can present reconciliation and resurrection, sin and redemption, without emptying them out or demythologizing them into a contemporary dominant discourse.

RESIDUAL ISSUES

In what I have suggested so far, several questions have been begged or sidestepped. They concern problems that have to be canvassed, but are not so refractory as to undermine the whole project. One concerns why English poetry matters at all, and I have no difficulty answering it. English poetry

---

6. Schama, *Embarrassment of Riches*.

matters because it is a supremely sensitive indicator in the context of a literary culture that, from marginality and obscurity on an offshore island, became one of most powerful, impressive, and influential in world history. Without any evident absurdity, those who in England supported the Moderns against the Ancients could point to Shakespeare and Milton as equal to Virgil and Homer, and, moreover, they could do so in a context that witnessed the earliest manifestations of the nation and the industrial revolution. The supremely sensitive indicator of English poetry remained culturally important even when partially supplanted by prose in the latter part of the eighteenth century, or partially displaced by the novel in the nineteenth century.

Another question concerns what is to count as a Christian poem rather than a poem about some aspect of Christianity, or a poem that is religious without being Christian. Helen Gardner's *The Faber Book of Religious Verse* (1972) includes non-Christian poets like Shelley, Hardy, Housman, and Yeats.[7] The latter sections of *The Oxford Book of Mystical Verse* (1917), edited by D. H .S. Nicholson and A. H. E. Lee, bring into sharp focus the issue of poems that are religious but not Christian.[8] Generalized mysticism, also understood in contemporary terms as spirituality, gains salience in the late nineteenth and early twentieth centuries. But there is also the complex case of Platonizing Christianity to be considered, whether in the sixteenth and seventeenth centuries or in the writing of Robert Bridges (1844–1930). This is a problem that resists resolution, because the Platonic element in Christianity can be seen as a perennial aspect of what it means to be Christian. In principle, it appears in the key normative texts of Christianity, for example the epistles of Paul and the anonymous epistle to the Hebrews. The distinction between *sarx* and *soma*, or spirit and body, is deployed by many of the writers of the New Testament, at the same time as they also resist such a fundamental division.

A further issue concerns quality rather than quantity: Keble's *The Christian Year*, written in 1827, counts very high on quantity and influence rather than on quality. There is a difficult tightrope to be trod between focusing on minor poets who are very influential, like Keble and some of his Tractarian successors, major poets that are not at all influential at the time they initially flourished, like Smart, Blake, and Hopkins, and poets now individually regarded as distinctly minor, like Young, but who belong to whole categories of poetic production once very influential.

---

7. Gardner, *Faber Book of Religious Verse*.
8. Nicholson and Lee, *Oxford Book of Mystical Verse*.

The choices of those who have compiled anthologies of Christian poetry raise other important questions, sometimes explicitly. Donald Davie, in his "Introduction" to *The New Oxford Book of Christian Verse* (1981) raises the awkward question of a generalized Christianity that informs the whole context of writing poetry, so that, even if a poem described immorality, at least it was recognized as sinful rather than categorized as maladjustment.[9] Davie is here pointing to a distinctive mode of secularization, whereby sin is redefined as maladjustment, and redemption as therapy. David Cecil, in his "Introduction" to *The Oxford Book of Christian Verse* (1940), hews a line quite close to Christian orthodoxy that is not without problems.[10] The inclusion of William Blake could be one of them, but in practice Blake has to be included, notwithstanding his major heresies. Blake is peculiarly interesting, because he can be understood as retrieving elements of Christianity, notably antinomianism, which no church could preach without courting social disaster, something that the apostle Paul recognized from the start.

A final problem concerns what exactly is to be included under the heading of English poetry, especially as this problem mutates from questions primarily relating to the other national cultures of the British Isles to questions relating to English as a global culture, more particularly in North America and the British Empire. There is increasing interchange of insular English with global, and especially American, English. Sometimes that interchange is very important, for example through the influence of poets like Whitman, Longfellow, and Emily Dickinson. There are also major poets like Les Murray in Australia and Derek Walcott in the West Indies. Both would be perfect for this kind of enquiry. Walcott is interesting given his Methodist background in the dominant Catholic culture of Santa Lucia; and Murray is interesting as a Catholic in an Australian culture affiliated to the English pattern of Protestant dominance. But I cannot violate my criteria just because particular cases would be so germane to my purposes. Emily Dickinson is equally tempting; but once I yield to temptation, the canvas becomes too big to handle. T. S. Eliot is included because he not only became assimilated to English culture but became Anglican. In the twentieth century I marginally loosen my criteria for exclusion and inclusion.

---

9. Davie, *New Oxford Book of Christian Verse*.
10. Cecil, *Oxford Book of Christian Verse*.

Chapter 2

Ninth to Sixteenth Centuries

Of course, Anglo-Saxon as a developed language long antedated the ninth century, as did the two poems I want initially to discuss; and the very idea of a distinct English people using that language derives from Bede in his *Ecclesiastical History* in the eighth century. The two poems have sources in oral tradition, and they are the product of a prolonged evolution. I choose the ninth and tenth centuries as my baseline, simply because the reign of Athelstan (c.894–939), following in the wake of the English political and cultural resurgence under his grandfather Alfred, saw England more or less unified under a single royal authority.

At roughly the same period, the monasteries became fully integrated into the power structure as sources of legitimacy for the exalted genealogy of kings, a mutual support that continued for the next half millennium. As a result of the fusion of old and new, pagan and Christian, people first committed murder and mayhem according to the old style. But then, once their ends were achieved, they were free to express penitence in the new style. They were now free to seek divine forgiveness, and to use wealth to ensure that perpetual prayers were instituted for their translation to heaven. From the point of view of dynastic succession, it was expedient to kill other plausible claimants. It made for social order. Leaving survivors, out of incautious clemency or Christian scruple, had its disadvantages. The demands of paganism and Christianity had both to be satisfied, in a contradictory mix. From the point of view of the original repertoire of the New Testament, this Christo-pagan version of the economy of salvation amounted to a conspicuous secularization. Another way to put this is to suggest that endemic brutality was modified (some time in the first renaissance of the twelfth century) with those ideals of chivalry and courtesy to be observed much later in Chaucer's idealized portrait of the "parfit gentil knight."

Endemic brutal conflict tempered by sacrifice and forgiveness provides the context of *Beowulf* and "The Dream of the Rood."[1] *Beowulf* lies firmly within the assumptions of the heroic cultures of pagan northern Europe, where honor and the feud are the default background of everything that happens. It is a site of a Darwinian and Nietzschean struggle for status, honor, and dominance. Then "The Dream of the Rood" introduces the radically different Christian themes of self-sacrifice, salvation, and forgiveness, but in such a way as to relate them to the preexisting cultural assumptions. Christianity is grafted on to paganism without replacing it, and that is because radical change is most successful when it works by slow subversion. One indication of that is the way the rood, or the tree of the cross, is itself an actor in the drama. The sacred tree of the pagan past, with jewels and gems, is now marked by the Christian sign of the blood that has been shed for the redemption of humankind. Moreover, Christ is the warrior who heroically ascends the cross as savior and conqueror of death. But this theme of triumph in mortal combat had already been present in Christianity for centuries as part of an assimilation to antecedent models in Latin culture, and constantly renewed. *Finita jam sunt proelia*: the battle has been won once and for all. *Vexilla Regis prodeunt*: the royal banners go forward. Half a millennium or so later, we find the Scottish William Dunbar, in his poem on the resurrection, representing Christ as a lion and as a giant removing the fangs of the tiger of evil.[2] A millennium and a half later, triumph in the warfare of the cross reappears in David Jones.

In the eleventh century, English receives a major Latinate injection by way of French and of monastic Latin through the Norman invasion, so that, by about 1300, it becomes a creole uniting the Germanic north with the Latin south. The former language focused on the everyday, the latter language represented courtly power; but they fused as people mixed. Chaucer's English varied its register with the topic: predominantly "Saxon" vocabulary for physical functions, French vocabulary for elevated topics, whether real, or else artfully simulated, as in "The Nun's Priest's Tale."[3] Macaronic poetry alternated monastic Latin with folk English.

English poetry also became another kind of creole by fusing the pagan and the Christian. Pagan yuletide ditties and Christian carols jostle each

---

1. Davie, *New Oxford Book of Christian Verse*, 1–4; Heaney, *Beowulf*.
2. "On the Resurrection of Christ," in Davie, *New Oxford Book of Christian Verse*, 21–22.
3. Chaucer, *The Riverside Chaucer*, 3–328.

other in different combinations. The outer vesture of Christianity in the Middle Ages encompasses a deeply embedded paganism, just as in the early Renaissance it encompassed alchemy and astrology. "The Boar's Head in Hand Bear I" is a macaronic pagan poem that jostles the Coventry carol celebrating the birth of Christ.

These are centuries in which folk poetry occasionally emerged as powerful artistic creations. The themes included the pure and holy mother nurturing the divine son who is present in humanity and wounded and abandoned for the good of humankind. A perfect example of a folk poem is provided by:

> There is no rose of swich vertu
> As is the rose that bare Jhesu. Alleluia.
> For in this rose conteyned was
> Heven and erthe in lytyl space. Res miranda.[4]

The "vertu" of Mary is not simply purity but more akin to the healing power of a plant; and some of the Latin phrases used come from the liturgical Sequence for Christmas, *Laetabundus*. "The Lyke-Wake Dirge" is an extraordinarily powerful poem composed anonymously that expresses the omnipresent sense of death and judgment.[5] It concerns the fate of the soul, and expresses the condign justice of God rather than his mercy, based on a severe interpretation of Matthew chapter 25. As we sow so shall we reap.

> If meat or drink thou ne'er gav'st nane
> *Every nighte and alle*
> The fire will burn thee to the bare bane;
> *And Christe receive thy soule.*

A powerful poem that might well represent the whole repertoire is "Quia Amore Langueo."[6] It picks up the theme of the divine lover despised and rejected. A man sits under a tree. He is a seemly man to be a king, yet he is wounded to his heart and from head to foot. He gave all his love for his spouse, for his dear sister, the soul of man, and this is how he has been requited. "I crowned her with blysse and she me with thorne." An equally powerful representative poem, by Richard Rolle, begins "My trewesst tresowre sa trayturly was taken."[7] Rolle hymns the passion and all its manifold griefs, to conclude with a plea that Christ "be beryd in my brest and bring me to blisse." He was a Cistercian mystic, drawing on literary models of

---

4. "The Trinity Carol Roll," manuscript held by Trinity College, Cambridge, Library.
5. Cecil, *Oxford Book of Christian Verse*, 33–34.
6. Cecil, *Oxford Book of Christian Verse*, 25–29.
7. Cecil, *Oxford Book of Christian Verse*, 1–2.

sublimated love developed by St. Bernard. Rolle was part of a succession endangering clerical power that erupted in Lollardry and eventually in the Reformation. He was remarkably influential, and in his train there followed ecstatic women who were easily seen and targeted as sources of potential trouble to the authorities. Sometimes, as in the case of Margery Kempe, they undertook astonishing pilgrimages, and were feared for the power exercised by their erotic emotionality.[8]

Another poem to be placed alongside "Quia Amore Langueo" is the *Pearl*, a work of astonishing linguistic virtuosity and symbolic and numerological complexity written in the East Midlands dialect.[9] *Pearl* is thought to be by the unknown author of three other poems, including the chivalric *Sir Gawain and the Green Knight*. He was a contemporary of Chaucer in the late fourteenth century, but his kind of vision and his theological meditations are remote from the humane observation of manners found in Chaucer. It seems generally agreed that the loss of the "pearl" has to do with the real loss of a young daughter, aged only two. I abridge the details, just to bring out the remarkable theology of a poet-narrator who may have been writing for clerics. Like Piers Plowman, he falls asleep and has a dream of a beautiful woman on the other side of a river whom he takes to be his lost daughter. She inhabits a paradisal landscape very like the landscape pictured in the much later visions of Traherne. She tells the poet-narrator that she is the Queen of Heaven, and shares with all the redeemed in the benefits of the shed blood of the Lamb in the shining city described by John the Divine in Revelation. All are equal in having obtained the "pearl of great price" that offers the key to the everlasting kingdom of bliss. They each receive the same "bonus" of grace enjoyed by all the laborers in the Lord's vineyard, whether they arrived early or late to do the Lord service. Underlying this, there is the perpetual problem of the equality of sin, presumably shared by all the "children of men" since Adam's disastrous fall, the myriad early deaths of those we deem innocent victims, and what is required for participation in the benefits of peace and bliss flowing from the wounded side of the Lamb. At times the querying skepticism of the grieving father confronted by the deft theological moves of the wondrous "pearl of great price" could almost be read as bemused reflection along the lines of the carol, where the Virgin's role as queen of heaven all depends on the fatal bite of the apple. There is no glory without transgression, no salvation history at all without the "fortunate fall," "as clerkes finden / wretyn in here book."

---

8. Beckwith, *Christ's Body*. Beckwith gives an account of the subversive anti-clerical power exercised by Margery Kempe.

9. Armitage, *Pearl*; Hatt, *God and the Gawain Poet*.

With Gower, Chaucer, and Lydgate, named and prolific authors, we shift to a very different atmosphere. It remains Catholic in ambience, but full of skepticism about the church as manifested in its local representatives, apart from Chaucer's "Poor Parson of the Town" who is praised for practicing the Christian life even as he taught it. The story of the unbelievable virtue of "Patient Griselda" in "The Clerk's Tale" reads like an ironic critique of female submission, while the "Prioress's Tale," about the fate of little St. Hugh of Lincoln, is marred by the ubiquitous anti-Semitism of the time. John Lydgate (1370–1451), a poet consciously writing in the wake of Chaucer, might be a monk and prior, but, on his own confession, he lived a profligate life, always on the verge of ecclesiastical censure. He wrote moralities, many of them political, narratives from the Greek classics, translations from French medieval literature, and many lives of the saints, including *The Life of Our Lady*.

Some of the most powerful poetry of the late Middle Ages, replete with intimations of Renaissance humanism and classical reference, was written in Scots. The best known names are Robert Henryson, William Dunbar, and Gavin Douglas. In his *The Bludy Serk* ("serk" means "shirt"), Henryson weaves an allegory around the knight Christ, rescuing us from the giant Lucifer by his saving death, and Dunbar writes major poems on the incarnation and the resurrection.[10] John Skelton (1464–1529) was, like John Lydgate, a clerk in holy orders, but in poems like *Speke, Parrot* he was linked to the Scottish tradition of religious and political satire. This was a form of courtly insult practiced, among others, by William Dunbar, in which contenders traded insults known as flytings. There was a European-wide fascination with Erasmian folly, and *The Ship of Fools*, (English translation, 1509) shared in this satirical tradition.

I have already suggested that the distribution of absences and presences in Christian poetry does not fall into the slots demarcated by the beginning and endings of centuries. To that must be added the fluidity of religious positions in the sixteenth century. At the same time, a fundamental break with the past has been accomplished by 1560, with at least the establishment of Protestantism, if not its universal acceptance. The continuity of a Catholic tradition has been carefully documented historically by Eamon Duffy and discussed by the literary scholar Alison Shell.[11] The liturgy of 1549, translating the Sarum rite, became the Protestant liturgy of 1552 under Edward VI. All this was reversed in the reign of Mary, until, at her death, her Protestant

---

10. Cecil, *Oxford Book of Christian Verse*, 19–23.

11. Duffy, *Stripping of the Altars*; Shell, *Oral Culture and Catholicism in Early Modern England*.

half-sister Elizabeth inaugurated the compromise liturgy of 1559. This process of rapid and disconcerting change, followed by total or partial reversal, and then further pressure to radical change, came to a startling fruition in the political upheaval of the Commonwealth. It was still working itself out in the American Revolution over a century later.

Yet Catholicism retained a real presence, and one that was feared throughout the seventeenth century and as late as the 1745 rebellion. Catholicism was seen as the subversive "privy paw" identified by Milton in *Lycidas*. Milton's magnificent apologia for liberty of opinion in *Areopagitica* (1644) did not include those he identified as its enemies, among them Catholics. The same is true of Locke's *A Letter Concerning Toleration* (1689), marking a shift from Christianity understood as the prop of state power, to Christianity understood as the personal practice of virtue. It is impossible to avoid such anticipatory reflections, because they are the persistent context of English poetry. Ben Jonson was converted to recusancy for a period, Donne wavered between the English Church and Catholicism, Crashaw converted to Catholicism to become a baroque poet in exile, Dryden became a Catholic, and Alexander Pope was a Catholic, of sorts. Perhaps it is worth noticing here, as my daughter Jessica Martin has pointed out, that Protestants long relied on Catholic devotional models, such as *The Imitation of Christ*, including contemporary examples. A similar point concerning Protestant recourse to Ignatian models of meditation was made by Louis Martz.[12]

In returning directly to poetry in the sixteenth century, one really needs to begin with the teetering ambiguities set in train in the terrifying reign of Henry VIII. David Cecil's *Oxford Book* offers nothing at all for this period, and Donald Davie's *New Oxford Book* next to nothing, except a poem by Thomas Wyatt on Psalm 130. This is a paraphrase, among others, of (mainly) penitential psalms composed, like those by his friend Henry Howard, under threat of execution. Likewise Ann Askew's extraordinarily moving paraphrase of Psalm 54: the sentiments of the psalmist are appropriated to express individual responses to personal extremity. Miles Coverdale's *Ghoostly psalmes* (c.1535) do not feature at all. But the Reformation once successfully established, we have in the 1590s the remarkable Sidney Psalms of Mary Herbert and Philip Sydney, drawing on Protestant sources, including Coverdale. Psalms were relatively safe, and authors were reluctant to commit themselves more explicitly in poems, when getting it wrong could have very serious consequences.

The case of Wyatt (1503–1542) indicates the complexity of the issue, and requires some brief exploration bearing on the practice of several poets

---

12. Martz, *Poetry of Meditation*.

in turning to the Penitential Psalms. Wyatt can be regarded as the first "modern" poet in English literature, and his context is the increasingly oppressive Henrician court, where opaque expression was a necessity of survival. As a poet influenced by Italian models, both in his secular and his religious poems, Wyatt finds a stimulus in the writing of Pietro Aretino. He follows through the psalms in sequence, with Psalm 51 ("*Miserere Mei*") providing a climax, treating them as the autobiographical work of King David. David is a sinner, guilty of adultery and treachery, who seeks after divine grace. The poems work through key themes of Protestant theology as they contemplate the divine hand upon David and his helplessness before grace. In the end sin fails and mercy prevails.[13]

Edmund Spenser (1552–1599) is a major poet writing in the 1570s and 1580s during the reign of Elizabeth. He is a Protestant who represents a syncretic theological middle way which takes marriage as normative rather than the Catholic privileging of celibacy. Here, according to Bonnie Lander Johnson in *The Language and Literature of Chastity* (2016), one has to recollect the persistent personal and political salience of chastity. It is Spenser who, for quality and quantity, needs to be weighed in the balance against the contention that this is a relatively secular century. His *The Shepheardes Calendar* (1579/1580) is mainly concerned with shepherds of the Lord's flock, whether or not they are hirelings. It is an essay in ecclesiastical polity, taking Virgil's *Georgics* and rendering them Christian. Here one has to emphasize, yet again, that a classical and classicizing background is throughout to be taken for granted as the universal basis of a Renaissance humanist education. Spenser's *The Faerie Queene* (1590s) is a very long and coded poem drawing on classical and Italian models that simultaneously recommends various moral virtues in the persons of Arthurian knights and exalts Elizabeth (Gloriana) while criticizing her. It sets out the proper moral qualities of the gentleman. It is religious to the extent that Chaucer's portrait of the perfect knight is religious.

What of the protean ambiguity of Shakespeare? "Sonnet 146" provides the single example in both David Cecil's and Donald Davie's anthologies. It is unique among Shakespeare's sonnets for its quasi-religious philosophising, but hardly unambiguous. It has to be set against other expressions, for example in "Sonnet 30," sadly recollecting friends lost in "death's dateless night." Arguably the sonnets carry weight as evidence because in them we are closer to Shakespeare's own voice than in the plays. In the plays, Shakespeare may be expressing either the hierarchical world view of the time, or else adopting particular voices, ventriloquized as appropriate to particular

---

13. Brigden, *Thomas Wyatt*.

situations, like Macbeth talking about life as a "tale told by an idiot . . . signifying nothing." Complexity is further increased by the Christian thematic materials of the late plays, notably forgiveness and resurrection, as discussed in Sarah Beckwith's *Shakespeare and the Grammar of Forgiveness* (2011). Beckwith explores how the late "post-tragic" plays fill the hiatus left by the abolition of the sacrament of penitence.[14]

Alison Shell explores the issue of "Why didn't Shakespeare write Religious Poetry?" in chapter 6 of a volume edited by Takashi Kozuka and J. R. Mulryne (2013). What she argues bears quite directly on the erotic secularity of the sixteenth-century verse, at least up to the closing years of the century. She takes off from the dedication of Robert Southwell's collection of verse containing "St. Peter's Complaint," a major example of "tears poetry," and exploring extreme emotions in the context of Christian contrition. It could be that Southwell had Shakespeare specifically in mind in his dedication, but that is less important than his plea for a reform of English poetics away from popular erotic profanities to divine subjects more proper to the poet. Alison Shell suggests that, while the Reformation did not completely kill off religious verse, it suspected the exercise of human imagination on divine topics, particularly because they added to Scripture. The unintended consequence of this suspicion was the secularization of verse. Catholics (and people of similar mind) for their part cited practices of verse-making (and singing) in the Bible to justify extra-biblical compositions, and so far succeeded that, by the end of the century, there was a shift to sobriety and religious poetry.[15]

Here we need to explore the marginality of Catholic poets like Southwell (c.1561–1595) and Crashaw (c. 1613–1649) to the English canon, as discussed by Alison Shell in *Catholicism, Controversy and the English Literary Imagination, 1558–1660* (1999), at the same time keeping in mind the potent role of English revenge tragedies set in corrupt and violent Catholic Italy as a form of anti-Catholic propaganda.[16] Catholic poets have not only been marginalized but excluded from the roll-call of approved victims,[17] partly because treated as un-English, even when, as in the case of Crashaw, they were still writing as "Anglicans."

Yet their work has a claim to importance alongside Donne and Herbert, above and beyond such poems as Southwell's "The Burning Babe" and

14. Beckwith, *Shakespeare and the Grammar of Forgiveness*.

15. Shell, "Why Didn't Shakespeare Write Religious Verse?" in Kozuka and Mulryne, *Shakespeare, Marlowe, Jonson*, 85–112. Alison Shell comments on the anti-Catholic prejudice of the British intelligentsia up until quite recently.

16. Shell, *Catholicism, Controversy and the English Literary Imagination*.

17. Gregory, *Salvation at Stake*.

Crashaw's "Hymn to St. Theresa," and they were at the time comparable presences. There is an English Catholic baroque, for example, a tradition of tears poetry long antedating the Reformation. The publication of Southwell's 1595 collection made non-biblical poetry increasingly acceptable, and helped stimulate the moral debates conducted by poetic theorists. Yet Southwell's collected poems, like Crashaw's, are out of print. It is as if Southwell's importance is merely as a recognized harbinger, when he was a continuing influence, for example on book three of Giles Fletcher's "Christ's Victorie" (1610). Herbert's and Vaughan's intolerance of secular verse derived from Southwell, and his poems met a devotional need which Protestants only tardily acknowledged on account of Protestant nervousness about imaginative literature as idolatry. In practice, the poems could be read indifferently by Catholics and Protestants. But educated Protestants took their time recognizing the value of imaginative literature, even though the theme of contrition, surpassing even the lamentations of Jeremiah and drawing on the penitence of David, helped recommend it. Alison Shell concludes that Southwell influenced Herbert's whole career, and that he challenges the conventional association of Protestantism with inwardness. She also concludes that ecstatic weeping in the tears tradition affected Southwell's two most important heirs, the Catholic converts William Alabaster and Richard Crashaw.

Chapter 3

Seventeenth and Eighteenth Centuries

Once we come to the seventeenth century, we have to be conscious of an approach to "the Metaphysicals" provided in the early to mid-twentieth century by T. S. Eliot, Herbert Grierson, and Helen Gardner, and of reactions to that approach. The Metaphysicals are not a group, but need at least to be separated into Donne and Herbert as belonging to an earlier period and the others to a later. One Metaphysical poet, Thomas Traherne, was virtually unknown until the twentieth century; and the term "metaphysical" was coined by Samuel Johnson as an expression of opprobrium. Nevertheless, David Cecil seems to take a view of them as a group for granted, with Donne indisputably the leading figure, and the "Caroline poets" trailing in his wake.

All things considered, it seems reasonable to see this period as an efflorescence of religious poetry. Moreover, this was a time, unlike succeeding centuries, when the minor poets, such as Wither, Quarles, Suckling, Carew, and Lord Herbert of Cherbury, could often write as powerfully as the major ones, and on precisely the same themes, of faith, devotion, love, and death.[1] Thomas Carew wrote indifferently numerous love poems and psalm paraphrases. Francis Quarles's mystical poem on the Song of Songs, "My beloved is mine and I am his" (set by Britten) is one the greatest poems in the language.

It is worth emphasizing that these Christian poets are mostly a twentieth-century rediscovery. Their writings, insofar as they were well known, were understood against the pervasive backdrop of the erotic poetry of

---

1. Howarth, *Minor Poets of the Seventeenth Century*.

cavalier court poets, like Ben Jonson and Thomas Carew, and for some parts of their lives they were very actively part of that world. John Donne represents a crux in every sense of the word. The "divine poems" share with his earlier erotic poems an obsessive concern with the flesh. They represent Christianity at a historical juncture in deploying a "modern" frame of reference that includes science, medicine, and the new world of discovery, but they can barely be understood apart from the cultural assumptions of Christianity in general, meaning incarnation, redemptive death, resurrection, second coming, and last judgment, and the very distinctive articulation of these central doctrines at that particular historical moment. Modern readers retaining access to Christianity, by upbringing or by literate education, are aware of what is both familiar and distant. The strenuous intellectual and emotional power of Donne's serious play with the central paradoxes of the divine humanity and the dying God still engages us. Yet the Christianity of a contemporary informed Christian is framed very differently, for example, with regard to "the kingdom of God" understood proleptically as poised in the eschatological future, and also with regard to what doom awaits us should we fail to respond to the offer of salvation. In the poetry (and prose) of Donne we encounter an onset of early modernity.

The point about prose matters, because poets like Donne, Milton, and Traherne, as well as writers like Lancelot Andrewes and Thomas Browne, write a kind of prose that often has the impact of poetry. Their prose had all the imaginative impact of poetry. There were also prose writers in the style of the "Cambridge Platonists," who stood between the Laudians and the Calvinists by following a biblical Wisdom tradition for which the light of reason was "the candle of the Lord." This was the great age of the sermon, reaching back to the major figures of the Reformation: the lineage runs back to Hugh Latimer. As in the case of poetry, so in the case of the sermon: nothing comparable emerges until the mid-nineteenth century.[2]

Donne and Herbert are the key poets of the efflorescence of religious poetry in the earlier phase. They embody an internal dialectic of sacred and secular, in that they both inhabited the secular world of the court and the sacred world of the church. Yet the contrast between the two worlds at this period is not so great as you might suppose from a reading of Izaak Walton's *Lives*, because Walton is keen to stress a change of heart which was in fact not all that much of a change of milieu, at least for Donne.[3] Of the two, Herbert has a smaller range, and his meditative devotional character enables us to appropriate him without so many disturbing wider questions. His poem

2. Sisson, *The English Sermon*; Seymour-Smith, *The English Sermon*.
3. Martin, *Walton's Lives*.

on "Prayer," with its cumulative cascade of images, conveys his sensibility and intellectual spirit perfectly: prayer is

> Exalted manna, gladness of the best,
> Heaven in ordinary, man well drest...[4]

Herbert is the progenitor of Vaughan and Crashaw, inasmuch as they both refer back very directly to his 1633 collection, *The Temple*. Because Herbert did not experience the vast disruption of the Civil War and Commonwealth, he represented harmony, stability, and order. Both Vaughan and Crashaw lived through those times as adherents of a proscribed tradition, and Crashaw, of course, became a Catholic priest before going into exile. Vaughan's most important poetic output carries a double meaning, one metaphysical, the other psychological. His references to the bliss of childhood, with Neoplatonic overtones, might seem to reach forward to Wordsworth's ode, "Intimations of Immortality from Recollections of Early Childhood," but they also refer back to the halcyon days before the Commonwealth. In a similar way, Vaughan's poem "Peace," evoking a secure realm of peace "beyond the stars," also refers forward to an almost unimaginable future where the old liturgy has been restored.[5] It also illustrates a characteristically Christian capture of military imagery, such as the secure fortress, the warrior sentry, and the child who "commands the beauteous files," for the beatific vision of peace.

Milton (1608–1674) is an outlier, because he is ultimately the most influential protagonist of Commonwealth ideals insofar as they promote conscience, freedom of opinion, and the separation of church and state destined to emerge finally in the USA. He is also a Renaissance humanist who not only facilitates a second influx of Latinity into English but constantly refers back to classical models in poems like *Lycidas* and *Paradise Lost*. In *Paradise Lost*, Eve is Venus and also Narcissus on an Ovidean model. Most of the poems best known today were written before Milton was thirty, and breathe a rather different atmosphere from his later work. They include the "Ode on the Morning of Christ's Nativity," which sounds like an orthodox celebration of the birth of the Savior and of his incarnation and self-sacrifice. Christ brings peace and blessedness in the conflict between Hercules as a type of Christ, and Leviathan, and completes a linear conclusion to history after many cycles. Other poems, for example "L'Allegro and Il Penseroso" (published 1645?) and "At a Solemn Musick" (1633–34) display an

---

4. Herbert, *Complete English Poems*. The classic study is John Drury, *Music at Midnight: The Life and Poetry of George Herbert*.

5. Davie, *New Oxford Book of Christian Verse*, 114.

appreciation of the cloistered life and of "service high and anthems clear" that might feed the idea of an early Laudian phase in Milton's life. In the masque *Comus* (1634), Milton celebrates chastity as a Neoplatonic victory of right reason over desire and the body. In "Lycidas" (published 1638) he uses a pastoral elegy in the classical vein to celebrate a friend untimely cut off who is a true shepherd of souls rather than an hireling.

Milton has been celebrated and denounced at different times, often on account of his republican politics. His portrait of Satan has been regarded as heroic, and his portrait of God as unattractive. It really is impossible to bring together the range of Milton's reception history, particularly as it developed in the twentieth century. Perhaps the most that can be indicated here concerns his view of the operations of Providence, especially given the recent analyses of the historian Alexandra Walsham.[6] According to her, the Puritan spirit both did away with the structure of mediation (as Sarah Beckwith also argues in relation to the sacrament of penance) and gave fresh prominence to the doctrine of providence.

It is this doctrine that lies at the heart of *Paradise Lost* (1667) and of "Samson Agonistes" (1667–70?). "Samson Agonistes" may be variously dated, depending on whether it is seen as a response to Milton's divorce or his blindness or the failure of the revolutionary cause. The critical consensus favors a late date after the royalist restoration. At any rate, both *Paradise Lost* and "Samson Agonistes" set out to "assert Eternal Providence and to justify the ways of God to man." The problem here, as Jessica Martin has pointed out, is that Milton, as a mere creature, asks whether he is really in a position to question what the "Dispose of Highest Wisdom brings about," though he knows there are many apparent reasons to doubt its operations.[7] In *Paradise Lost*, the divine Son volunteers himself to undergo a humiliation that will satisfy God's justice and release his mercy. In "Samson Agonistes," the protagonist wrongly impugns God's justice until he realizes by painful steps of slow illumination how he is to work that out in his own sacrifice. In both poems, against the background of a landscape that is both biblical and Classical, there is a fundamental critique of the kind of heroism represented by Satan, and of the unregenerate physical power of Samson, in favor of patience, faith, and love.

Andrew Marvell (1621–1678) also lived through the Commonwealth period, but he partly conforms to the regime, and he is in any case an ambiguous and transitional figure. Given that I have had a relatively small acquaintance with Marvell, apart from "To His Coy Mistress," and that he has

6. Walsham, *Providence in Early Modern England*.
7. Martin, *John Milton*.

been the subject of vast critical controversy, especially since the nineteenth century, I rely on an unsigned essay, published by the Poetry Foundation, which provides an interpretation of his ambiguity including its implications for the secularization of the public sphere.[8] This interpretation would point forward to Locke's *Letter Concerning Toleration* (1689) on religion as personal virtue rather than as a vehicle of political domination, but it takes off more immediately from Hobbes's *Leviathan* (1651), as arguing, in Machiavellian mode, that power is its own justification. There are two secularizations here, both momentous and neither based on how many people practice or believe.

The poems under particular scrutiny include the "Horatian Ode" of 1651, "The Garden" (1668?) and "Bermudas" (1654). Marvell initially composed lyrics that combined metaphysical wit with cavalier grace. But in his "Horatian Ode," looking back to the victory of Augustus at Actium, he became the first panegyrist of the Protector as embodiment of the will to power and historical necessity, and also his satirical critic in the later style of Dryden and Swift. Marvell's "Ode" signals a transition throughout Europe from a medieval Christian society, with its notions of ancient rights, to modern secular society. This entails a split between the raw exigencies of public life and what is possible by way of individual withdrawal to "The Garden," understood as an enclosure and a prelapsarian Eden. This brings into play the tension between the exigencies of the political discussed earlier in the introduction and the Christian visionary imagination. In "Bermudas," the route to Eden symbolizes individual withdrawal and implies a Puritan critique of the earlier transfer of love poetry to devotional poetry as an idolatry of our "devices and desires." As in the discussion of the sixteenth century, this critique secularizes the sphere of art and culture by leaving it to the occupation of the profane. But this is a very specific type of secularization: one associated with a particular viewpoint that is not generalized to become a universal social condition. The poem itself has been endlessly discussed with regard to the veracity of the account given of an extraordinary expedition, establishing the first Anglophone republican commonwealth in the New World. An article in *The Times Literary Supplement* (January 13, 2017) by Jonathan Sawday provides firm evidence for the accuracy of the account.[9]

The eighteenth century, whether or not seen as the so-called "long" eighteenth century, has often been regarded as rationalistic and hostile to

---

8. "Andrew Marvell," www.poetryfoundation.org/poems-and-poets/poets/detail/andrew-marvell, accessed September 2016.

9 Sawday, "A Kinder Isle?" 15–17.

religious poetry. There is a great deal to be said for that viewpoint, and it is built into my argument. Perhaps one could say that, in the seventeenth century, even prose emulated poetry, and, in the eighteenth, even poetry emulated prose. But there are other major currents and they need to be explored. At any rate, the eighteenth century needs to be broken up. Its earlier years saw religious poetry written by Alexander Pope, for example "Messiah" (1712), referring back to Virgil's Fourth *Eclogue*, and by Joseph Addison, in compositions like "The Spacious Firmament on High." For Addison, writing from the perspective of latitudinarian optimism, our situation might be miserable, but it was nevertheless alleviated by the operations of a divine providence including the hope of immortality. For Pope, poetry was mainly a medium for elegant moral reflection, as in *An Essay on Man* (1733–34).[10] *An Essay on Man* belongs to the category of a moral epistle and it reflects on man's position on "this isthmus of a middle state," in one way obviously powerful, especially through science and reason, but also confused and vulnerable, in a world where "whatever IS, is RIGHT." The *Essay* is religious in the very general sense of taking up Milton's attempt to "justify the ways of God to man," and its eventual reception (for example Voltaire's satire of it in *Candide*) suggests that it fails in this optimistic enterprise. It is a failure that presses on either to skepticism or to a more orthodox Christianity.

Samuel Johnson's *The Vanity of Human Wishes* (1749) is religious in the same general sense, reflecting, rather in the manner of Old Testament Wisdom literature, on the profound frustration of human desires, ambitions, and aspirations. Johnson's poem is one of the pinnacles of English literature, and reminds us yet again of the ubiquity of classical reference in English poetry. It is a reworking of Juvenal's Tenth Satire on the futility of human projects, substituting Charles XII for Hannibal but expressing pity for the fallen hero, rather than mockery. Johnson, in philosophic vein, concludes that Christian values are central to virtuous living.

James Thomson's *The Seasons* (1726–30) was a remarkably influential poem, and its popularity lasted for at least a century. It again illustrates the ubiquity of classical reference as a Latinate version of Virgil's *Georgics* relocated in England. Thomson was saturated in the biblical world of his Scottish Christian upbringing, but moved towards a more generalized religious understanding. *The Seasons* has been seen as deistic in its approach, as well as owing a great deal to science, including optics, to illuminate its understanding of the unity and harmony of nature. For this approach, Newton was the visionary prophet unveiling the majesty of God in Nature and providing what turned out to be the last guarantee of an underlying ontological

---

10. Pope, *An Essay on Man*.

harmony. But there is another viewpoint that sees Thomson's work as part of a pervasive sensibility known as the "Religious Sublime," now to be discussed through an analysis persuasively set forth by David B. Morris in his *The Religious Sublime: Christian Poetry and Critical Tradition* (1972).[11]

Morris accepts the broad characterization of the eighteenth century as secular. He accepts the idea that, in general, the century lay between the explicitly religious poetry of much of the seventeenth century and the religious preoccupations of the nineteenth. He reminds us that this was the time of expanding commercial empire, of growing nationalism, and of the emergence of the common reader. Yet he regards much of the eighteenth century as characterized by the "Religious Sublime." Morris fastens in particular on John Dennis, a contemporary critic who provided a theory of the sublime as so rooted in the passions that it enabled poetry to restore the harmony of an inward paradise. In such a conception we have another early anticipation of Wordsworth. Dennis promoted the idea that religion represents the highest form of sublimity, especially the Christian religion, and above all as exemplified by the poetry of Milton. The highest poetic good rested on some combination of the Christian, the biblical, and the Miltonic, all three contributing to the sublime. This idea was remarkably influential, and it was associated with a great quantity of poetry, often ambitious in scope, though not often distinguished by quality. It dealt, for example, with the attributes of God, the infinite, and the four last things. Samuel Boyse actually wrote a poem in 1739 simply titled *Deity: a Poem,* and even Christopher Smart adopted the sublime style in his 1753 winning entry for the Seatonian prize, "On the Power of the Supreme Being." Jonathan Swift subjected the whole genre to ridicule, as illustrating human hubris, and Samuel Johnson was equally dismissive, ridiculing any human attempt to encompass the infinite. The influential viewpoint of Johnson will be picked up below.

Morris discusses three important poets representing the religious sublime: Joseph Addison, James Thomson, and Edward Young. Addison's contribution to devotional poetry is less important than his critical discussions illuminating the context of Thomson and Young. Of course, Addison praised reason as offering access to God, otherwise we fall into mere "enthusiasm," but reason also required imagination and Revelation. Imagination is appropriate for the exercise of devotion, since its sensory and visual character relates it to the passions. His poem "The Spacious Firmament on High" did not so much extol reason as exalt imagination for its ability to sustain religious convictions through the experience of God as manifest in Nature and "the spacious firmament." Reason was rendered persuasive

---

11. Morris, *The Religious Sublime.*

by the feelings in the strengthening of faith. The clearest expression of Addison's view emerges in Edmund Burke's treatise on the sublime, where he claimed that, when God intended we should be affected by anything, he did not rely on the precarious operations of reason, but rather endued reason with the resources of imagination.

For Thomson, in *The Seasons*, the poetry of natural description was more than mere painting in words but led rather though Nature to God.[12] In the tradition of Philip Sidney, citing scriptural practice as a justification for poetry, Thomson defended poetry as a divine art practiced from Moses to Milton. Morris comments that the storm in "Winter" reflects Thomson's understanding of sublimity in the form of terror. Though Thomson's religion contained deistic elements, he was not a rationalist physico-theologian. He believed that Nature and a providential God were mysteriously terrible, as well as benevolent. God "rides upon the storm," and also manifests himself in all the beneficent felicities of the world around us. Poetry stimulates faith and devotion, because it communicates an imaginative perception of Nature. The hymn that concludes Thomson's poem is appropriate, and, like the morning hymn of Adam and Eve in *Paradise Lost*, it is modeled on Psalm 148. It ends in "expressive Silence" simply because language cannot contain divinity.

Edward Young (1683-1765) was as influential as Thomson, and in his long poem "The Complaint: Night Thoughts on Life, Death and Immortality," (1742-46) he explored the "religious sublime." John Wesley and Coleridge both drew sustenance from his work. Apart from accepting the proper claims of reason, Young held that sense, passion, and feeling facilitated access to the truth. Among these facilitating sources, terror and sheer astonishment at the spectacle of a final dissolution played a major role. For such aids to faith, prose is inadequate, because only poetry can express the mystery of faith. All this, suggests Morris, implies that "the ethics of moderation and limitation were no longer adequate to sustain the religious and literary aspirations of a great many readers."[13] Limitation and resignation were giving way to an aspiration to soar to the divine. A new view of man's place in the scheme of things was emerging. Feeling and the sentiments of the heart became the key criteria in a way that paralleled Evangelical fervor. And sentiment was closely related to sentimentality. Here the popularity in England of Klopstock's *The Messiah* suggests an appetite for sensation and pathos. Morris comments that "only a reading of the religious literature of

---

12. Chalker, *The English Georgic*.
13. Morris, *The Religious Sublime*, 152.

the sentimentalists" assures one of the justice of Samuel Johnson's dictum that to describe the divine is to diminish it.[14]

Morris comments that there were other more promising possibilities for rejuvenating the sublime, to be derived from the treatment of biblical sublimity in the Hebrew Scriptures by Robert Lowth, especially Job, the Psalms, and the Canticles. This treatment had to do with the infinity of God, admiration of his manifold works, and gratitude for his favor. Lowth argued, in a manner reminiscent of Dennis, that this "conventional" mode of sublimity derived from strong passion in the Hebrew poets, and their ability to arouse such passion in others. For Lowth, as for Isaac Watts, Hebraic sublimity was essentially lyrical, based on passionate feeling in the poet and on the natural language of the heart. This unrivalled natural language was embedded in the nature of Hebrew versification. It was magnificently plain and simple, as befitted a primitive culture, and without recourse to restraint and artifice. There was a link between the primitive and the sublime, as well as a link with the Gothic, including the ghostly. Vijay Mishra in particular has pointed to manifestations of "the Gothic sublime."[15] Morris comments that a popular gusto for "Gothic machinery" implied a debasement of the taste for the supernatural. Edmund Burke added the element of obscurity alongside terror to the character of the sublime. A clear idea was a little idea, whereas obscurity offered scope for the imagination.

Christopher Smart was a distinctively Anglican poet. His best work is found in "A Song to David" (1763) and "Jubilate Agno," started in 1759 but not published until 1939. The immediate context is, again, Robert Lowth's analysis of the structure of Hebrew poetry: hence the genuinely Hebraic spirit of Smart's poetry in deploying biblical parallelisms governed by sense rhythms. For Morris, Smart viewed the world in almost Franciscan terms. He was a fool for Christ's sake. His supposed madness licensed his role as prophetic interpreter of God and even licensed his pregnant obscurity. The poet does not, in the more usual eighteenth-century manner, imitate nature, but feels an inner compulsion to serve as an intermediary to the spiritually unawakened. The widest diversity of created things is included in the mystery of God, the singular, the small or even the ridiculous. Things of little account, like the flea and the mouse, are to God singularities of infinite moment. All nature was of God, whether vast or minute, brutish or angelic, and shared in God's spirit. Whereas the physico-theologian is a spectator of God's finished handiwork, "Smart is a communicant of the mystery of God's

---

14. Morris, *The Religious Sublime*, 159.
15. "The Gothic Sublime," in Punter, *New Companion to the Gothic*, 288–306.

continuous presence in nature."[16] "Jubilate Agno" is a hymn to creation and all its variegated creatures that deploys the Bible from Genesis onward, and sounds like a supplement to the *Benedicite*. In his poetry, Smart is specifically Christian in rejecting the terror manifested in the tempest to celebrate power realized in meekness, peace, and prayer.

Smart also devised hymns that followed the liturgical cycle in a high Anglican tradition of fast and festival that went back to precursors like Thomas Ken, George Herbert, and George Wither. However, Smart's hymns were not suitable for congregational use. They were imaginative poems based on a complicated scheme of allusion, which went even beyond the Bible and the Prayer Book. They focused on mystery, miracle, sacrament and revelation rather than the universal and naturalistic frame of reference created by Newtonian science. Like Charles Jennens, in the epigraph for Handel's *Messiah* (1741), they consciously took their stand on the text from 1 Timothy 3:16, "Great is the mystery of godliness." Beyond that, they picked up a tradition of the English nation as a new Israel, found for example in James Thomson, and the view of the English Church as supplanting Rome.

Here I pick up an important argument put forward by Morris about the eighteenth century in general. He asks why eighteenth-century religious poetry differs "so markedly from that of the previous century."[17] According to a standard explanation, it was the age of reason that constricted religious and poetic emotion. For both Cleanth Brooks and W. K. Wimsatt, it was impossible for poetry and religion to unite without mutual dilution. Morris comments that this argument posits an impersonal force constraining individual writers, with the result that secular literature was suffused by pious religiosity, and explicitly sacred writing underwent a curious process of secularization.

Morris canvasses an alternative approach, starting with reference to the sermon as a forum of protean public debate rather an exhortation directed to the devout. We can see this as secular *if* we take Donne's *Holy Sonnets* and his sermons as our criterion of the religious. Morris says that we are rarely challenged to ask how the Addisonian mixture of secular and religious could create a work like *Robinson Crusoe*, oddly mixing economics and religion. Certainly, there was a lowering of religious temperature whereby clerics engaged, and engaged successfully, in rational polemics against the menace of free thought. In other words, rationalism by itself cannot explain the poetry of the period.

---

16. Morris, *The Religious Sublime*, 171.
17. Morris, *The Religious Sublime*, 198.

Morris turns instead to the means of expression, specifically the significance of print. A sermon by Whitefield to the uneducated represented a mode of oral interaction inimical to the sweet rationalism of a printed sermon by Tillotson. For the same reason, from the viewpoint of polite literature, the hymns of Charles Wesley were so much "spiritual Billingsgate" (as the contemporary insult had it) not written primarily for printed reproduction. Yet this was a century witnessing an explosion of printed media without parallel. Quite literally, print created the prosaic modern man of letters who was "the most lasting contribution of the eighteenth century to modern culture."[18] The prosaic character of contemporary religious literature was in part due to the press.

But then Morris also introduces an argument concerning changes in sacred poetry that turn on the poetics of Samuel Johnson as touched upon above. Johnson held that neoclassical poetry was inimical to the nature of religious ideas. What hampered religious poets was the imagination's necessary recourse to pictures, a view based on the analogy of painting. The poet required a subject capable of graphic representation. But omnipotence cannot be exalted and it is literally impossible to imagine or grasp heaven, God, or the last things. Beyond that, eighteenth-century poetry failed to explore personal religious experience, except through the broad contours of the congregational hymn. It ignored the conflict and resolution of sin and redemption, and the drama of choice, in favor of the didactic and of what inspired awed attention. Only when the influential analogy of the visual and painterly was replaced by the analogy of the oral and musical in the Romantic era could the blockage be overcome.

But the Evangelical and Methodist hymn writers did indeed explore personal religious experience, the drama of choice, and the conflict of sin resolved by redemption. They have acquired proper recognition only recently through the critical writings of Donald Davie (*The Eighteenth-Century Hymn in England* [1993]) and his inclusion of many examples of their excellence in his *Oxford Book of Christian Verse* of 1981.[19] A classic earlier appreciation of their work is found in Bernard L. Manning, *The Hymns of Wesley and Watts* (1942).[20] Manning emphasized the way Charles Wesley (1707–1788) deployed dense scriptural reference to create a tight theological argument in verse. Wesley focused above all on the progress of the soul in struggling to find redemption, for example in his major poem or hymn "Wrestling Jacob" (1742). The sequence of his hymns followed the progress

---

18. Morris, *The Religious Sublime*, 208.
19. Davie, *Eighteenth-Century Hymn*.
20. Manning, *Hymns of Wesley and Watts*.

of the soul from penitence to justification and sanctification rather than the sequence of the liturgical year. At the same time, there was a Eucharistic emphasis that even revived an ancient orthodoxy, as in the hymn celebrating the centrality of the epiclesis:

> Come, Holy Ghost, Thine Influence shed,
> And realize the sign,
> Thy life infuse into the bread,
> Thy power into the wine.[21]

The emphasis on the Spirit, experience and sanctification became part both of Methodism and Pentecostalism. Love, sometimes framed in erotic imagery, was central to his writing, for example, "Jesu, Lover of My Soul" and "Love divine, all loves excelling," in part a Christianization of Dryden and Purcell's "Fairest Isle." Charles Wesley believed in converting the secular, both in poetry and in music, to godly purposes. Apart from his classic preaching, missionary, and educational work, resembling the work of Franke in Halle, his brother John (1703–1791) introduced German hymns into English through several magnificent translations. "Ich habe nun den Grund gefunden" becomes (1740) "Now I have found the ground wherein / Sure my soul's anchor may remain." This is "experimental religion" influenced by Pietism and the Moravian brethren. The emphasis on feeling and experience, as well as reason, fits with broader shifts to sentiment and has even been understood as proto-Romantic. That point will be picked up later in discussing Romanticism.

Isaac Watts (1674–1748) was the "Father of English Hymnody." A product of a Dissenting Academy, he was learned in the classics as well as a logician. He sought to inform worship with devotional passion and to provide hymns that made the psalms of the biblical David speak like a Christian, for example in *Hymns and Spiritual Songs* (1707) and another collection in 1719. This meant, among other things, that his writing not only hymned the crucified Savior, but also celebrated the whole realm of nature. Wesley, by contrast, focused more exclusively on the soul and its redeemer: "My heart is full of Christ / And longs its glorious matter to declare." Not everyone recognized Watts's transformation of psalms into hymns, for example, the transformation of Psalm 90 into the classic hymn "O God our Help in Ages Past."

William Cowper (1731–1800) was a major poet as well as a hymn writer. As a hymn writer in the Calvinist tradition, he is best known for the *Olney Hymns* (1779), co-authored with John Newton, and as a poet he is

---

21. Rattenbury, *Wesley's Legacy*, 184.

best known for "The Negro's Complaint" (1788), reflecting the humanitarian concerns of many Evangelicals, and "The Task" (1785). This last-named work included scenes from everyday English country life that anticipated the concerns of the Romantic poets. In his later life, Cowper both engaged with the beauties of the external world and (for some commentators) suffered a devastation of his inner world as having committed the unpardonable sin that puts you beyond God's mercy. God was, in Cowper's own phrase, "His own interpreter," and had made it plain that Cowper was a lost soul. His suffering as "the stricken deer" anticipated a modern existential condition of inner chaos and outward dissolution. But that is not the only interpretation: his own hesitations and fears are met by an unchanging love, and the inexhaustible fountain of the Savior's blood washes away all his "guilty stains." In his *Moral Satires* (1780–81) such as "Truth" and "The Progress of Error" he both attacked the subversion of Christianity by reason and science, and set out the artless scheme of salvation.

This brings me to Marilyn Butler's classic discussion of the poets of a period well into the eighteenth century, from Gray and Collins to Macpherson and Chatterton, in her *Mapping Mythologies: Countercurrents in Eighteenth Century Poetry and Cultural History* (2015).[22] None of these poets was Christian, not even, it seems, Gray as author of the "Elegy Written in a Country Churchyard" (1750), but they were either indifferent to Christianity or directly opposed. Laurence Sterne in book 6 of *Tristram Shandy* (1760s) gave Christianity only a very few decades to survive. There was a "country" or provincial party interested in antiquarian pursuits, including bardic and pagan elements and the Welsh language, which set itself against the polite metropolis represented by people like Warton. Indeed, major figures in the literary world like Joseph Ritson and Thomas Spence were provincial, oppositional, politically radical, and atheist. That is precisely why I select the late eighteenth century as my baseline to bring out the second great efflorescence of Christian poetry, alongside the seventeenth century, in the Victorian period.

---

22. Butler, *Mapping Mythologies*.

Chapter 4

The Nineteenth Century
The Early Romantics

I begin with Blake, even though he is partly situated in the eighteenth century. For that matter, so is Wordsworth, and my problem here has already been mooted. It is that centuries are not particularly useful for the purposes of periodization, even though such distinguished scholars as Basil Willey have written books on literature treated century by century. I also need to slow the pace of my argument very considerably, because we are now in a time often considered proto-modern in its special problems of faith and doubt, and its embrace of subjective apprehension, of the historical perspective, and of what Coleridge (with a proper sense of linguistic roots) called comprehension.

I turn first to the specific problems and opportunities for an alternative secularization narrative presented by William Blake (1757–1827) and William Wordsworth (1770–1850). These are, of course, pivotal figures in any account of the course of English poetry. Blake was little known in his own lifetime, and (like Smart and Cowper) considered mad, but he reaches back to the radical religious anarchist and antinomian wing of the seventeenth century revolution. And the reception of his protean writings reaches forward to the Beat generation of the nineteenth-sixties, and also to twentieth-century English composers—indeed the use of poetry by these composers, especially Britten, is worth consideration in its own right. On one reading of Blake, he is an eccentric radical Christian, opposed to church and state. At the same time, in poems like "The Everlasting Gospel," he brought out aspects of the New Testament all too frequently overlain with conventional morality and Pharisaic legalism. Jesus embodies the sheer humanity of God, and he releases sinners from chains of suffocating moral condemnation that emanate from the Antichrist and Jehovah. On one reading, this is only a hair's breadth away from the classical Evangelical gospel. Blake expresses his understanding of the incarnation (perhaps without the definite article) in the lines "Thou art a Man, God is no more; thine own humanity learn to adore . . ."[1] On another reading, this is a radical humanism very close to the kenotic Christianity of God's self-emptying. Blake also showed the way to escape "warlike pomp," "The Miser's net and the Glutton's trap," and, in that way, revived sectarian social radicalism and anticipated the intellectual social critique furthered later by Ruskin. A major clue lies in Blake's aphorism, written on his engraving of *Laocoön*: "If Morality was Christianity, Socrates was the Saviour." In this, he identifies a first order category-mistake that vitiates rationalistic critiques of Christianity. For him, these critiques misunderstand faith as a set of falsifiable propositions. On the contrary, Christianity is a mode of interpreting lived experience. Blake fills this out in his negative attitude to all those kinds of understanding that rely on generalized abstractions, whether in the physics of Newton, the philosophy of Plato, or the paintings of Reynolds. Christianity is a work of the imagination and akin to the insights of art rather than the generalizations of science. The act of praise with which we daily greet the luminous marvel of the sun is a whole world different from any process of rational appraisal. The sun is not a "golden guinea" but a revelation of the whole angelic host.

This understanding of poetry and Christianity alike turns on the famous lines from "Auguries of Innocence" (1803), where Blake sees "a world in a grain of sand . . . and eternity in an hour."[2] Wordsworth expressed a similar viewpoint in 1798 in "The Tables Turned": "We murder to dissect."[3] For Blake and Wordsworth alike, whatever the vast differences between them, the organ of their understanding is imagination, so that both religion and poetry deal in wholeness, in particularity, in the projection of potential worlds lying in wait, and in the idea of visitation through what Blake called "the doors of perception."

Max Plowman, in his "Introduction" to the 1927 edition of Blake's *Poems and Prophecies*, claims that Blake's subject is the soul, an "unreasoning super-sensuous entity, divine in origin and destiny, whose perception and desire are infinite." "The god of the eighteenth century was Rational Behaviour,"[4] and the worship of that god radically reduced the emotional

---

1. "The Everlasting Gospel," in Blake, *Poems and Prophecies*, 350.
2. "Auguries of Innocence," in Blake, *Poems and Prophecies*, 333–37.
3. Wordsworth, *Selected Poems*, 202.
4. Blake, *Poems and Prophecies*, xii–xiii.

range of poetry. Blake had to choose between Spenser's *Faerie Queene* and the Blatant Beast of Pope's *Essay on Man*. The *Songs of Innocence* concern the childlike and undivided unity of our early heaven while the *Songs of Experience* concern the hell that presages disillusion, the divided self, cruelty, and mortality. "Awake, we live in Eternity, asleep, we exist in Time."

According to Marilyn Butler, the mystery of Blake is why he is only radical up to a point, "radical but not populist, apocalyptical but not revolutionary."[5] Though clearly opposed in principle to the church, property, war, the law, matrimony, and monarchy, he did not engage in active subversion, and his victims, foundlings, chimney-sweeps and prostitutes, belong as much to literary culture as real life. For Butler, his mature work begins with prophecies and creation myths in the Old Testament manner that are really about England as a tyrannical state warring against French and American revolutionaries. His manner was biblical, and, like Smart's, it followed on Lowth's analysis of the nature of Hebrew poetry. But his poem, *Jerusalem* (for which read London), is a British Bible, which, in the febrile atmosphere of the time, dangerously combined the language of religion with the idea of the popular nation. That part of the "Preface" to *Milton: A Poem*, set to music by Parry in 1917 under the title "Jerusalem," has become the British national song, embraced alike by radicals and conservatives, is far from surprising. But, unlike writers in the mold of the Welsh radical Iolo, who appealed to an ancient people as a natural constituency and launched a bardic grassroots nationalism, Blake wrote as an isolated individualist. His was the kind of artistic genius, identifiable from the prophet Ezekiel to today, that can reinvent the sacred texts. As a result the radical Chartists ignored him in favor of Shelley's *Mask of Anarchy*. In a wider perspective, perhaps, one may see Blake as participating in a shift to a horizontal transcendence, based variously on the kingdom about to come on earth through the nation and on the radical political fraternity, or else, as in Wordsworth, through Nature. His enthusiastic reception on the British left after the Second World War had much to do with his idealistic utterances on "artistic autonomy and personal fulfilment" ("Damn Braces, Bless Relaxes").[6]

Here I introduce a reading of Blake by Stephen Prickett that provides a bridge to Wordsworth and Coleridge at the point where the major changes associated with Romanticism in Western Europe are also present in England. I spend time on the transitions brought about by Romanticism because they are of singular importance. Stephen Prickett again picks up on the influence of Robert Lowth regarding the superior quality of biblical poetry. Just at the

5. Butler, *Mapping Mythologies*, 162.
6. Butler, *Mapping Mythologies*, 190.

point where the position of Christianity was weaker than ever before, the prestige of the Bible as literature was higher than ever before, and effectively displaced the ancient classics in esteem. The context here is Tom Paine's attack on Christianity, in particular the unfortunate stories attributed to Moses, as defaming the Almighty God revealed by Nature. Blake responds as a Bible believer and professed Christian to confute natural religion, disown these stories, and celebrate a Christ murdered on a cross for revealing a loving heavenly Father. He defends the doctrine of the Fall and sees natural disasters like the famous Lisbon earthquake of 1756 as due to sin.

Stephen Prickett regards Blake as to this extent biblical and orthodox. The natural religion against which Blake rails is a symptom of the late eighteenth-century shift whereby nature and history become part of divinity. The Fall is rejected, and the gap between God and Creation eliminated, a move that makes possible the perfectibility of man and inaugurates the bloody history of earthly utopia. Art (including poetry and music) becomes caught up in biblical aesthetics. "Aesthetics" is a new word that morphs into the sublime character of biblical poetry and the idea that Christianity is Art, as in Blake's "Great Code of Art." Aesthetics is, in this way, a prime vehicle of religion rather than ethics. Rephrased by Wordsworth and Coleridge, we are cocreators of all we experience through the Imagination. This fits entirely with Schleiermacher's rephrasing of religion as direct personal experience rather than the acceptance of doctrines on the basis of authority and the church. To acquire faith on the basis of tradition is not to have understood what faith truly is.[7]

There is more to the influence of Lowth, and it bears directly on the advent of Romanticism in England, and for that matter in Germany. It relates to what was earlier said about sublimity. Lowth's approach to poetic expression in the psalms and the prophetic books stressed what the reader brought to the text rather than what was innately present in the text. That immediately undermined straight appeals to its authority, rather as the Reformation idea of its plain and perspicuous meaning had earlier given rise to many rival interpretations. Lowth also undermined the idea that the Bible was inelegant and crude compared to the classics, so that whereas the classics had defined the heights of appropriate expression in 1700, by 1800 that eminence was occupied by the Bible. The Bible spoke in the unadorned accents of the ordinary humanity to which it was addressed, and it did so with "enthusiasm," meaning the emotionality for which the Methodists were held in such contempt.

---

7. Prickett, *Words and the Word*, 197 ff.

From enthusiasm and the common people, it was a short step to the engaged and active Imagination of the "Preface" to *Lyrical Ballads* (1798) and everyday language. As already suggested, there is a line running from John and Charles Wesley, first from "experimental" (or "experiential") religion to Wordsworth, and second from Methodism to Romanticism. But there are other mutations that lead to Shelley and Coleridge. In his "Defence of Poetry" (1821) against the skeptical animadversions of Thomas Love Peacock, Shelley revised the relation between Revelation and poetry to become the revelation brought by poetry understood as a vehicle of the divine. It lifted the veil lying over creation, and lent wonder to what had been merely familiar. Coleridge argued that the translucence of poetry in expressing revelation was realized in the psychological resonances of potent symbolism.[8] The Scriptures, as Stephen Prickett argues in *Romanticism and Religion*, are for Coleridge the channels of the imagination.[9] They convey universal truths in the special and particular, simultaneously ideals and pictograms. An imaginative symbol is stereoscopic in focusing science and art, the outward revelation and inward assent, the world of things and our intuitive selfhood with its moral awareness and judgment, the realm of necessity and the realm of vision. We do not live in a divided world, but one in which the parts are to be read in the context of the whole. This transcendent whole is realized and comprehended not in spite of language but through language and its living powers.

Marilyn Butler links Wordsworth's poetic doctrine back to the "country poets" discussed earlier. Hazlitt might regard Wordsworth's high estimate of the wisdom and speech of the poor, rustic, and humble, in the "Preface" to the *Lyrical Ballads* (1798), as uniquely egalitarian. But its source, alongside Percy's rediscovery of the ballad and Blake's primitivism, was above all Ritson's work on the songs of the common people. It is worth recalling in parenthesis that the extraordinary achievement of John Clare (1793–1864), only properly recognized in the second half of the twentieth century, was not only rooted in those songs, and in acute observation of a local natural world and its vanishing way of life, but presented to the literary world as the poetry of one who really was of "the poor."

Wordsworth's high estimate of the wisdom of the humble poor can easily be seen in his "Resolution and Independence," oddly included in Davie's *Oxford Book,* since the Christian element is at best tangential. The sophisticated poet, suddenly subject to inexplicable melancholy, even

---

8. Prickett, "Robert Lowth's Biblical Poetics and Romantic Theory," in Cohen and Berlin, *Interpreting Scripture*, 309–25.

9. Prickett, *Romanticism and Religion*.

though absorbed by impressions of uplifting natural phenomena, meets a sick old man, a leech-gatherer. On being accosted by Wordsworth he replies in words of such "lofty utterance" (like "religious men," says Wordsworth) that the poet felt in touch with a source of "stately" security and thereby rebuked. Wordsworth's complementary belief in the wisdom of Nature is most famously expressed in the lines from "The Tables Turned" (1802 and after) in the *Lyrical Ballads*:

> One impulse from a vernal wood
> Will teach you more of man,
> Of moral evil and of good
> Than all the sages can.[10]

Whatever the singular dubiety of this sentiment, Wordsworth, in common with Coleridge, is taking from Nature what he as an active organizing mind (rather than a bundle of passive impressions) puts into it.[11] Wordsworth's difference from Coleridge is that Coleridge very directly invokes the spontaneous activity of the Creator as the model of human creativity as well as rejecting the preference for the language of the common man. For Wordsworth the imagination rejects the generalized and urbane in favor of non-conceptual knowledge, and to that extent he resembles Blake. This knowledge is (in the famous phrase from the "Preface" to *The Lyrical Ballads*) the "spontaneous overflow of powerful feelings." It is found in intimations of the sublime distilled in tranquillity and in a "wise passiveness." But there is a constant oscillation between the "philosophic mind" keeping watch over man's mortality, and the renewal of childlike apprehensions of immortality that can be traced in the "Lines Written above Tintern Abbey" and in the Immortality Ode. There is a melancholy of loss and there is a return of perpetual benediction; there is a sad perplexity and there is a tranquil restoration.

The Immortality Ode raises the question as to whether Wordsworth is Christian, and does so in a way that contrasts sharply with the same question raised concerning Blake. The New Testament frequently contrasts mortality and immortality, for example in Paul's First Epistle to the Corinthians chapter 15, but the governing concept is that of resurrection. Wordsworth rarely turns to the core vocabulary of Christianity, and is credited with a statement made on his deathbed that he had no need of a redeemer. There is neither reference to resurrection nor to salvation from sin, atonement, or

---

10. Wordsworth, *Selected Poems*, 201.

11. For Wordsworth's approach, especially in *The Prelude*, it is important to consult Jarvis, *Wordsworth's Philosophic Song*; see also Prickett, *Romanticism and Religion*, especially chapter 3.

incarnation. In *The Prelude* (1805, 1850) where Wordsworth reflects on the French Revolution, men are not only born equal but they naturally aspire to fraternity, apart from the machinations of regressive tyrannies. At the same time there is a respect for the monastic impulse threatened by revolution, and (in a visit to the Grande Chartreuse) a respect for the cross as a sign of the dedicated, self-giving life. The cross exists in a sacred landscape rather as it does in the painting of Caspar David Friedrich, except that in Friedrich there is a more direct reference to the efficacy of salvation. There is also, in later Wordsworth, a sense of the importance of the ecclesiastical institution as a material representation of the sacred. The poem "Inside of King's College Chapel" (1820) precisely expresses this sense, and it also expresses an ethical desire (earlier expressed by Wordsworth in his sonnet, "The World is Too Much with Us; Late and Soon") to go beyond "nicely calculated less or more."[12] This ethic chimes closely with the generosity recommended in the gospel.

One poem in particular expresses Wordsworth's particular and partial mutation of Christianity into generic religion. In his "Devotional Incitements" (1832–1835) he first invokes the aspirations pleaded by the cathedral spire before regretting that "the sanctities combined / By art to unsensualise the mind" decay and languish like creeds in the storms of secular fanaticism.[13] He then recollects with relief that kindly Nature still keeps open "a heavenly door" with "mute harmonies," and "every day should leave some part / Free for a Sabbath of the heart." There is also in Wordsworth, for example in *The Prelude*, a desire to offer praise to the almighty giver in terms that parallel the *Benedicite*. It would be worth comparing the passages hymning the Creator in *The Prelude* with similar passages in Christopher Smart. The object is the same, and the source is biblical, but the tonality is very different.

Perhaps Wordsworth is generically religious while rather rarely being specifically Christian. By contrast, among his fellow Romantic poets, Coleridge is specifically Christian in subjective mode, though maybe more obviously so in prose than in verse, where he often focuses on extraordinary states of mind. Key exceptions might be "A Christmas Carol" (1799) and "My Baptismal Birthday" (1833), a poem in which he speaks of gaining true life by being Christ's child "by adoption," in a clear echo of Paul to the Romans, chapter 8, verse 15.

Keats embraces a fragmentary spirituality beyond the restrictive protocols of consecutive rationality, where the poet is himself an imaginative

---

12. Wordsworth, *Collected Poems*, 307.
13. Wordsworth, *Collected Poems*, 269.

seer celebrating a visionary power of insight into the holiness of love. Except in the despair of his final illness, there is also in Keats a belief that this life, understood as "a vale of soul-making," comes to fruition in an afterlife. Shelley is famous for his early essay on "The Necessity of Atheism" and for his early poem "Queen Mab," where he assaults the clergy, Christianity, and Christ as unique sources of violence, persecution, and oppression. But in "Adonais," his threnody for the death of Keats, he expresses a faith that wavers between theism and pantheism. It concludes with

> The soul of Adonais, like a star,
> Beacons from the abode where the Eternal are.[14]

Byron might seem the most insistent of the early Romantics in his rejection of Christianity and religion, especially the Anglican Church, which he despised as the (Whig) establishment at prayer. Yet the reality is more ambiguous. Though he doubted the historicity of the Bible and could make no sense of the atonement or the damnation of those who had never, or could never have heard the saving message, he remained haunted by the demons of the Calvinist upbringing he vehemently rejected. Shelley despaired of persuading him to make a clean break. If we take into account Byron's explorations in other religions, in orientalism, in paganism, and dualism, we have in these poets of early English Romanticism (as in German Romanticism) a strong reinforcement of the idea that religion or rather "spirituality" is individually appropriated and constructed. We also have a conspicuous reinforcement of the related idea of religion as individually chosen *or rejected*, a development built into the very idea of Protestant conversion *or its absence* since the Reformation. The way is also prepared for shifts to more Catholic ideas that begin in the 1820s. These reinforcements of personal choice represent a long-term trend, not a late modern development as has often been argued, because the seeds of late modernity have been flowering, often luxuriantly, over centuries.

---

14. Shelley, *Selected Poetry and Prose*, 505.

Chapter 5

The Mid-Victorians

A PROGRAMMATIC ANTICIPATION

So far I have traced through poetry the engagement of Christianity with paganism, Renaissance humanism, Enlightenment, and Romanticism. At this point I have to be programmatic and outline the future course of my argument, taking account of the massive changes in the Church of England as it roused itself from religious torpor in the second quarter of the nineteenth century. That arousal provides a context for much of the poetry of the period. I then comment on several massive poetic presences: the Brownings, Hopkins, and Tennyson, all deeply engaged by Christianity. I have a special interest in Elizabeth Barrett Browning's critique of the abstractions of social science. I also have to canvass explicit repudiations of Christianity, beginning with Arnold, who provides a major and exemplary focus of attention, but then discussing in turn a succession from Clough to Swinburne, Hardy, and Housman. At this period, there is also a shift to mystical apprehensions outside the ambit of Christianity. The same shift can be traced in European painting, so it is far from an English phenomenon. A minor English poet like Edwin Arnold, the author of *The Light of Asia* (1879), might suggest what I am talking about. There is a further shift away from what is held to be a life-denying Christian morality to more integral, joyful, aesthetic and life-celebrating paganism now lost. In Schiller's classic formulation, "Schöne Welt, wo bist du? Kehre wieder . . .": a lament for the lost world of classical beauty.

The turn to the aesthetic, explored earlier in the discussion of Lowth, does not necessarily have to be a turn to the world of classical beauty. It can appeal to various sources, including Catholicism. It is a theme that weaves in and out of Romanticism from the outset, and poetry often provides its vehicle. Because poetry by this time was a mainly private activity consumed in silence rather than a read performance, as earlier, the shift is most easily grasped in the context of music. Music is a public as well as a private (or chamber) art, and, in the early Romantic period, the public performance of works of genius was treated as an intimation of the divine through beauty, realized in the concert hall, which was regarded as a temple of profound seriousness. Music was prayer (mostly) without words. Of course, genius was a key Romantic category, and throughout the Romantic period one needs to hold together genius and intimations of the divine through beauty and the imagination. This is part of the appeal of ritual even for those of little or no faith: it fed the aesthetic imagination as a form of collective poetry.[1]

Of course, whatever the rival forms of religion emerging at this period, Christianity continues to provide the accepted frame of what is to count as faith, and there continue to be Christian poets, some of them marking a significant shift to Catholicism broadly understood: Christina Rossetti, Coventry Patmore, Alice Meynell, and Francis Thompson. These writers seem not concerned with the sort of questioning found in Robert Browning. Coventry Patmore is interesting as a Pre-Rapahelite who celebrated marital love, and, after his wife's death, wrote his best poem, *The Unknown Eros* (1877), on love, death, and immortality. Perhaps the shift to Catholicism has to do with the apodictic authority of the kind of religious experience found in Thompson's "The Hound of Heaven" and "The Kingdom of God." It is not so much a question of scrutinizing faith, item by item, asking what can be believed, as of responding to enriching experience as fostered within the holy community of the faithful. Eliot later expressed this approach in his essay on Pascal,[2] where he does not begin by asking about a particular doctrine, but by asking about the viability of a religious approach.

In the nineteenth century there is a version of Catholicism, or at least of Catholic sensibility, associated with a group of writers that includes Lionel Johnson, Aubrey Beardsley, Dante Gabriel Rossetti, Ernest Dowson, and Oscar Wilde. This sensibility is sometimes linked to the kind of "decadence" represented by J.-K. Huysmans, as it is also influenced by Baudelaire and Verlaine. These people, whether converts or simply attracted by the culture of Catholicism, were not so much engaged by dogma as by the appeal of

---

1. Dahlhaus, *Between Romanticism and Modernism*.
2. Eliot, *Essays Ancient and Modern*, 137–60.

Catholicism to the sensuous, the emotional, and the imaginative. The path to this sensibility had been laid down by the Pre-Raphaelites and the Tractarians, as well as by John Henry Newman, in spite of his strenuous intellectuality. According to Claire Masurel-Murray, the context was provided by the joint impact of Renan and Darwin, the one impugning the biblical witness to God and the other undermining Nature's witness to God.[3] The Catholic converts reacted generally against the desiccated picture of the world provided by science, and particularly against the scientific ideology of positivism. The Church of England, in its role as the national church, was too parochial to engage their loyalty, and also too affected by the adjustments to modernity sought by liberal Protestantism. The Church of Rome appealed by its universality, by being un-English, and by its firm stand against the corrosions of the age. Unlike Protestantism, it did not posit a gulf between transcendence and the mundane, but offered multiple mediations of transcendence in the mysteries of rite and sacrament, as well as the re-enchantments of monasticism, mysticism, and the Gothic. Of course, this was not the faith of the many thousands of Irish migrants in the newly constituted Catholic Church in England. But that did not undermine the appeal of aesthetic fantasy to a literary elite.

Catholicism of any kind was a minority faith compared with Protestantism, even though the Catholic literary genealogy was continued later by Belloc and Chesterton. Newbolt, Kipling, and Masefield were extremely popular poets who expressed a generalized and undogmatic Protestant view of the world, while Bridges expressed a refined Neoplatonic Christianity for a much smaller constituency of readers. In a poet like Kipling, with a huge constituency of readers, we encounter a popular male activism consonant with the "muscular Christianity" of the late nineteenth and early twentieth centuries, and even perhaps reacting to what was elsewhere seen as the feminization of Christianity and the mostly very minor poetry associated with it.[4] Kipling's very well known poem "If," with its celebration of stoic level-headedness, and Newbolt's perhaps equally well known poem "Vitaï Lampada" on sportsmanship and playing the game, fitted perfectly with the sporting ethos fostered by the YMCA.[5] Each of these poets requires some serious attention as the last of their kind.

Exactly when generalized Protestantism fell on hard times, apart from a negative residue persisting to this day in the exaltation of inward sincerity over ritual form, is for social historians to debate. But at some time in the

3. Masurel-Murray, "Conversions to Catholicism."
4. Gray, *Christian and Lyric Tradition in Victorian Women's Poetry*.
5. McLeod, "La Religion."

twentieth century there occurs what Eliot and David Jones describe as a momentous break in the succession where poets increasingly define themselves as Christian or as non-Christian. Donald Davie, in his *Under Briggflatts: A History of Poetry in Great Britain, 1960–1988* (1989), even places this change as late as the publication of *Milton's God* by William Empson in 1961.[6] In his comments on "The Religious Dimension," Davie also sets what is for him a critical moment within an interesting context.[7] He says that Empson's repeated attacks on Christianity represented a break with what had been a compact of mutual and perhaps contemptuous tolerance between believers and unbelievers. Empson sought to revive the old anger at the infamy of Christianity, and thus restored the issues of belief to the center ground.

"The Break," or whatever is meant by Eliot's comment about something having happened that has "never happened before," marks the point at which I look at poets who take traditional Christianity and its liturgy seriously, beginning with Eliot's conversion to Anglo-Catholicism in the 1920s, but proceeding as late as Geoffrey Hill and Michael Symmons Roberts. Just as the shift to Eastern mysticism is visible in European painting, for example, Kandinsky, so this shift to the liturgical is visible in European music, for example Messiaen and Poulenc even in the secularist context of France. These are pan-European shifts in consciousness.

So far I have set out the further reaches and broad outline of my program. As for the critical literature dealing specifically with the Victorian period (which is strictly several periods, given that Victoria reigned from 1837–1901) we need to question a still influential secularization narrative for which these years are mainly defined by doubt in the context of the industrial and scientific revolutions and biblical criticism. For those who take this approach, George Eliot is an exemplary heroine, and key examples can be found in works of the 1960s such as Joseph Hillis Miller, *The Disappearance of God: Five Nineteenth-Century Writers* (1963), and A. O. J. Cockshut, *The Unbelievers: English Agnostic Thought, 1840–1890* (1964).[8] Of recent years this narrative has been put under critical scrutiny by important voices in Victorian studies, for example Kirstie Blair and Karen Dieleman, as well as by the intellectual historian Timothy Larsen, in his *Crisis of Doubt: Honest Faith in Nineteenth-Century England* (2008).[9] After all, this was the time

---

6. Davie, *Under Briggflatts*.
7. Davie, *Under Briggflatts*.
8. Miller, *The Disappearance of God*; Cockshut, *The Unbelievers*.
9. Blair, *Form and Faith in Victorian Poetry*; Dieleman, *Religious Imaginaries*; Larsen, *Crisis of Doubt*. It is important to read Larsen on the ways in which the notion of a crisis of faith gained momentum, just as one should read John Brooke on how the crisis of faith and science gained momentum. A corrective to the crisis of faith idea can be

of the Oxford Movement and of the massive influence of Evangelicalism. In the fundamental perspective set out here, it really is implausible to treat the year 1850 as marked by accelerating doubt compared with 1790. The position is precisely the reverse. At the same time, the central role of faith needs to be placed in counterpoint with the problems raised by a revolutionary period, politically, socially, and intellectually, that lend verisimilitude to a secularization narrative and to the idea that we are dealing with *the* crisis of incipient proto-modernity. All this means we need to pay prolonged attention to the poetry of the time, both to its currents and to its countercurrents, to its massive belief and incipient doubt, and in what follows I focus first on the Tractarians, and then on the religious preoccupations of major figures like Robert and Elizabeth Barrett Browning, Christina Rossetti, Hopkins, and Tennyson.

LEANING TO FAITH?

I begin with the work of John Keble, especially in the enormously popular *The Christian Year* (1827), as progenitor of the Oxford Movement, which I treat from the perspective provided by Kirstie Blair in her *Form and Faith in Victorian Poetry and Religion* (2012).[10] Keble is a minor poet, but a major influence, and he represents the Tractarian espousal of external form, in particular liturgy, but also form and appropriate formality. Outward exercises performed and internalized as a matter of duty within a community of worshipers provided a proper foundation for inner sanctification and a prophylactic against insidious doubt and unruly passions, as well as the enthusiasm associated with Evangelicalism and Dissent. Keble, like Christina Rossetti decades later, advocated the banking-up and channeling of potentially fluid devotion. For Tractarian poetics, poetry is the handmaid of faith, mediating emotions stemming from the love of God. Acts of devotion, understood as fixed, repetitive, controlled, directed, and rhythmic, were themselves a form of poetry. In every sense of the word, poetry should be "measured." Form and faith interacted, and notably in the calm, comforting, regular, and reassuring cadences of *The Christian Year,* conceived as God's music and as a gloss on the liturgical sequences of the Book of Common Prayer according to a model provided by George Herbert.

Similar considerations apply to Isaac Williams's highly popular 1844 volume *The Baptistry,* in which poetry was linked to the related arts of music and of architecture, above all the architecture of the Gothic Revival, to

---

found in Hilton, *The Age of Atonement.*
   10. Blair, *Form and Faith.*

provide a unified, carefully ordered, and richly symbolic environment for worship. This was supported by a wider strand of poetic discourse, which includes Wordsworth and Elizabeth Barrett Browning, focused on architectural symbolism and its emotional effect, Gothic being itself a similitude of the sublime forms of Nature. Kirstie Blair points out that Wordsworth, in "The Excursion," not only explored relations between worship and the natural world, but in his "Ecclesiastical Sonnets" he also produced a discourse of English architecture as integral to the landscape and contrasted with Rome and Dissent. In the last of these sonnets, Wordsworth desires more ritual rather than less, and, concerning the Book of Common Prayer, wishes that "our scrupulous Sires had dared to leave / Less scanty measure of those graceful rites / And usages." (Other poets felt the same even more intensely more than a century later: for example, Donald Davie, Charles Sisson, and W. H. Auden.)

The formality espoused by the Tractarians contrasted with the dissenting informality and rough-hewn quality espoused by Robert Browning (1812–1889). Browning is particularly significant, because he engages quite directly with key religious issues such as dissenting religion, spirituality in the specific forms of spiritualism and mesmerism, with geological and cosmological science—and with biblical criticism. Browning is the most acute poetic intellect of his time, dealing in penetrating detail with many of its key issues, as well as issues flagged up as important by the present analysis, such as the religious status of music. In my view the issue of music matters because music shares with poetry a special, if contested, proximity to religion. Of course, Browning poses difficulties because his use of dramatic monologues enables him to assume different voices that may not express his own views, but the difficulties are not so intractable as they are in Shakespeare. The poems I have in mind are "A Death in the Desert" and "Abt Vogler" from *Dramatis Personae* (1864), "Bishop Blougram's Apology" (1855), "Saul" (1855), and "Christmas Eve" and "Easter Day" (1850).[11]

I take "Abt Vogler" first because it is the most carefully considered statement in English poetry of the relation of music to religion, with clear implications for poetry as the sister-art of music. There is inevitably a context here which goes back centuries to Shakespeare, Milton, and Dryden, and this at least needs to be indicated, since Browning is not coming from nowhere. The context includes two of the greatest odes in English: Milton's "Ode on the Morning of Christ's Nativity" and Dryden's "Ode to Saint Cecilia." Shakespeare set the scene by invoking a traditional view of music as the heavenly harmony of the music of the spheres bringing peace and

---

11. Browning, *Poems*, 639–49; 634–36; 136–53; 26–32; 499–526.

order, as provoking the various passions and moods, and as inducing melancholia and disordered affections. Milton and Dryden express variants on this. Wordsworth, however, simply used the words "harmony" and "music" generically, without much specific reference to music as an art form. What we encounter in Browning is a distinctly personal commentary on the implications of the structure of music from the viewpoint of a performer. He subjects this structure to a religious interpretation feeding off aspects of the traditional view: for example, the idea of the C major chord as the concluding resting place of a spiritual journey. There are numerous references to the all-creating finger of God, the builder of a house "not made with hands," lying behind the lawful structure of music, which is in turn creatively worked upon by the artist and sent back up to God. Browning concludes, in what is surely his own voice, that eternity will affirm "the conception of an hour." Life is replete with dubiety and grief but the musician is the confidant of the divine.

Browning also wrote two other poems on music, "A Toccata of Galuppi's" and "Master Hugues of Saxe-Gotha" (both 1855),[12] also deploying his grasp of standard musical theory, but with a different emotional tonality. The first of these is set against a Venetian background that facilitates reflections on evanescence, decadence, and death, while the second contemplates a "huge house of sound" emanating from the organ loft but leaving only a sense of unresolved complexity. No previous poetic commentaries on music in earlier centuries exude such a negative atmosphere.

Neither of the poems made much of a mark at the time, though they pose no obvious problems, and it has been suggested that this marks a transition to a period where socioeconomic critiques gained public primacy and poetry was confined to the sphere of private meditation. If so, this proposal echoes, or maybe anticipates, a standard theory about the privatization of religion. Moreover, it can be supplemented by the privatization associated with the growing influence of the novel, given that novels were consumed in solitary silence. This is yet another version of "the Break," and one which links the privatization of religion, a standard trope of sociology, to the privatization of poetry, an issue ignored in sociology. Below I return to the public space regained by poetry with the help of new technology from the nineteen-sixties on, for example, the BBC and Poems on the Underground. My sense is that poets are indeed heard and absorbed through new media, but that Auden was right to say, in his poem "In Memory of W. B. Yeats," that poetry does not make anything happen, even though the iron will of the unjust is constantly confronted by visions of transfiguration.

12. Browning, *Poems*, 18–19; 50–53.

"A Death in the Desert" presents Browning's response to contemporary biblical criticism, which he wrote a year after reading Renan on the life of Christ according to John.[13] The setting is arcane, because it focuses on John portrayed as the sole Evangelist still living and confronted by questions concerning the veracity of his Gospel. One of these questions touches on the propriety of inventing miracles to lend adventitious authority to a basic message about the primacy of love. There are numerous confusions here, but the underlying issue has to do with a misplaced demand for empirical proof in contemporary Victorian society where no such proof is to be had, especially when a truth which may be known today may be differently known tomorrow. Browning is regretting the sundering of faith from enlightened reason when the insights of faith are in reality validated within the human heart, and the power of Christ is in any case a human projection. For him the truth struggles through earthly forms to find itself gloriously in the faculties of man and not in outward manifestations: something akin to Wordsworth's concept of Imagination.

In "Bishop Blougram's Apology," Browning uses a Catholic bishop in the context of the restoration of an English Catholic hierarchy in 1850 to articulate a multiply ironic commentary on problems of belief and unbelief.[14] Bishop Blougram is a sophisticated hierarch in conversation with Gigadibs, a sceptical journalist with multiple unexamined secular faiths. There are many possible ways of interpreting the text, including one which sees it as an attack on Blougram for his blatantly honest hypocrisy. What matters here is that Browning inverts the convention whereby faith struggles with unbelief to posit a situation where the unbelief of a bishop officially committed to the dogmatic certainties of Rome (not Peter's creed but Hildebrand's!) struggles with the awkward possibility of faith. It seems he has to guard his unbelief against varied intimations of faith: his consciousness is invaded by the "Grand Perhaps." The key sentence, presumably characterizing the situation in which Victorians (like Browning?) find themselves, is:

> All we have gained then by our unbelief
> Is a life of doubt diversified by faith
> For one of faith diversified by doubt.

Bishop Blougram is clear, first of all, that faith and doubt are by their nature mutually implicated, in which case there is nothing so very new about present dilemmas, and, second, that this mutual implication does not apply simply to religion but to the mythical structures that keep society itself in

---

13. Browning, *Poems*, 639–50.
14. Browning, *Poems*, 136–53.

being. Our social being, and its legimations, depend in part on potent myth and pretence. Here Blougram turns the tables on those who believe in the rationality of the public sphere by adopting a sociological account of the central role of myth in keeping society in being. To this he adds, with a distinctive Pascalian touch, that the supposed revelation in Nature is testimony to a hidden rather than a revealed God. *Vere tu es Deus absconditus.* It comes down to a question of choice not evidence:

> Like you this Christianity or not?
> It may be false, but will you wish it true?
> Has it your vote to be so if it can?'
> *Quod petit?*

To this Blougram proposes an account of secularization based on a collapse of faith before intellectual assault, citing all those words with Greek endings, like "cosmology," "ethnology," and "geology," that spell the death of a faith. He appends a sociologist's charter explicitly taken up by this sociologist with matching irony. The background is the supposedly faithful Middle Ages, where men truly believed while enthusiastically killing, robbing, and fornicating: so much for real Christian commitment in that so-called "Golden Age of faith." And the current problem is:

> You'll say the old system's not so obsolete
> But men believe still: ay, but who and where?[15]

Here we have a foundation charter for the sociology of religion. There is nothing like this intellectual *tour de force* in the whole corpus of English poetry, and only the fringe has been touched upon here.

"Saul" is a poem with the same problems of voice but one which also breaks through with Christian affirmations so direct as not to be easily set up for deconstruction. One concerns the Christian paradox of law and love, so that love and law are mutually implicated: "All's love yet all's law." God's ultimate gift is to offer a new law that places the fear and trembling of the Mosaic dispensation in the context of confidence and acceptance. In terms that anticipate the theology of Paul Tillich, we are accepted. The other affirmation concerns the Christian paradox of godhead realized through self-emptying into humanity. Much of "Saul" consists of the different kinds of music sung and played by David to soothe Saul's troubled spirit. But Saul remains in the valley of the dry bones, until, in section 18, David turns to a higher theme and a "new harmony." This is the final gift of unconditional grace, brought by one who bore most by manifesting his "strength

---

15. Browning, *Poems*, 148.

in weakness." "The gates of new life" are thrown open to Saul, as he finds himself beloved by one with "a face like to my face."

"Christmas Day" and "Easter Eve" can be read as a single poem, and they are often printed as such. Taken as a unit, it tells us much about Browning's relation to his dissenting background. In some ways, it is a response to the dissenting faith he shared with his new wife, and it takes the form of an autobiographical meditation. Browning enters a chapel and is disturbed by the banality of a dissenting sermon made up of clichés that have lost touch with inner spiritual meaning, as well as marred by meanness, ignorance, and stupidity. At the same time, he compares the simplicity of Dissent favorably with the sumptuous seductions of Rome, and with the aridity of contemporary rationalism and biblical criticism. The context here may be both the conversion of Newman to Catholicism and the biblical criticism of David Strauss. Browning confesses his own belief in the inward nature of faith and in the divine power evidenced in the work of love, such as he also confesses in "Saul" and in the related poems, "Cleon" and "Karshish," published in 1865.[16] "Cleon" introduces Christianity at the last moment, commenting ironically (in words voiced by an Arab doctor) on how implausible its message is, while "Karshish" uses the resurrection of Lazarus and the crucifixion of Jesus to proclaim the divine power of the message of love. With "Cleon" we are not far from Tertullian's paradox about believing the absurd.

Before turning directly to Elizabeth Barrett Browning, it is worth summarizing the argument in Karen Dieleman's *Religious Imaginaries: the Liturgical and Poetic Practices of Elizabeth Barrett Browning, Christina Rossetti and Adelaide Proctor* (2012).[17] Dieleman has clearly had to grapple with extensions of secularization theory in Victorian studies that, first of all, assume that religion is not important, and, secondly, hold that insofar as it retains any salience its effects are regressive. She turns above all to Charles Taylor's notion of the "social imaginary" to combat these assumptions. Dieleman argues her case with great sophistication, drawing on sociological and even neurobiological understandings to argue that distinctive poetic voices emerge from the liturgical experiences of her three Christian poets, one Congregational, one Anglo-Catholic, and one revivalist Roman Catholic. Their different poetic voices are shown in attitudes to the poet's role, in approaches to Scripture, and in the place accorded the church. Their faith is not subordinate to their gender as a shaping medium, and their faith in no way inhibited their creativity. In all three women faith generated social concern.

---

16. Browning, *Poems*, 153–58; 117–22.
17. Dieleman, *Religious Imaginaries*.

Elizabeth Barrett Browning adopted the role of poet-preacher rather than prophet, striving to bring together intelligence and feeling. For Christina Rossetti worship was more a manifestation than a proclamation, influenced as she was by ecclesiology and Tractarianism. This bred an aesthetic culture of reception where sacrament and mystery were as important as the preached word. Adelaide Proctor was influenced by different experiences of the Roman Mass in different churches, one of them based on control, the other based on emotional enthusiasm. She accepted authority, but at the same time her responses were autonomous.

I turn now to the poetry of Elizabeth Barrett Browning (1806–1861), paying particular attention to her verse novel, *Aurora Leigh* (1856), a work she described as conveying her "highest convictions."[18] Before looking at this masterpiece, it is worth saying something about her long poem, "The Seraphim," as equally conveying her convictions concerning the incarnation, the crucifixion, and the resurrection.[19] It may be that some of the poem's more obscure celestial machinery reflects Elizabeth Barrett Browning's interest in Swedenborg, but I am no more capable of detecting it than I can detect it in William Blake. The machinery I pick up most clearly is from *Revelation*.

Two seraphs are in colloquy about the difference between heaven, where they dwell, and earth. In heaven, they stand before the throne engaged in what Milton called "the angelic symphony" surrounding the Presence. *Paradise Lost* hovers above the poem throughout, and the two seraphs are aware of how, through disobedience, humanity lost the perfection of paradise. One of them has, however, visited the ruined earth with the promise of peace and goodwill when *He*, the sometime crowned Son, walked in the clay that he created. He became vulnerable to death, to the bitter herbs, to the mystery of tears and human treachery. By doing so, he reversed and sweetened the bitterness and poured blessing on humanity through the shedding of his blood. The victim-king entered in at the city gate, until, within a few days, three crosses stood outside the city wall, and a woman stood beside them weeping. The One who gave Nature its flowers received in return a thorn; and no answer comes to his cry of desolation. Yet the cry of the "orphaned One" and the slain victim is a cry of victory and of the completed work of redemption. Heaven's unperturbed perfection is dull and meaningless compared with the spectacle of God's love issuing from the crucible of human woe. The sound of a new song rises from the sinful who have been redeemed, to which merely perfect angels have no access. The skies that turned to darkness at his death heralded his rising at the break of

---

18. Browning, *Poetical Works*, 561–740.
19. Browning, *Poetical Works*, 113–40.

day and the onset of summer. The poet affirms that "*CHRIST IS RISEN*," so that the weak, "like me," "should walk in white."

Aurora Leigh is in verse, perhaps because novels were superseding poetry as vehicles of serious public reflection, and, were this essay differently focused, that would lead us to consider Christian themes (say) in the novels of Gaskell and Dickens. In this essay I am particularly interested in Elizabeth Barrett Browning's critique of the French sociological abstractions in which Aurora Leigh's cousin, Romney Leigh, casts the social concerns they both so passionately share. Other poets have contrasted the nature of both poetry and religion with the abstractions of natural science, but Browning does so in relation to the abstractions of social science. After all, for her, poetry and faith are mutually implicated. It is the application of these abstract sociological theories that brings disaster on her cousin because he sacrifices humans to principle, and the humans resist. Aurora Leigh rejects his proposal of marriage because he would enlist her in his enterprises in the subordinate female role of an emotionally motivated woman, by contrast with the informed theoretical grasp of a man. I am incidentally assuming that Aurora, is in large measure, Elizabeth Barrett Browning herself, even though she never enjoyed the fully independent life she attributes to Aurora. This near-identity applies to the theological understandings Aurora expresses as much as to her articulation of the contemporary problems of the female public intellectual and poet speaking authoritatively in her own voice.

Aurora Leigh is saturated in biblical as well as classical references, for example, the truncated reference to Colossians chapter 3, verse 3 in the phrase "hid with God." The poem begins with Aurora rejecting the Tractarian ideas of female duty, emotional reserve, and proper deference to forms and formularies proposed by her English guardian, following the deaths of her mother and her father. Here it is worth recollecting that EBB shared with her husband a dislike of forms and formularies insofar as their articulation by "ritualists" implied exclusive access to the Spirit. On this matter, the Brownings were dissenting partisans of tolerance and inclusion in the body of Christ, however and wherever that body was manifested. Their view was a version of what Charles Wesley affirmed about the sufficiency and centrality of Christ beyond all the divisions fostered by "names and sects and parties."

Aurora recollects the color and wildness of her native Italy, as contrasted with the manicured mildness of the English scene, but nevertheless communes with the Unseen and its blessings through Nature. Then there is the world of books opening up before her. Here it may be difficult to distinguish between seers and conjurors, yet something quickens in the obscurity, enabling her to discern "oracles of vital Deity / Attesting the Hereafter." The Lord who cares for each sparrow as it falls will not cease to care for fallen humans in the Hereafter.

Poetry frees her spirit and quickens it with a sense of life and love. Love is the lesson taught by the Lord, and also taught to Aurora by her beloved departed father. A divine finger "convicts" her of the "great Eternities." Poets are the only genuine truth-tellers, beyond all relative and temporal truths. She cherishes a spiritual sense that beyond each common flower lies an archetypal counterpart. The God who took human flesh breathes into humans a spirit that aspires to that other realm. We work with God as the heavenly vision is realized in poetry, pictures, and music. We take God's word and pass it on, just as we pass on the sacramental bread from one to another. To quote Keble: "Two worlds are ours." Romney Leigh may heed the moral and intellectual call of social theory and systems, but Aurora has her own vocation to be an artist and to show she can span the "whole octave" of humanity. This includes her concern for the supposedly "fallen woman," Marion Erle, whom Romney proposes to marry out of a mistaken sense of duty. (The question of the humanity and status of Marion Erle is a major theme of the poem/novel, but not directly relevant to concerns here.)

On her long European itineraries, Aurora sees France as the dreamer among nations who succeeded in creating a nightmare. In Italy, back now in the Florence of her birth and her earliest experiences with her father, she sees women "writhing" towards the divine in Catholic rituals. But compassion compels her to remember that God feeds the ravens when they cry: so why should he not also feed them? It is only as we recognize with Moses that we are on holy ground that we take off our shoes and realize that:

> Earth's crammed with heaven,
> And every common bush afire with God.

Christina Rossetti (1830–1894) pursued a career in many respects like that of Elizabeth Barrett Browning. She too was disregarded by twentieth-century modernism, until she attracted critical interest in the latter part of the twentieth century, in part motivated by feminist concerns. She too suffered from disabling illness, was profoundly attracted by Italy, wrote love poetry, explored the position of the female writer, and espoused social concerns, including the plight of "fallen women." All her work has a religious resonance deriving from her original Evangelicalism and her later Tractarianism.

Her poetry explores the hardships of the journey of faith. Doubt interrogates faith. It is worth giving some examples, all published in her collected

1862 volume.[20] In her poem "The World" she envisages a dangerous female who offers attractive fruit and flowers but is by night a Medusa figure.[21] In her most famous and innovative poem, "Goblin Market," she is again tempted by erotic fruits and flowers, but nevertheless finds salvation.[22] In "A Better Resurrection," she looks to Christ to restore her brokenness and unite her with the divine.

> My life is like a frozen thing,
> No bud nor greenness can I see:
> Yet rise it shall—the sap of Spring;
> O Jesus, rise in me.[23]

In "A Birthday" the theme is once more the brokenness of her life until her divine lover comes to her, and in "Up-Hill" she traces, like Bunyan, the trials of the journey and of the Hill Difficulty before achieving a depth of true heavenly vision.[24]

Gerard Manley Hopkins (1844-1889) only emerged as a major poet after the First World War, largely following the advocacy of Robert Bridges. He came of a wealthy Anglo-Catholic background, where his artistic, linguistic, musical, and poetic talents were lovingly fostered. At Oxford, he encountered religious ferment, and his subsequent conversion to Roman Catholicism caused a break with his family, with lasting personal costs and consequences. In his poem on "Henry Purcell" he not only praises the composer for his "abrupt rehearsal of self" but hopes that he might on that account be accorded the special favor of salvation, in spite of the fate properly reserved for Protestants.[25]

In his conversion, Hopkins was particularly drawn to the doctrine of the real presence which brought the incarnate Christ directly into a contemporary world that had been "smeared" and "bleared" with the depredations of industrialism in spite of "the dearest freshness deep down things."[26] For Hopkins the metaphor of presence participated in the reality. A rather similar conception of incarnate immanence seems to underlie his poem comparing the Blessed Virgin to the "air we breathe." The Virgin is "World-mothering," and one might here make a comparison with Hopkins's

---

20. Rossetti, *Complete Poems*.
21. Rossetti, *Complete Poems*, 70-71.
22. Rossetti, *Complete Poems*, 5-20.
23. Rossetti, *Complete Poems*, 62.
24. Rossetti, *Complete Poems*, 30.
25. Hopkins, *Poems*, 80.
26. "God's Grandeur," in Hopkins, *Poems*, 66.

poem, "Pied Beauty." Here Hopkins praises a God who "fathers forth" all the infinitely varied and changeful beauties of the natural world, while himself remaining the beauty beyond change.

Hopkins also had strong ascetic leanings that drew him towards the celibate life of a religious. In this he was influenced by Christina Rossetti, herself already elevated by her circle as an icon of the Blessed Virgin, and someone who recognized the overriding imperative of the religious vocation. His sense of the supreme demands of faith resulted in an abnegation of his aesthetic and poetic sensibilities, to the point where he felt obliged to embrace artistic silence and be "lovely-dumb" in the "heaven-haven" of his religious obedience. He recognized the real but dangerous attractions of beauty in people and poetry, but sought rather to refuse its enchantments, in order to give beauty back to the divine giver and seek "God's better beauty, grace."

It was his reading of the Scotist doctrine of "haeccitas" or a unique and especial character in the world, above all as realized in people and their unique selfhood, that released him from that silence. He now felt able to express his response to unified form, or "inscape," in Nature as the book of God, to be read alongside the book of revelation, in the sacraments, and in the depths of the self. Nature was for him both a revelation and a pointer to transcendence in the starry citadels and "bright boroughs" above.

He admired the God of Nature and in Nature, for example, as the "master of the tides / Of the Yore-flood, of the year's fall" in the narrative of the "The Wreck of the Deutschland" (1875–76, first published 1918).[27] At the same time, he recognized the destructiveness of "God's cold" and of the "passionless wet" as the ship and its precious cargo of humanity foundered. I find his conventional Catholic theodicy of the heavenly feast enjoyed by a faithful nun with the Blessed Virgin profoundly unconvincing. For me, he fails to justify the harvest of souls that was garnered in that "shipwrack" by the action of "lovely-felicitous Providence." In the same way, he fails to justify his own spiritual trials in the sonnet "Carrion Comfort," where a fierce devouring God lays "a lion-limb" against him so that his "chaff might fly." For a period, he became seriously depressed, to the point where he felt abandoned by God and expressed this abandonment in the "terrible sonnets," before appearing to recover hope and faith in a poem that concluded by celebrating the resurrection.

According to Daniel A. Harris in *Inspirations Unbidden: The "Terrible Sonnets"* (1982),[28] there is a sequence to be observed here whereby Hopkins

---

27. Hopkins, *Poems*, 51–63.
28. Daniel A. Harris, *Inspirations Unbidden*.

first finds Christ immanent in the world, for example in the sheer beauty of a bird in flight, as in "The Windhover," a poem dedicated "To Christ our Lord." But then, for complex personal reasons, he loses his sense of God, or at least finds it only intermittently, a condition documented in the "Terrible Sonnets." In an echo of Newman in "The Dream of Gerontius," he half concedes "I can no more," before saying "I can, / Can something, hope, wish day come, not choose not to be."

Finally, when immanence fails, as further recorded in the poem on the comfort of the Resurrection dealing with the loss of everything, including the wonder of Man, in the "enormous dark" of death, he turns suddenly to Pauline eschatology. At the last trump, all is reversed in Christ. Man, who is seemingly no more than a "Jack, joke, poor potsherd, matchwood" is revealed as "immortal diamond."[29]

A brief aside is necessary here on John Henry Newman as another convert and poet, even though his poetry, notably "The Dream of Gerontius" (1865), is more significant as an index of the shock then administered to Protestant beliefs than as poetry. That we are, for the most part, not shocked now, is an index of a modern tendency to assimilate quite specific religious dogmas to any number of manifestations of spirituality. For many contemporary commentators, "beliefs" are the merest adiaphora: indifferent ways of responding to the axes of life and, in this case, of death. The governing category is existential depth and entirely alien to the specific content of what Newman wanted to express as the considered conclusion of a notably cerebral quest, even though one supported by the powers of the imagination. Content is bracketed in order to immerse the soul (interpreted as selfhood) in the flow of minatory and consoling messages, which are now mostly provided by Elgar's eloquent setting of 1902. Purgatory can be reinterpreted as a psychiatric concept.

It is worth remembering that the nineteenth century, like the seventeenth, was a period of great preachers, among them Newman, Spurgeon, Kingsley, MacDonald, and Maurice: that published repertoire provides another set of "signs of the times"—for example, the decline of providential warnings.

Alfred Tennyson (1809–1892) is a major progenitor of a tolerant and diverse Broad Church Christianity, seeking the principles underlying the creeds, along with others, for example F. D. Maurice, Dean Stanley, Benjamin Jowett, and F. W. Robertson, as well as Coleridge. This Broad Church contrasted with the Dissent of the Brownings and with the various

---

29. "That Nature is a Heraclitian Fire and of the Comfort of the Resurrection," in Hopkins, *Poems*, 105–6.

Tractarians. Here I lean on Kirstie Blair's analysis where she focuses on *In Memoriam* (1849) and "Akbar's Dream" (1892).[30] She takes off from Tennyson's embrace of a faith beyond forms, in one instance not going beyond silence and listening to organ music in sacred space in the service of a larger and inexpressible truth. That contrasts with his sense that poetic and affecting forms, such as the Anglican liturgy, were sustaining and helpful, provided that they were not promoted dogmatically as the sole channel of salvation. This makes it interesting that Tennyson's own poetic practice depends so much on repetitive and stable form, as did his private devotions. Indeed, Tennyson's "In Memoriam" could itself be seen as continuous with Anglican forms of worship, beginning with the lines in the "Prologue" about our wills being ours "to make them thine." This sounds like a clear echo of the Book of Common Prayer.

Tennyson was not strongly engaged by the sacraments, though he received communion, and his reference to man as having built "fanes of fruitless prayer" appears despairing. But it is redressed by a reference to "beyond the veil," suggesting that we cannot measure the efficacy of prayer. There are other channels of grace beyond the controversial language of formal services, like the celebratory call of church bells signifying a presence at the heart of every community. Though Tennyson appears at times to evoke a terrifying vision of an unstable world crumbling into dust in the vast spaces of geological time, he contrasts this instability with the eternal form of truth and God's ordering presence.

> And all is well, tho' faith and form,
> Be sunder'd in the night of fear;
> Well roars the storm to those that hear
> A deeper voice across the storm.[31]

For Kirstie Blair, Tennyson's poem "Akbar's Dream" is an unambiguous statement of his kind of faith. The poem is part of a final volume where Tennyson was expressing anxieties and hope about the future of religion. Maybe all the differing faiths of the world expressed similar principles. Tennyson was interested in comparative religion of the kind pursued by Max Müller, and in Eastern religions along the lines of Edward FitzGerald in the *Rubaiyat*, where he intuits God's secret presence beneath local changes, chances and external forms. "Akbar's Dream" takes off from a shared idea of the unity of God beyond all claims to exclusive truth. Yet Akbar's universalism does not negate the need for forms as regards "The Spiritual in Nature's

---

30. Blair, *Form and Faith*, 163–96.
31. Tennyson, *Poems*, 110.

market place." That is especially true among the vast crowds of humanity, even as it might also be necessary to venture and mold new forms. Tennyson unsettles the notion that the Highest necessarily refers to the Christian God. Maybe there are many truths.

Perhaps it might be worthwhile citing some of the most well-known of Tennyson's poetic utterances. In section 96 of "In Memoriam," beginning "Strong Son of God, immortal Love," after speaking of "believing where we cannot prove," he writes:

> There lies more faith in honest doubt,
> Believe me, than in half the creeds . . .

Tennyson here questions the quality of any faith untried by doubt. Faith and religion are not coextensive. God is greater than "our little systems." "They have their day and cease to be." He is a greater light and a "beam in the darkness . . ." Perhaps this might be described as a kind of para-Christianity.

In the early poem (written 1839, published 1842),

> Break, break, break
> On thy cold grey stones, O Sea,

the poet sees the action of the sea and human action as equally pointless. In the late poem "Crossing the Bar" (1889), which Tennyson regarded as something like a valedictory statement, he writes, evoking St. Paul, of hoping to

> see my Pilot face to face
> When I have crossed the bar.

AVATARS OF DOUBT

I now turn to the counterpoint of doubt as it plays against the various expressions of faith just canvassed, beginning with Matthew Arnold as the original and most important exemplar. Matthew Arnold (1822–1888) raises important and recurrent questions for this analysis, particularly because he explicitly claims to be articulating the spirit of the age from the elevation of cultural critic and seer. Such a claim exercises a pressure on any analyst to decide whether what he has to say about religion in his poetry, and more explicitly in prose works like *Literature and Dogma* (1873), belongs all too obviously to its own time, or anticipates what many believe to be the modern condition. But the example of Arnold raises wider questions, bearing directly on the objectives and the assumptions of this book. At least one of his poems, "Dover Beach," is regularly taken to be symptomatic of the mid-century as well as prophesying the future. No other poem, apart from Yeats's "The Second Coming," has this status, and its import is very different. Arnold's poem is read as a bellwether of precisely the secularization thesis this book sets out critically to scrutinize. Indeed, a Roman Catholic theologian, Nicholas Lash, thought it his vocation to do theology as though on Dover Beach.[32] Other poems by Arnold, such as "The Scholar Gypsy" (1853), "The Forsaken Merman" (1849), and "Thyrsis" (1867) express an alienation from the spirit of the times in a way that is taken to foreshadow much later forms of alienation. That forces us to ask in what way the industrial civilization of 1850 was in its moral temper worse than the world in 1750 or 1650. We have at least to question what a man with Arnold's particular history and background tells us either about the mid-century or much later or indeed about the past, beyond exhibiting some of the standard attitudes of privileged intelligentsias to their environment. After all, his predictions include an important role for poetry as a central element in culture, and they envisage personal cultivation as taking over the role of religion. In this he is perhaps anticipating F. R. Leavis. But he is plainly deluded, as the word "culture" has largely lost its connotation of acknowledged excellence and qualitative difference to succumb to politicized versions of the sociological meaning of culture whereby all tastes and judgments are just lifestyle choices. When Bentham said, "Pushpin is as good as poetry," he was a more prescient prophet than Arnold. In seeing Arnold as a prescient seer, we may be succumbing to the assumptions about avant-gardes descrying the future before it arrives. Looking back, we may see that sometimes they do, but maybe we screen out the cases where they do not.

I spend time on Arnold because he is so central to my specific concerns. I discuss two other projects of Arnold, because they are implicated in the notion of culture serving as a future substitute religion. One concerns the Bible and the other science. Arnold seeks to release the unconscious poetry of the Bible from the outdated and pre-scientific husk of its outer form. Of course, the Bible is "unscientific" in all kinds of ways, for example, in not conforming to criteria of historicity, and specifically in not putting forward scientific hypotheses. It is a group of intersecting *narratives* concerned with a journey from the paradise garden to the celestial city and from exile to homecoming. In the New Testament it moves from descent to ascent, bondage to liberation, and death to resurrection, and it does so through all the encounters of the imminent and immanent kingdom of God climaxing at

---

32. Lash, *Theology on Dover Beach*.

Golgotha. You cannot lift moral sentiments out of the narrative any more than you can lift out the miracles, because the narrative of the generous gift is totally embedded in (say) the feeding of the five thousand, or in the wine at Cana, or in the anticipatory and actual offerings of the body in love in the Passion narrative. This leads directly to the issue of science. None of this can be reduced to statements that conform to the criteria of science, any more than can Arnold's views of poetry and the nature of a classic or his concept of impersonal fate. Redemptive narrative and science are incommensurable discourses, as Eliot clearly saw in his classic essay on Arnold.[33]

I aim to provide a context for three key poems bearing on religion, but in the case of Arnold I can only attempt that by reference to the prose. Moreover, there are many variations on his views, in part due to their incoherence but also due to varying opinions at different times in his life. I take distinguished treatments by Basil Willey, Stephen Prickett, and Kenneth Allott and place them in apposition or opposition. They are not in the chronological order in which they appeared.

In his classic *Nineteenth Century Studies: Coleridge to Arnold* (1949), Basil Willey holds that Arnold is a harbinger of modernity and an eminent example of what I call an "avatar of doubt."[34] He begins by quoting Arnold on the difficulty of doing without Christianity, and the equal difficulty of doing with Christianity as it is. For Willey, Arnold is the quintessential middle-man, one for whom religion was what mattered most, and therefore it was necessary to purge it of elements vulnerable to scientific criticism. The spirit of the times and progressive opinion would awaken the English from their provincial slumbers. So Arnold's project was to provide for serious-minded people what the Cambridge Platonists had done for an earlier age: a sober rational piety.

In Arnold's case, that meant self-abnegation, or *metanoia*, achieved in loving community with others rather than individual isolation. This piety was to rest on the basis of verifiable experience, understood as that which elevates and sweetens human nature. Here we have, first of all, a triumph of the moral (broadly understood) over the aesthetic. Second, we have an almost Kantian triumph of the moral over the theological, in terms of frameworks of interpretation, including eschatological anticipation, built from the start into the Gospels themselves and into Paul. Christianity was to be attenuated to "morality tinged with emotion" and promoted for its beneficent social consequences. What Arnold appears to anticipate is the

---

33. "Matthew Arnold," in Eliot, *Use of Poetry*, 103–9.

34. Willey, *Nineteenth-Century Studies*. Willey, though himself a Methodist, gave impetus to the loss of faith idea as *the* Victorian pattern.

replacement of religion by education in "culture," which is another way of recommending culture as the civil religion of the future and Arnold as its prophet. He is privileged to annunciate modernity. The Bible had its value as a kind of unconscious poetry, and the poet was a seer best able to interpret it for the coming age.

Stephen Prickett treats Arnold in *Romanticism and Religion: The Tradition of Wordsworth and Coleridge in the Victorian Church* (1976).[35] In the course of his chapter 8, focused on issues of demythologizing and mythmaking, it is clear that the underlying issues are complex to a degree, so I simplify by drawing only on pages 219–222, hoping that I do not too much misrepresent. Prickett argues that Arnold's project of demythologizing Christianity is undermined by his reliance on the poetic tradition of Wordsworth, Coleridge, and Keble. Arnold does not recognize that the whole project of a poetic interpretation of Scripture rests on the premise that poetry expresses what cannot be expressed in some other way. For Wordsworth, Coleridge, and Keble form and content are indivisible. Paraphrase impoverishes because a poetic or religious symbol *resists reformulation in abstractions*. It follows that the critical method in the German higher critical style can destroy faith, but cannot retrieve it, because it lacks the vital life of the original. Whether in Scripture or poetry, the poetic, apparently elevated by Arnold to a new eminence, has been radically devalued. What Arnold takes to be the outer husk that in unenlightened ages protected the essentially moral meaning cannot be jettisoned by a more enlightened age without losing the heart of the matter. What the imagination once obscurely groped after cannot be expressed in terms amenable to verification.

Kenneth Allott contributed an often quoted introduction to his edited volume *Matthew Arnold: A Selection of his Poems* (1954).[36] He suggests that Arnold's relatively brief period of writing poetry has been overshadowed by his far more extensive prose, for example in Lionel Trilling's *Matthew Arnold* (1939). His crucial argument claims that, apart from his Victorian window-dressing, Arnold is our contemporary in teaching us how to feel and live with our feelings as people who live in a world where the bloom has faded and life has been infected. He was peculiarly gifted in expressing the disenchantment induced by our time-ridden sensibility. His vocation was to express disenchantment and do so independently of faith or doubt. T. S. Eliot said he had no serenity, merely an impeccable demeanor, but demeanor is a virtue and at least he tried to be truthful.

35. Prickett, *Romanticism and Religion*.
36. Arnold, *Matthew Arnold: A Selection*, 7–24.

The first poem I select has to be "Dover Beach" (1867). It is based on the pathetic fallacy, so that the natural scene, initially invoked as calm and serene, is then invoked as both restless and a sign of the decline of faith and the loss of all human meaning. All that remains is the (temporary) sharing of love. The poem is sometimes seen as a response to the displacement of the mystery of faith (God is not mentioned) by the mundane spectacles of science following Darwin. It can also be seen in the context of the restless movements of the earth revealed by geology. The beach at Dover is a liminal place viewed at a liminal time. It is the shore where England ends, looking towards France as the light across the channel gleams just briefly before giving way to complete darkness. We are standing on the cusp of change and (to invoke another Arnold poem, "Requiescat") of "the vasty halls of death."

"Stanzas from the Grande Chartreuse" follows in the wake of Wordsworth's poem on the same theme, but with a more negative inflection. It was written in 1855 and may be the first poem of Arnold's married life, and it reflects his belief in religion as morality shorn of the divine presence. He is an agnostic

> Wandering between two worlds, one dead,
> The other powerless to be born.

To the liberal Protestant Arnold, the monks are the otherworldly relics of a dying faith now incarcerated in a "living tomb" and he looks at them with the curiosity of one stumbling across the enigmatic remains of outworn superstitions. Arnold is one who has felt the pull of Newman, but rejects it in the name of truth and integrity. At the same time he is not satisfied with the frigidity of reason.

In his poem "Resignation" (1849) Arnold revisits the Lake District with his sister, as Wordsworth revisited Tintern Abbey with his sister, and this is a parallel poem in which Arnold says farewell to Wordsworth's vision of nature. In contrast to passionate natures enthralled by great labors, the poet seeks freedom from the passions. He adopts a viewpoint far above the rural and the urban scene, and the poet is one whose mighty heart subdues his impulses to contemplate the human condition and the "general life." He cultivates a Stoic attitude that gains in width what it may lack in depth. The poet concludes that the "mundane spectacle" of the world in which we live and move outlasts all human emotions and death itself. Love and power are alike transitory. We can expect no gifts from chance, and only thus can we gain freedom and a victory over fate. Perhaps this seems less than heroic, but it has its own sterling virtue of detachment through immersion in "the general life." Perhaps it is possible to lend a voice to nature, but, in contrast to Wordsworth's vision, that is all. Our "iterated" prayer does not penetrate

"Fate's impenetrable ear," nor is much gained for humanity if commitment to dizzying action allows our spirits to forget "The something that infects the world."

Arthur Clough (1819–1861), Arnold's close friend and intimate correspondent, was unable to share his stoicism, and hesitated over even a partial approach to religious truth, though (like Arnold) he retained an affection for Anglican ritual, for the Book of Common Prayer, and for church music. It was, after all, part of his environment, and, like Thomas Hardy later, he was at home in it. At Oxford he had been (like Arnold) attracted to Tractarianism, but later lost faith in Christian doctrines to the point where he felt obliged to resign his fellowship at Oriel College. After a period at University College, London, he again resigned: he even found the Unitarians too dogmatic. He exemplified skeptical nostalgia and a split consciousness while being radical in his religious doubts, his politics, and his attitude to sexuality. His political radicalism sent him to Rome in 1848 to support Mazzini, only to find himself confronted by the French takeover of the city in 1849. Unlike Matthew Arnold, he took a Byronic, rather than a Keatsian, view of religion, but like Arnold, he felt that the English were provincials who had failed to notice that advanced countries on the continent had already given up belief in heaven.

His religious doubts were expressed in several lapidary poems.[37] One, "The Latest Decalogue," satirized the hypocritical morality of Victorian society. Another, "There is No God" (1850), suggests that religion only flourishes under unhappy conditions, concluding:

> And almost everyone when age
> Disease or sorrow strike him,
> Inclines to think there is a God,
> Or something very like Him.

The poem on "Easter Day—Naples 1849," has the refrain "Christ is not risen" and declares:

> Eat, drink and die, for we are souls bereaved,
> Of all the creatures under heaven's wide scope
> We are most hopeless who had once most hope,
> And most beliefless that had most believed.

Algernon Swinburne (1837–1909) is another poet initially influenced by Tractarianism, but he nevertheless takes the discussion into quite different territory. According to the Poetry Foundation's essay, he was a preeminent symbol of transgressive practices aimed at subverting Victorian

---

37. Clough, *Poems*; see also Kenny, *Arthur Hugh Clough*.

values.[38] Sexual imagery became part of his public image. Yet his real preoccupation was with the nature of poetic beauty. "The most important and conspicuous quality of Swinburne's works was an intense lyricism." He was identified with the principle of art for art's sake.

In what follows I lean on Sara Lyons's *Algernon Swinburne and Walter Pater: Victorian Aestheticism, Doubt and Secularisation* (2015), which has the particular merit of dealing with the secularization thesis.[39] Her arguments in her second chapter, "'Though Hearts Reach Back and Memories Ache': Melancholy, Religious Doubt and Swinburne's Strenuous Joy," are particularly helpful. They elucidate Swinburne's position, and also show how Swinburne takes issue with poets already discussed like Browning, Tennyson, Arnold, and Clough. Sara Lyons points out that by the time Swinburne embarked in earnest on his poetic career with the publication in 1865 of *Atalanta in Calydon*, Tennyson was already a cultural monument, in particular in his role as intercessor between science, notably Darwin, and faith. His "honest doubt" chimed with Browning's belief that believers should "mix uncertainty / With faith." For Swinburne, such consolations were empty. He defined himself as a radical critic of earnestness, and excoriated the carefully caught regrets of unbelievers afflicted by nostalgia.

In his poem addressed to Christ, "Before a Crucifix," he appears, in the manner of Shelley, to debunk any favorable sentiment towards Christianity, especially European Catholicism, in the name of the wretched of the earth and republican liberty. Swinburne honors political compassion above Christian compassion, and therefore repudiates Christ as one whose name is tarnished by all the oppressions it has sanctified. Here he is attacking the genre of the "agonistic tourist poem" written by those who have moved well out of range of a religious response, and yet fall back on the gentle nostalgia of the tourist. The seminal poem of this kind is Arnold's "Stanzas from La Grande Chartreuse" (1855), but other examples include Clough's "Easter Day, Naples—1849" (1849), Hardy's "The Impercipient" (1898), and Larkin's "Church Going" (1954). For the agonistic tourist, the evanescence of Christianity can foster an intensified aesthetic experience and a musing regret, rather like that of Wordsworth for the glory that was Venice. In Arnold's poem modern people may overhear the distant noise of the approaching secular future, but they remain enchanted by a secret childhood space of reverie and prayer. For Clough, the alienation induced by Strauss's demythologizing of Scripture makes the stained glass glow ever

---

38. "Algernon Charles Swinburne," www.poetryfoundation.org/poems-and-poets/poets/detail/algernon-charles-swinburne, accessed September 2016.

39. Lyons, *Algernon Swinburne and Walter Pater*.

more brightly. Swinburne congratulated himself on having denatured this pose of pathos and he was determined to set aside Romantic responses to picturesque ruin in favor of a realistic view of Christianity as malignant and cankered. At one and the same time it was deservedly and unequivocally dying *and* managing to thrive in its own rot to the general detriment.

In "Before a Crucifix" Swinburne exploits an anti-Catholic rhetoric through images of grotesque Eucharistic consumption, priests as vampires, and the church as a leprous bride. Sara Lyons remarks that Swinburne's willingness to exploit the rhetorical luxuries of anti-Catholicism, treating Catholicism as a metonym for Christianity, parallels the willingness of other Victorian secularists to exploit anti-Semitism to debunk the Old Testament. It introduces jarring instabilities into his approach: he is nostalgic for the battle cries of French secularism against a monolithic church when the religious landscape of England in which he actually lives is quite other. The trope concerning a Christianity that is on the way out but surprisingly vigorous in its malignity has been revived today by the new atheists. No doubt the battle is won in principle. Great is truth and will prevail. At the same time, all good men and true must fight manfully against the malignity of religion. Only thus can we ensure the arrival of a future where the poisonous source of all our woe is finally exterminated. The answer is to be found in a disinterested and politically committed secularism.

But for Swinburne the disinterested stance is yoked to a sanguine affirmation of nature which not only seeks to overcome Christian doctrine but also the enervating hopes and despondencies that he identified with a liberalized modern Christianity. He sought to dismantle the very assumption that grief, melancholy, and contemplation are proper responses to mortality. Reverent agnosticism is out. The desire for immortality is, like sexual desire, no more than a form of hedonism, destined for disappointment and therefore to be preempted. Sara Lyons suggests that Swinburne's sadomasochistic poetics go beyond the urge to shock, in order to achieve an immanent conception of life that guards itself ascetically against the temptations of metaphysical desire.[40] She also suggests that, while Swinburne's *carpe diem* poems ally aestheticism with anti-transcendent worldliness, and seem to declare art's freedom from the burden of polemics, they are in fact polemical: in the very act of celebrating the gratuitousness of song, they polemically recommend an anti-transcendental model of art's value.[41]

After an impressive analysis of "By the North Sea" (1880), a poem concerned with the amoral power of nature in its endless flux as a sign

---

40. Lyons, *Algernon Swinburne and Walter Pater*, 91.
41. Lyons, *Algernon Swinburne and Walter Pater*, 92.

of a secular future without providential safeguards, Sara Lyons turns to Swinburne's *Tristram of Lyonesse*. This poem is an attempt, grander than *By the North Sea*, to posit an atheistic sublime. A passionate surrender to a radically deterministic and post-Darwinian materialism is "heroism of a kind: a heightened receptivity to the inexorable affords a blissful sense of freedom."[42] At the same time, though Nature takes no account of our desires, "it pulsates with something akin to those desires."[43] This pulls against Swinburne's criticism of Christian anthropomorphism and "recuperates a Romantic perception of a benevolent intelligence at work in nature, a view that Swinburne elsewhere often seeks to dismantle." There is here an emergent evolutionary sentience, rather than Thomas Hardy's nescience. Swinburne does not entirely ignore the problem of pain, nor seek to abolish the tragic, but he does "press his sado-masochistic imagination into the service of a grand cosmic 'yes.'" Sara Lyons concludes that "*Tristram of Lyonesse* is the epitome of Swinburne's counter-elegiac secularism . . . it strives to imagine the secular as an intoxicating love affair, and thereby to dissolve the identification of poetry with religious doubt, intellectual ambivalence, and disenchantment that had come to seem so natural to Victorian culture."[44]

It is worthwhile returning to "Before a Crucifix" to consider Swinburne's attitude towards, and understanding of, Christ, before comparing it with the understanding of Oscar Wilde, as another major proponent of art for the sake of art—and, incidentally, someone with serious reservations about Swinburne's emphasis on perverse behavior. Swinburne suggested that, had Christ really cared for the redemption of humankind, he would have come down from the cross, sacrificing his symbolic potency and dying an ordinary death with no resurrection. Then there are Swinburne's famous lines from his "Hymn to Proserpine" (1866), based on the supposed sentiments of the emperor Julian: "Thou hast conquered, O pale Galilean; the world has grown grey with thy breath." This mode of understanding Christ is very different from Oscar Wilde's understanding in *De Profundis* (written 1897, published 1905). Wilde envisages Christ as the supreme life-affirming Romantic, lover, poet, and individualist, giving to Man a Titan personality, rising above all the constraints of legalistic regimes. The obvious comparison here would be Blake's antinomian reading of the Gospels. There is clearly a study to be done of images of Christ in English poetry, starting with the suffering Christ who emerges from the shadow of God the Father in the twelfth century. In the specific context of a comparison with Greek drama,

---

42. Lyons, *Algernon Swinburne and Walter Pater*, 121.
43. Lyons, *Algernon Swinburne and Walter Pater*, 127.
44. Lyons, *Algernon Swinburne and Walter Pater*, 129.

Wilde not only claims that classical drama does not begin to compare with the Passion narrative but adds: "When one contemplates all this from the point of view of art alone one cannot but be grateful that the supreme office of the Church should be... the mystical presentation, by means of dialogue and costume and gesture even, of the Passion of her Lord."[45]

At the same time, when we read Wilde's poems we seem to find a pantheism and humanism inflected by Christian imagery, as in "E Tenebris," "Panthea," and "Humanitad." In "Humanitad," he writes:

> O smitten mouth! O forehead crowned with thorns!
> O chalice of all common miseries!
> Thou for our sakes that loved thee not hast borne
> An agony of endless centuries,
> And we were vain and ignorant nor knew
> That when we stabbed thy heart it was our own real hearts we slew.[46]

Here it is useful briefly to draw attention to Thomas Carlyle's estimate of the role claimed by the artist-poet, as presented by Trevor Hogan. According to Hogan, Carlyle (1795–1881) saw the emphasis laid by the artist-poet on the inward vision as not in itself capable of bridging the abyss separating subject and object, self and nature. Artist-poets simply expressed inward withdrawal, whingeing and giving vent to social alienation. For his part, Carlyle in *Sartor Resartus* (1833–34) sought a total view of the world uniting the science of consciousness with the science of knowledge, and presented "both the semiotic science as a poetic because symbolic mode of knowledge and the *Lebensphilosophie* as a philosophy of feeling" to be "experienced, believed, willed, enacted."[47]

Thomas Hardy (1840–1928) was a poet who rightly described himself as "churchy." He loved the church's liturgy, loved its music as it had once inhabited his early memories, loved and cared about its architectural presence at the heart of each huddle of habitation. He knew the Bible intimately. Yet he rejected the narrow morality with which the church was often associated, particularly with regard to marriage and "fallen women," and he was horrified by the ubiquitous god of war. Beyond that, he wrote poetry (and novels) that consistently rejected any trace of an ultimately benevolent Providence in favor of a principle of fatalism, variously attributed to the President of the Immortals and, following Schopenhauer, to the Immanent Will. The same approach informs his vast poetic drama, *The Dynasts*, on the Napoleonic wars. Before its opening scene the "Shade of the Earth" asks the "Immanent

---

45. Wilde, *De Profundis*.
46. Nicholson and Lee, *Oxford Book of English Mystical Verse*, 397.
47. Hogan, "Modernity as Revolution," 378.

Will" of its designs and is answered in terms of "Eternal artistries in circumstance" working unconsciously in rote-like patterns, indifferent to consequence and incapable of checking its clock-like laws.[48]

I have an investment in Hardy, because I have intimate personal acquaintance with his regional setting in Dorset as an adoptive maternal landscape from the Iron Age to Romano-Britain and medieval England, and also know the North Cornish coastline and West London scene that are so important for his poetry and his biography. This investment is supplemented by an intimate sense of the world of Hardy's near-neighbor, the dialect parson poet, polymath extraordinary, and protagonist of "Saxon" English, William Barnes (1801–1886), about whose funeral procession Hardy wrote a moving poem, "The Last Signal."[49] If you know the spirit of the place and understand its religious habit in its Anglican and Methodist forms, even though the 1930s are far away from the1830s, you have access to the nostalgia and sense of loss that pervade Hardy's poetry even as he expresses the mindless workings of universally destructive Fate.

Hardy was always the inveterate preacher. He echoes the preacher in Ecclesiastes on the depredations of Time and the loss of all that makes life worthwhile well before the body returns to the dust from whence it came. The zest of life has been exhausted even before our vain and vaunted human projects come to grief. The biographer of his London years, Mark Ford, suggests that this pessimistic anticipation of failure was already a settled psychological propensity and a rhetorical strategy in his earliest writings, including his first treatments of erotic dreams and his wooing of Emma.[50] The poem that eloquently expresses much of his pessimism in its philosophic form (marvellously realized in Britten's musical setting) is "Before Life and After."[51] In this poem, Hardy speaks of the happy state of nescience before consciousness "germed" and disturbed primal unknowing rightness with the knowledge of wrong, hope frustrated, and love lost. In a biblical phrase, he concludes by asking "how long, how long?" before unconsciousness brings the tally of human sorrow to an end.

Hardy has his own theory of secularization, based on the assumption that no one can any longer accept Christianity with intellectual honesty. He expresses this in his poem "God's Funeral" (1908–10), which provides the title of a book published by A. N. Wilson in 1999 on precisely the problem

---

48. Hardy, *Poetical Works*, 2:1–525.
49. Hardy, *Complete Poems*, 473.
50. Ford, *Thomas Hardy*.
51. Hardy, *Complete Poems*, 277.

of doubt in the "long" nineteenth century up to 1914.[52] Hardy sees a funeral procession slowly and sadly bearing a mysterious form, and immediately intuits whose funeral this is and meets it with his own answering sadness. What follows suggests how closely a concept of secularization is linked to a particular concept of God, in this case the project (and projection) of a Figure "we can no longer keep alive." God, our creation, was progressively endowed with justice and compassion. But rude reality supervened. Our myth collapsed in oblivion and the Maker of our own making "quavered, sank: and now has ceased to be." Clearly sympathizing with those who cannot accept the death of God, the poet does not fail to recollect how much he himself "once prized" what he now mourns for. There remain a few who still point forward, like Bunyan's pilgrim, to "yonder shining light," but the poet knows there is no break in the universal darkness. Hardy is blind to what others claim to see, and always remains "The Impercipient" (1898):

> Why thus my soul should be consigned
> To infelicity,
> Why always I must feel as blind
> To sights my brethren see,
> Why joys they find I cannot find,
> Abides a mystery.[53]

I could supplement this with Hardy's poem "The Respectable Burgher: on 'The Higher Criticism,'" where the poet marvels at the range of things reverend doctors are prepared to disbelieve, but maybe I can best illustrate Hardy's feelings about the church, the clergy, and above all church music from "The Choirmaster's Burial" (another Hardy poem set by Britten).[54] The choirmaster hopes that, when he too comes to his last resting place, the church musicians with their viols will play the old tune "Mount Ephraim" over his grave. However the vicar decrees "a read service quicker" in chill weather. This casual disrespect engenders a story about how the lack was remedied at night when bright seraphim foregathered by the choirmaster's grave to sing "the ancient stave." Hardy signals his approval of the old church music and its musicians and his disapproval of the insensitive vicar.

Hardy's sense of a vanishing village culture and its music needs to be set in a wider context. Merryn Williams provides that context in his *Thomas Hardy and Rural England* (1972).[55] For him the situation of people in ru-

52. Hardy, *Complete Poems*, 326; Wilson, *God's Funeral*.

53. Hardy, *Complete Poems*, 67.

54. "The Respectable Burgher," "The Choirmaster's Burial," in Hardy, *Complete Poems*, 159, 534–35.

55. Williams, *Thomas Hardy and Rural England*.

ral Dorset was one of starvation, illiteracy, illegitimacy, depopulation, and exploitation, and this was not new, even if further exacerbated in the nineteenth century. Hardy's writing really belongs in a long tradition going back to Goldsmith's *The Deserted Village* (1769), Crabbe's *The Village* (1783), and the poetry of John Clare, for example, *The Village Minstrel, and Other Poems* published in 1821. Hardy recreates this rural proletariat as real people, with, at the same time, a sympathetic concern for those who have begun to aspire to an intermediate class but are fated to experience frustration. This is the context against which the Immanent Will weaves its unconscious designs and where humans, unfortunate enough to be equipped with consciousness, suffer and experience loss. There is a complementary aspect to this explored in Mark Ford, *Thomas Hardy: Half a Londoner*, where the author discusses how Hardy, the inveterate auto-didact, church goer, and reader of the Greek New Testament, as well as aspiring metropolitan socialite, carefully constructed the image of a Dorset Arcadia lost and corrupted by the advent of the railways and London mores.[56]

With A. E. Housman (1859–1930) we encounter an adamant atheism that echoes Swinburne in its preference for classical paganism. The classical world easily outbid Christianity and its moralistic monotheism in its attractions. Housman arrived at doubt and then at atheism in adolescence, moving by inexorable degrees away from what he described as the best form of religion available to him: high church Anglicanism. Perhaps there is a study to be done of how high Anglicanism can precipitate doubt among a certain kind of highly sensitive humanist. In fact, Housman had no relish for the cautious regrets of honest doubt. For analytic help I turn to an address by Angela Leighton given in Trinity College Chapel in 2009[57] and some comments by Peter Howarth in *The Cambridge Companion to Twentieth Century Poetry*, edited by Neil Corcoran.[58]

Housman shared with many other humanist atheists a sense of the inferiority of humane modes of understanding compared with the rigor and cognitive power of the natural sciences. But his waspish vehemence had other and deeply emotional sources in the secret wounds inflicted by unrequited homosexual love. That required him to downgrade and trivialize his emotional life, including his poetry, by comparison with the rigors of textual classical scholarship. When it came to his activities as an exact and exacting classical scholar, he could appeal to secure criteria: in that avocation he

---

56. Ford, *Thomas Hardy*.
57. Leighton, "God and A.E. Housman."
58. "Fateful Forms: A. E. Housman, Charlotte Mew, Thomas Hardy and Edward Thomas," in Corcoran, *Cambridge Companion to Twentieth-Century English Poetry*, 59–73; 62–63.

was safe from the painful vagaries of impulse. Those vagaries could then be explored at a safe distance in self-indulgent poetic bagatelles that did not seriously matter and could be airily dismissed as tone of voice or stylistic preference. If so, the deepest sexual desires and the sufferings they invite are inconsequential. As a minor but nevertheless influential and accomplished poet, Housman could be, as Peter Howarth puts it, "a connoisseur of misery as Pater was of sensation." Howarth goes on to suggest that the same blend of satisfaction and self-scorn informs his blasphemous attacks on Christianity. The best known of Housman's poems dealing directly with Christianity is the "Easter Hymn" (1936), with sentiments that might be compared with Clough's poem on the same subject. It is in the conditional, almost as though alternatives were available.

> If in that Syrian garden, ages slain,
> You sleep, and know not you are dead in vain,
> Nor even in dreams behold how dark and bright
> Ascend in smoke and fire by day and night
> The hate you died to quench and could but fan,
> Sleep well and see no morning, son of man.[59]

The second verse explores the merest possibility that maybe the ascended Christ might sympathize with the morass of human misery, and so "Bow hither out of heaven and see and save." The expression is as perfect and easy as the understanding is shallow. It is shallow in the supposition that Christ died to reverse human violence and in the supposition that anything could turn on a heavenly intervention that canceled human freedom forever and reestablished a static original Eden bereft of meaningful and dynamic activity. It would be worthwhile comparing the easy sentiments of Housman about Christ's fanning "the flames he died to quench" with equally easy sentiments in Hardy, noting that two thousand years of reciting the mass have brought us no further than poison gas. Both Housman and Hardy assume that Christianity is a failed version of social amelioration. It seems beyond them as purveyors of this conventional wisdom about the consequences and nature of faith, to see Christianity as emblazoned in "the intolerable shirt of flame" that engulfed Christ—so that, in Eliot's words, we could only be "redeemed from fire by fire." In Housman and Hardy alike, one encounters a fundamental misapprehension of Christianity as a failed scheme of secular improvement that makes possible easy observations about the lack of progress after two thousand years of it.

---

59. Housman, "Easter Hymn," www.chiark.greenend.org.uk/~martinh/poems/housman.html#MPi, accessed July 2016.

The melancholy pathos of a perfectly formed but minor poetic production in *A Shropshire Lad* (1896)[60] becomes an arena for exploring emblems of male comradeship, of the free flow of encounters without consequence, and of the break-up of heterosexual relationships, waste, despair, and death. For Housman, the only viable motive for action is to capture such brief pleasure as may be possible. As in so much poetry of this period, this melancholy and despairing pose is given deeper and prophetic resonance by musical settings, for example by George Butterworth's song cycle, composed in 1912, with the added overtone of male comrades who go off to death in war.

> On the idle hills of summer,
> Sleepy with the flow of streams,
> Far I hear the steady drummer,
> Drumming like a noise in dreams.

---

60. Housman, *A Shropshire Lad*.

Chapter 6

The Early Twentieth Century

The twentieth century, taken as a whole, includes a whole series of major changes. They include the consequences of the explosion of print, of new modes of communication creating new readerships, and of poetry written outside the circle of the metropolis and the ancient universities, as well as universal education, the spread of English as a global medium, and crucial influences from other global cultures, notably France and North America. But for the discussion of the early twentieth century, these changes simply provide the background. The poets I want to discuss often lived substantial parts of their lives in the nineteenth century, though they also flourished in the early twentieth century. Some anomalies are unavoidable: Thomas Hardy has been already discussed in the previous chapter, even though much of his poetry, as distinct from his novels, was written between 1900 and 1928. One also has to remember that Hardy is a major poet of war in poems like "Men Who March Away," but he is not in any sense a war poet, and his perspective includes the Boer War and the Peninsular War. The poets I discuss here may live well into the century of total war, but their primary and formative experiences are mostly acquired decades earlier.

The poets I have in mind are, firstly, "popular" poets like Newbolt, Kipling, and Masefield, but including Bridges, who is a major poet, but hardly popular. These poets are selected because they are the last representatives of Protestant cultural dominance, even though they represent mostly a popular, or demotic, rather than a carefully grounded faith. The rather eclectic group of poets discussed in the remainder of the chapter are all post-Protestant, but they serve to foreground different modes of post-Protestant religion, Belloc and Chesterton in their pugnacious Catholicism,

Lawrence in his celebration of a powerful immanent principle, and Flecker and Waley as illustrating two forms of "orientalism."

I take Henry Newbolt (1862–1938) and Rudyard Kipling (1865–1936) together, because there are important similarities when it comes to their particular kind of Protestant nationalism, but with very significant differences when it comes to contemporary reception. Archbishop Rowan Williams preached a commemorative sermon about Kipling, but it is difficult to imagine his preaching such a sermon on Newbolt. T. S. Eliot took Kipling seriously as a writer of extremely eloquent verse, but as far as I know showed no interest in Newbolt. Presumably Newbolt lies permanently in the critical shadows because dismissed as entirely a period piece and as someone who purveyed what is now unacceptable sentiment. But in his time he was extremely influential and left a serious mark. I, like so many others, read him innocently, not yet knowing he was a despised relic. Moreover, Newbolt is a more complicated case than one might suppose, given that he was a Liberal and that he lived nearly up to the Second World War.

One or two of his poems were extremely well known, such as "Drake's Drum" (1896), "Clifton Chapel" (1908), and "Vitae Lampada" (1892). These poems convey ideas of above all else playing the game fairly, indifferent to whether you win or lose, and ideas of warfare, particularly naval warfare, as a chivalrous and honorable vocation, whether on one's own side or the side of "the enemy." Newbolt, rather like Rupert Brooke, apostrophized those who died for the imperial cause and whose bodies are buried on distant frontiers, quoting the lines that Wilfred Owen stigmatized permanently as "the old lie: *Dulce et decorum est pro patria mori.*"

Newbolt represents precisely the same popular Protestant Ethic and popular Protestant patriotism as Kipling represented, except that there was a different class location. Moreover, as I suggested above, this kind of Protestant sentiment infused and suffused a large swathe of English life at least up to the catastrophe of the First World War: there are still traces of it in the early part of Siegfried Sassoon's *Memoirs of a Fox-Hunting Man*.[1] Perhaps it is worth remembering Thomas Hardy's enthusiastic support for the war, and pondering why it has not invested him with the same negative aura that surrounds Newbolt and that still complicates the reception of Kipling. The same holds for H. G. Wells, who execrated "The Hun" just as much as Kipling did. Perhaps in the case of Newbolt it has something to do with the relatively narrow range of his writing, or at any rate the narrow range of what is now remembered, if remembered at all, whereas, in the case of Kipling, it has to do with just one or two very well known and distinctly unfortunate lines

---

1. Sassoon, *Memoirs of a Fox-Hunting Man.*

about "lesser breeds" and taking up the "white man's burden." Inevitably these lines are taken out of the overall context of Kipling's very extensive writing. Beyond the negative aura they attract, there is a very wide-ranging and complicated body of poetry that can still deliver an emotional punch to contemporary readers if they care to take the trouble.

One point is puzzling. Because Kipling was an active Mason, with religious sympathies ranging beyond Christianity, he is thought to be a deist on the margin of Christian faith, if Christian at all. Yet while it is true that he was not all that much concerned with specific Christian teaching about Son of God and Son of Man, his kind of biblically saturated Protestantism probably approximated what most Britons took to be a standard contemporary version of Protestant sentiment. You have only to remember the kind of psalmic sentiment that later informed the massed choral singing of Kipling's "Non nobis Domine" to have a sense of the tenor of this kind of biblical faith.

> And we confess our blame —
> How all too high we hold
> That noise which men call Fame,
> That dross which men call Gold.[2]

To reinforce this point, which has relevance to the whole secularization thesis, quite apart from Kipling, I point to some more important examples, and begin with the patriotic poem called "The Children's 'Song'" from *Puck of Pook's Hill*.[3] The first verse, repeated as the last verse, might confirm the negative stereotype:

> Land of our Birth, we pledge to thee
> Our love and toil in the years to be;
> When we are grown and take our place
> As men and women with our race.

But thereafter it appeals to the grace, strength and judgment of God to:

> Teach us the Strength that cannot seek,
> By deed or thought to hurt the weak;
> That, under Thee, we may possess
> Man's strength to comfort man's distress.

"Hymn before Action" (1896) is wary of the physical and moral perils of empire in a way that anticipates the famous "Recessional" of 1897, but it also includes sympathetic concern for those of other faiths who fight in the

---

2. Kipling, *Works*, 512.
3. Kipling, *Works*, 573.

British ranks and (perhaps more surprisingly) invokes the Blessed Virgin in an echo of the *Stabat Mater*:

> Ah, Mary pierced with sorrow,
> Remember, reach and save
> The soul that comes tomorrow
> Before the God that gave![4]

Perhaps it should here be said that if this scrutiny of poetry "proper" were extended to the kinds of poems and hymns that make up the warp and woof of popular faith, then the most influential sources would extend along a broad spectrum from the Evangelical hymns of Cecil Frances Alexander like "There is a green hill far away," "All things bright and beautiful," and "Once in royal David's city," to the hymn "Dear Lord and Father of mankind" by the American Quaker John Greenleaf Whittier (1807-1892). The question of popular hymnody must come up again in discussion of Robert Bridges, as it has already come up in relation to Watts and Wesley.

John Masefield (1878-1967) is yet another poet who achieved a wide popular following, for example the almost universally known poem sung in schools titled "Cargoes" and also "Sea Fever," set by John Ireland. These poems celebrated the world of ships and the life of seafaring, as offering adventurous wandering and independence. One of the most popular poems of Masefield was "Reynard the Fox" (1920), which, in a graphic narrative (worth comparing with Sassoon's *Memoirs of a Fox-Hunting Man*) attacked the cruelty of hunting. Many of his poems (as well as his plays) have Christian themes. The fact that his plays on Christian themes encountered objections on their exposure to the media gives some indication of the aura then surrounding and protecting the sacred. The most famous of his religious poems, "The Everlasting Mercy" (1911), was constantly quoted and anthologized, especially the section beginning "O Christ who holds the open gate." It has a Eucharistic reference and concerns the change that came about with the conversion of the reprobate Saul Kane on his encounter with the everlasting mercy.

Robert Bridges (1844-1930) was an explicitly Christian poet, but not one who achieved any extensive popular readership. Perhaps he is best remembered for his advocacy of the poems of Gerard Manley Hopkins. His most famous work was his "Testament of Beauty," published in 1929, in which he apostrophized beauty as the "eternal spouse" of the divine and "angel of God's presence" in all creation. We come to Wisdom through the door of Beauty rather than reason. Christ, the true vine, with his ethic of

---

4. Kipling, *Works*, 324.

happiness, was at the heart of all our friendships: "self-expres'd in not-self." Bridges also had a Platonic sense of the radiant openness of childhood to divine impressions, which he referred to as the springtide miracle of a child's nativity.

Bridges had a passionate attachment to England and its church which comes out in his poem "Noel: Christmas 1913," where he speaks of

> the tow'rs
> that crown England so fair,
> That stand up strong in prayer
> unto God for our souls;[5]

Mellowed and transfigured, he hearkens to the seasonal bells in "the aspect of th'eternal silence." This sense of England as homeland, and as a country imbued with Christianity, came out passionately in the course of the First World War. Perhaps his most lasting achievements lie in the reform of English hymnody, beginning with the Yattendon hymnal of 1899, which provided the link between Victorian and early twentieth-century hymnody. His translations, like "All my hope on God is founded," are remarkable for their nobility of diction.

With G. K. Chesterton (1874–1936) and Hilaire Belloc (1870–1953) we encounter a different world and one informed by vigorous, theologically informed, and often polemical Catholicism. Their later years included the occlusion of the taken-for-granted popular Protestantism of Kipling and Masefield. To understand the social theory behind their positions, one needs to know that sometimes they saw little difference between capitalist society and its anti-democratic opponents. They sought to bypass the polarity of capitalism and socialism in what they called distributivism. Catholic intellectuals were a minority within a minority and one has to recognize a wider vision in the historian Christopher Dawson and a later development in thinkers like Maritain. The Catholicism of Chesterton and Belloc entertained a vision of a kind of Christian civilization that was the inspiration of European culture and was untroubled by the issues that inspired doubt in some Victorians, in particular biblical criticism. For Chesterton, the propagation of eugenics was a symptom of cultural crisis and loss of faith. For Belloc, that same loss of faith meant that the humiliation of Islam would not outlast the temporary technical superiority of the West. For both Chesterton and Belloc, the tradition of the church bypassed the issues which troubled Protestants. As for Belloc's religious poetry, for example on the Mysteries of the Virgin, it had little popular impact. Chesterton fared much better, for

---

5. Cecil, *Oxford Book of Christian Verse*, 503–4.

example his poems "Lepanto," "The Donkey," "The Rolling English Road," and "O God of earth and altar," included in the 1906 *English Hymnal*.

D. H. Lawrence (1885–1930) wrote a great deal of poetry as well as novels and travel works, and his first essays in print in 1909 were poems. His writing owed a debt to the unembellished and free modernist style of the imagists and was distinguished by its appeal to the unconscious, mysterious inner forces, to the primitive and the sexual, as well as by opposition to war and Protestant Puritanism. But these well-known and stereotypical characteristics have obscured his highly creative approach to religion motivated by saturation in the Bible as a child in the Nottinghamshire coalfield regularly taken to the Congregational church. He remembers this childhood with intense nostalgia in his poem "Piano." A powerful memory unmans him, stirred by his mother and by the tinkling of a piano as she played hymns on Sunday evenings.

His free and imaginative approach was also stimulated by his anger as he abandoned Christianity in his early twenties at the narrow literalism of "parsons and Sunday-school teachers." He sought to release the richness and the multiplicity of the biblical text from the restrictive lens of the literal meaning. According to Terence R. Wright he wanted to develop a religious alternative both to skepticism and to what he saw as outworn belief.[6] He regarded Nietzsche as having demolished Christianity as it then stood, and as providing a path to a reformulated faith in non-metaphysical terms. He was also influenced by late-Victorian and Edwardian forms of esoteric thought like the Fellowship of the New Life and theosophy, as was W. B. Yeats. He sought the ancient wisdom in the Bible, including intimations of sacred sex, for example in "Genesis." These intimations were half buried by the Puritanical God for whom the body and its instincts were the source of sin and who induced guilt and the need for penitence and forgiveness. His poem "Shadows," anticipating his own death, uses the word "God" to signal an immanent principle whereby we go down into the earth with all its seeming irretrievable losses to discover unexpected blossomings and the creation of a new man.

James Elroy Flecker (1884–1915) is worth some consideration because he brings into view two "exotic" elements. To begin with, Flecker had a Jewish and Eastern European ethnic background. His grandparents were Polish Jews who converted to Christianity and came to England for safety. In England his grandfather was a Baptist minister and his father practiced as an Anglican priest and schoolmaster. He sent his son to Dean Close

---

6. "Rewriting Genesis: The Nineteenth-Century roots of D. H. Lawrence's Religion," in Woodhead, *Reinventing Christianity*, 119–26.

independent school, Cheltenham, prior to studying classics at Trinity College, Oxford. At Oxford, James Elroy Flecker acquired a lifelong philhellenism, was attracted by aestheticism, and influenced in what may have been a homo-erotic relationship by the classicist Jack (later Sir Jack) Beazley. He was further influenced by the poetry of Baudelaire, whom he saw as a sin-haunted moralist, haunted, like himself, by demanding parents.

There is also Flecker's role in the Near East as a British official. In that capacity he acquired the relevant languages. To understand the background here and the slow literary and poetic apprehension of the Near East in Britain, I am using C. E. Bosworth's authoritative survey of an "orientalist" tradition in English literature, with particular reference to poetry.[7] This tradition does not begin with Shelley's "The Revolt of Islam" (1817), which is really a vehicle for an attack on Christianity, and an analysis of the paradoxes of secular revolution. It begins instead with works of derivative evocation like Thomas Moore's *Lalla Rookh* and Matthew Arnold's "Sohrab and Rustum." Richard Burton is a key figure here, as someone who cashed in on a vogue for agnostic pessimism and hedonism notoriously fed by Edward Fitzgerald's *The Rubáiyát of Omar Khayyám* (1859).

A proper understanding of the Arab, Turkish, and Persian Near East did not emerge until the early twentieth century, and the poetry of James Elroy Flecker was a major conduit of this understanding. Between 1907 and 1915, (when he died early of TB in Switzerland), he produced numerous poems, of which the best-known is "The Seven Gates of Damascus." Flecker was by no means besotted by the Near East, and, indeed, yearned for Oxford, the Dorset heathlands, and the Cotswolds, as well as taking an increasingly favorable view of English life and Christianity. But he thoroughly understood what he cordially disliked and successfully evoked it. Throughout he retained a sensuous delight in the present even as he conveyed a genuine sense of alien Near Eastern traditions and spirituality. His final major work was *Hassan . . . on the golden journey to Samarkand*, a poetic drama of disillusion touched with sadism, which anticipated the poetic dramas of Christopher Fry and T. S. Eliot. Due to the onset of war a performance of *Hassan* was delayed until 1923, when it scored a major success with music by Delius and ballet by Fokine.

Arthur Waley (1889–1966) was also Ashkenazi by background, but his "orientalism" concerned the Far East rather than the Near East. At King's College, Cambridge, he was influenced by the aesthetic philosophy of G. E. Moore and eventually lived a hermit-like existence working in the oriental section of the British Museum. He became the main conduit of Japanese and

---

7. Bosworth, "James Elroy Flecker," 363–64.

Chinese culture and poetry into English literary culture, influenced to some degree by Ezra Pound and mixing with the Bloomsbury Group. Several of his poems were set by Benjamin Britten in 1957. Perhaps one should see him as part of the interchange initiated by global contact, including western economic and political power in the course of cultural encounter over two centuries. This begins with figures like the Indianist and minor poet Edwin Arnold, and exercises an influence sufficient to help a poet like Rabinadrath Tagore, or even a writer like Khalil Gibran, inform aspects of western spirituality. I have already mentioned Delius and Britten, but it is also worth remembering that one of Mahler's greatest works, *Das Lied von der Erde* (1909), set translations of Chinese poems by Hans Bethge and initiated a change in the western sense of temporality also signaled by W. B. Yeats.

Chapter 7

War Poets; Pacifists and Marxists; Poets of Wars Post-1945

This is a key chapter, because the "century of total war" brings into high relief a fundamental question raised at the beginning of this book about the incompatibility of primitive Christianity with the dynamics of politics, especially retributive violence. In my initial treatment in *Pacifism* (1965),[1] and subsequent elaborations up to the present, I identified the oscillations in Christian history between pacifist withdrawal and revolutionary violence. In the modern period these oscillations were reproduced in both religious and secular forms.

The issues of war and peace did not come to a head in the nineteenth century, though there were anti-war movements in the Crimean War, notably expressed in the eloquent speeches of John Bright, and in the Boer War, and there was a current of pacific feeling dating back to the Peace Societies formed at the end of the Peninsular Wars. But the early twentieth century was a time of political questioning and intensified theorizing about the causes of war and about the establishment of international peace. The experiences of the First World War provided an even more intense lens about the causes of war and generated sentiments and hopes about a world where mass slaughter was to be outlawed. These same problems of war and peace occupied sensitive minds, including poets', throughout the twentieth century. In my writings on this issue over more than fifty years, I tried to map various responses to the extraordinary violence unleashed in the World Wars, and extending into the Cold War, following the dropping of the atomic bomb, and the conflicts of colonialism.

1. Martin, *Pacifism*.

Within the religious sphere there was a set of responses that moved between strict pacifist withdrawal, generalized pacific internationalism, and analogies between sacrificial death as understood by Christianity and sacrificial death in solidarity with comrades and countrymen. I also identified the same oscillation between withdrawal and revolution throughout Christian history replayed in the secular context and the parallel analogy of self-sacrifice made for the sake of the secular nation or revolutionary Marxist ideology. At the same time, there was, under the pressure of war, a move back to a fundamentally Christian understanding of violence which combined an understanding of sacrifice with a horror at the inhumanity involved in mass slaughter. A surprising number of poets deployed Christian imagery or became explicitly Christian, and frequently Catholics.

In this chapter I initially have in mind the group defined as war poets because they actually engaged in the fighting or enlisted, such as Brooke, Thomas, Owen, Sassoon, Graves, Gurney, and Rosenberg. These are selected in part because they can be so illuminating about the moral paradoxes inherent in war, notably its pitiable waste in the context of political drives and the call of solidarity, especially the solidarity with comrades so evident in Sassoon. This chapter also includes two groups of pacifists and Marxists, considered as alternative forms of political radicalism, as well as some poets responding to the prolonged aftermath of the Second World War, including the wars of the end of empire. The last poet discussed, James Fenton, provides an opportunity to develop some general thoughts on poetic rhetoric and the nature of political responsibility.

Rupert Brooke (1887–1915) is another poet associated with place, in his case Dymock in Gloucestershire and the area around Cambridge described with some ambivalence in his poem "The Old Vicarage, Grantchester." This well-known poem was written with nostalgia in Germany and concluded with an invocation of the village, asking "stands the church clock at ten to three / And is there honey still for tea?" At King's College, Cambridge, Brooke was a hedonistic neo-pagan who participated in the Cambridge Apostles. He enjoyed the company of the Bloomsbury Group, and was sufficiently confused about his sexuality to have something like a breakdown in 1912. He is regarded as a barometer of patriotic feeling in the period 1910–1915, before the onset of disillusion, in particular his poem "The Soldier." Although he was commissioned, he died, like Byron, in Greece, succumbing to an infection. Rupert Brooke belongs to a group of mostly minor and mainly pastoral poets, like de la Mare, Edmund Blunden, and W. H. Hudson, loosely linked together as "Georgian." He collaborated with Edward Marsh in the first of several collections, *Georgian Poetry* 1911–12.

Edward Thomas (1878–1917) came from London of a Welsh background, and his association with place included both the Wiltshire of the nature mystic Richard Jeffries, and Hampshire, the scene of his many intensely observed poems about wandering in its landscape. Although for years a prolific prose writer and acute literary critic, he only turned to poetry in 1914 under the personal influence of Robert Frost. The poems he wrote in the years immediately following are about his profound love of natural beauty rather more than about his war experiences. He enlisted, though he could have claimed exemption, and was killed in 1917 soon after arriving in France. He felt the war was beyond mere "petty right and wrong."

Thomas's poems are the works of a man for whom personal relationships were difficult, and they point towards a kind of modernism in their intense sense of solitude and existential isolation. His short poem "In Memoriam (Eastertide 1915)" brings together the countryside and the depredations of war:

> The flowers left thick at nightfall in the wood
> This Eastertide call into mind the men,
> Now far from home, who with their sweethearts, should
> Have gathered them and will do never again.[2]

His poem "Rain" brings present war experiences and past memories together. He speaks of himself as one who has

> no love that this wild rain
> Has not dissolved except the love of death,
> If love it be for what is perfect and
> Cannot, the tempest tells me, disappoint.[3]

Siegfried Sassoon (1886–1967) was the son of a mixed marriage, dissolved when he was only four, between a Jewish Baghdadi merchant and an English Anglo-Catholic mother. He was brought up in Kent, and in his three volumes of semi-fictionalized memoirs, he described his passion for the "tremendous trivialities" of hunting and cricket, his delight in the Wealden countryside, and his passionate attachment to male friends.[4] He brought his nervous determination to excel at sport to his role as an army officer and was decorated for conspicuous bravery. The memoirs are in several volumes, and are, of course, in prose, but in prose as eloquent as his poetry. They reveal a man of acute sensitivity coping with a gradual realization of the nature of the First World War and veering between moral shock and a

---

2. Thomas, *Annotated Collected Poems*, 80.
3. Thomas, *Annotated Collected Poems*, 105.
4. Sassoon, *Complete Memoirs of George Sherston*.

wild desire to prove himself in battle to the point where death seems almost desirable. Up to 1916, Sassoon had shown no particular engagement with Christianity beyond the most conventional and intermittent churchgoing, and he is aware that the soldiers under his command have no engagement with Christianity whatever. He mentions just one exception on hearing soldiers sing "How sweet the name of Jesus sounds" and recollecting, ruefully, how the name of Jesus is usually employed in military parlance. To the soldiers around him the Lent and late Easter of 1916 meant nothing, but then something burgeons in Sassoon very like the Christian sensibility that later burgeoned in Owen and also underlay David Jones's account, as an ordinary soldier, of the same Somme battle lines as those experienced by Sassoon. Away for a month on an army camp, Sassoon is instructed in the necessities of killing in so chilling a manner that he recognizes just how profoundly this ethos of death contradicts Christianity. As in the case of David Jones, this crisis of moral sensibility makes his later conversion to Catholicism entirely understandable.

Here it is important to read the poetry written in the war years, for example in *Siegfried Sassoon: The War Poems* (1983),[5] because they reveal different preoccupations from those dominant in the memoirs. In the memoirs the points of spiritual reference are music and literature, for example Tolstoy, whereas the points of reference in the poems are music and religion, in spite of Sassoon's self-description as a non-practicing and anti-clerical Christian. It becomes clear that he is in a totally irreligious environment but is visited with a moral crisis marked by major religious dimensions.

While Sassoon was on the western front he formed a close relationship with the writer and poet Robert Graves, and became further disillusioned with the patriotic rhetoric of war. Graves encouraged him to explore a kind of "gritty realism" about the way things actually are that looked towards modernism. Invalided home, he made a declaration against the conduct of the war and its corrupted aims which led to his being sent to Craiglockhart psychiatric hospital. Here he met Wilfred Owen and became for Owen "Keats, Christ, and Elijah." His poem "Counter-Attack" (1918) provided Owen with poetic resources for the realistic evocation of intolerable carnage:

> The place was rotten with dead; green clumsy legs
> High-booted, sprawled and grovelled along the saps
> And trunks, face downward in the sucking mud.[6]

---

5. Sassoon, *The War Poems*.
6. Sassoon, *The War Poems*, 94.

Some of Owen's finest poetry was inspired by this encounter. Thereafter, Sassoon turned to his memoirs, married, and also engaged in a number of relationships with males. Towards the end of his life he converted to Catholicism. Something of the extraordinary intensity of his inner life emerges in the lines:

> Alone . . . . . . The word is life endured and known.
> It is the stillness where our spirits walk
> And all but inmost faith is overthrown.[7]

Wilfred Owen (1893–1918) is today regarded as the foremost poet of the war, though his poems were little known until the nineteen-sixties when they were rediscovered and given wider resonance by their use alongside the Latin text in Britten's *War Requiem*. He came of a lower-middle-class background, and was brought up a devout Evangelical Anglican. For a while as a young man he assisted in a parish, but then, somewhat disillusioned, he took classes at the (then) University College, Reading, and taught English. In 1915 he enlisted and became an officer. After many traumatizing experiences he was sent to the Craiglockhart hospital. Here, as already mentioned, he met Siegfried Sassoon, and this meeting transformed his poetry into what eventually became a definitive understanding of the First World War. His words about the "pity of war" were inscribed on the Westminster Abbey memorial to the sixteen poets of the war generation. He died in the final stages of the war after he had returned to the front and had been decorated for gallantry.

His poems have inscribed the biblical image of the father's slaying the sons on the imaginative map of the conflict. Moreover, this biblical reference and the horror of mythic sacrifice based on the story of Abraham and Isaac (reappearing in another form in Rosenberg) comes into fuller view when we read his massive correspondence with his devout mother. He tells her quite explicitly that he has become more and more Christian in adopting a position on violence very close to the Sermon on the Mount. Above all, perhaps, he drained war of its rhetoric, for example in "The Send-Off" and "Insensibility."[8]

Isaac Rosenberg (1890–1918) was the author of some of the most impressive poetry of the war, notably his *Poems from the Trenches*. He was the child of Jewish parents from the Baltic States, and went to school in Stepney in London's Jewish East End. From there, he attended the Slade School of Fine Art at University College, London, where he met artists like David

---

7. Larkin, *Oxford Book of Twentieth-Century Verse*, 280–86.
8. Larkin, *Oxford Book of Twentieth-Century Verse*, 285, 280–81.

Bomberg, Mark Gertler, and Dora Carrington. After migrating to South Africa on account of poor health, he enlisted in 1915, with no particular patriotic commitments except a wish to get it all over. He was killed in the German spring offensive of 1918. His "Break of Day in the Trenches," with its overtones of mythic sacrifice, is regarded by some as the finest poem of the war.

Ivor Gurney (1890–1937) was remarkable, partly on account of genius to some extent thwarted by a bipolar mental illness exacerbated by the war, and partly because he crossed over seamlessly between music and poetry. His unusual potential has been underlined in a careful critical essay by Geoffrey Hill.[9] He came of humble origins in Gloucester and early showed promise, becoming a chorister at Gloucester cathedral where he was befriended by the composer Herbert Howells. He then went to the Royal College of Music, where he was taught by Stanford, also the teacher of Vaughan Williams, someone who shared Gurney's Gloucester roots. This illustrates the intense attachment to place in England shared by so many of the war poets. It further illustrates the extent to which composers set the work of English poets: Gurney set poems by Housman, W. H. Davies, and Edward Thomas, and his masterpiece "Sleep," from his *Five Elizabethan Songs*, was a setting of John Fletcher.

Gurney joined the Gloucester regiment in 1915 and wrote a series of remarkable poems, "Severn and Somme," that were published in 1917, a period of the war when he was both wounded and gassed. However, he had had a breakdown in 1913, and in 1918 he suffered a further breakdown. From that time on till his death in 1937 he was in psychiatric hospitals, while continuing to write poems and compose.

Robert von Ranke Graves (1895–1985) was born in Wimbledon to middle-class parents and attended several preparatory schools before getting a scholarship to Charterhouse and, later, a classics exhibition to St. John's, Oxford. He only took this up after the First World War, having early on volunteered for service. He was badly wounded in the battle of the Somme and misreported dead on August 6th, 1916. As already mentioned, he influenced Siegfried Sassoon in writing about the realities of the war, though what Graves himself wrote at the time often looked back to the innocence of childhood and the peaceful English landscape. Much of his writing about his experiences in the war, whether in poetry or in prose, came much later. During the interwar years, he broke up with his wife and moved to Majorca with the poet Laura Riding, who had considerable influence on his writing.

---

9. "Gurney's 'Hobby,'" in Hill, *Collected Critical Writings*, 424–47.

Graves's later writing included speculations on Christian origins and *The White Goddess* (1948),[10] which had an influence on popular understandings of both poetry and religion, even though largely the product of a fusion between his classical scholarship and his luxuriant imagination. These popular understandings fed into ideas of Celtic religion and neo-paganism and also affected the thinking of Ted Hughes and Sylvia Plath.

Graves thought the writings of early anthropologists like Frazier provided the bridge between poetry and science. He supposed there to have been a primal goddess who preceded the unfortunate delusions of aggressive male monotheism and who was the prototypical source of poetry and religion. Of course, the idea of a mother goddess is quite a standard scholarly supposition and has had an influence on feminist theology, but Graves built on it his own fantasies about the way her rituals were the main source of the myths, legends, and dogmas of Christianity. He believed that the prototypical source of the cult of the mother goddess was magical, shamanistic, and primitive in the way that the imagination of the child and literature for children is primitive. The child is a kind of poet combining the magical and the wildly insightful as in Edward Lear and Lewis Carroll. In the poem "Babylon," he wrote:

> The child alone a poet is
> Spring and Fairyland are his,
> Truth and Reason show but dim.
> And all's poetry with him.[11]

David Jones (1895–1974) was a major artist, writer, and poet. He was of Welsh background on his father's side, and Wales and its legends and history came early on in his life to provide him with a passionate identity, but he was born in Brockley in South-East London. His biography is extremely complex, and begins with his relation to his father, who was an open-air preacher. This meant that Jones was saturated in the Authorised Version of the Bible, and exposed to such papers as *The Christian Herald*. The background also introduced him to a culture that induced a strong sense of sin as well as redemption. All of this is intimately familiar to me in memories of my own childhood, though I recollect the millennial revivalism more than any culture of sin. But the genealogy on David Jones's mother's side was high church and quite disjunctive. This too I recollect, not because my intelligent (though formally uneducated) mother was high church, but because she encouraged my reading and aesthetic interest in poetry and music. For

---

10. Graves, *The White Goddess*.
11. Graves, *Fairies and Fusiliers*, 11.

David Jones, his disjunctive background involved chronic sibling rivalry and the deployment of his poor health as a reason for retiring to bed to read voraciously. It also involved following his intellectual mother in precocious drawing at a very early age before early attending Camberwell School of Art. Here he accepted celibacy as the price of vocation.

David Jones did not complete his great prose poem, *In Parenthesis*, on his experience of the war in the Royal Welch Fusiliers, until 1937.[12] As an extended evocation of an experience running from mobilization to near annihilation, and one which called on the vast background of recent and historic conflicts, it is unequalled. Dai Greatcoat, as he described himself, celebrated the tenderness of comradeship of soldiers under intense strain. In 1921 David Jones became a Catholic, as a result of this experience and of a particular epiphany at the front, when he accidentally came upon a priest celebrating Mass with some French soldiers. Some of his most beautiful artworks are found in the lettering he devised for prayers, often in Latin. He spent some years with Eric Gill in religious communities in Ditchling in Sussex and the Black Mountains where he developed his craft and the art, or indeed almost the religion, of making. He was the archetypal visionary outsider: Blake, Stanley Spencer, Samuel Palmer.

In 1932, David Jones suffered a serious breakdown prior to completing his masterpiece. He sets his poem in the context of the saving sacrifice of Christ and of the liturgy. The liturgy and the long history of warfare provide the governing framework of an amazing performance, demotic, allusive, and incantatory. It has to be read aloud. It was followed in 1952 by *The Anathemata*,[13] seeking to ravel up the disparate voices of British history. This is a difficult work, described nevertheless by Auden, on the back of the Faber reprint of the book, as "probably the finest long poem of the twentieth century." It would not be too much to say that the work of David Jones as artist, engraver, writer, and poet is signal evidence of a return to the framework of liturgy among both the composers and poets of the modern era. His picture, "Vexilla Regis" (1948), of the tree that gives life gives some idea of the depth of cross-reference in all his writing and art.

Vernon Scannell (1922–2007) was a poet of the Second World War. He was born of a poor family in Lincolnshire, who constantly moved about till they settled in Aylesbury. Leaving school at fourteen, Scannell discovered poetry at fifteen, especially de la Mare and Hardy. He enlisted in 1940, and fought in North Africa and Normandy. He hated the army, and twice deserted in disgust before teaching English (and, as a semi-professional boxer,

---

12. Jones, *In Parenthesis*.
13. Jones, *The Anathemata*.

encouraging boxing) at a preparatory school in Surrey. His drunkenness and violence probably reflected the trauma of his war experiences. His best-known poem is "Walking Wounded" (1965).[14] It evokes "vehicles made mythopoeic by their mortal freight," and is marked by his mordant sense of mortality and the pains of memory and desire.

I include Edith Sitwell (1887–1964) here because she responded to experience of the air bombardment of the Second World War as well as the dropping of the atomic bomb. Edith Sitwell was an eccentric aristocrat who represented a modernist *avant garde*. This led to a famous public confrontation with Alfred Noyes, a poet who felt relegated to a despised traditional past. Oddly enough, Sitwell and Noyes both appealed to tradition, just as Eliot himself also appealed to tradition.

Edith Sitwell explored the artificiality of life and its underlying barbarism in "Gold Coast Customs" (1929), and the relation between poetry and music in *Façade* (published in 1922 in the same year as Eliot's "The Waste Land"), with music by William Walton and decor by John Piper. Her most famous poem, set by Britten as his *Canticle III*, was "Still Falls the Rain." It followed on the London Blitz and concluded with the lines lamenting human culpability:

> Blind as the nineteen hundred
> And forty nails
> Upon the cross.[15]

Sitwell's "The Shadow of Cain" is a poem of complex symbolism, the first of three following on the dropping of the atomic bomb and eye-witness accounts of the terrible consequences. Lines towards its conclusion run:

> And the fires of your Hell shall not be quenched by the rain
> From those torn and parti-coloured garments of Christ, those rags
> That once were Men. Each wound, each stripe,
> Cries out more loudly than the voice of Cain—
> Saying 'Am I my brother's keeper?'[16]

The underlying theme concerns destructive and internecine impulses that generate a second Fall and stimulate apocalyptic potentials. There is an echo here of the deep sense of human culpability in the imagist and modernist poet and art critic, T. E. Hulme (1883–1917). Hulme translated Sorel's classic *Reflections on Violence*, and was fully aware of the pity and horror of the war; indeed, he was killed at the front in 1917. But he also had a strong

---

14. Stallworthy, *New Oxford Book of War Poetry*, 322.
15. Sitwell, *Collected Poems*.
16. Larkin, *Oxford Book of Twentieth-Century Verse*, 224.

sense (for example, in his *Speculations*, brought together by Herbert Read in 1924)[17] of the key religious themes of moral ruin and sacrifice by way of contrast to the kind of superficial progressivism he identified in Bertrand Russell and Clive Bell. Edith Sitwell was received into the Catholic Church in 1955. Alfred Noyes also converted.

As a postscript to the war poets, I touch on a group of radical anti-war poets who were pacifist rather than just skeptical of the patriotic rhetoric of war or preferring peacefulness to bellicosity. I follow them with a group embracing the other radical option of Marxism. The first of the pacifists is Laurence Housman (1865–1959), the socialist brother of A. E. Housman, and like him a homosexual. Housman was member of the Society of Friends and deeply influenced by the life of St. Francis, which he brought to life in drama. His portrayal of biblical (and royal) characters on stage put him athwart the censor. He was a sponsor of the "Peace Pledge Union," a co-founder of the "Men's League for Women's Suffrage," a member of the "British Society for the Study of Sex Psychology," and of the Order of Chaeronea, a secret society for homosexuals.

Basil Bunting (1900–1985) was a modernist poet influenced by Ezra Pound. He was brought up in a Quaker family in Northumberland, and, towards the end of the First World War, was imprisoned as a conscientious objector. Thereafter, he lived a colorful life, as summarized by Christopher Spaide in *The New Yorker* for August the 2nd, 2016. "By the age of fifty, he had been a music critic, a sailor, a balloon operator, a wing-commander, a military interpreter, a foreign correspondent, and a spy. He had married twice, had four children, lived in three continents (and one boat), survived multiple assassination attempts, and been incarcerated throughout Europe."[18] Then, in his sixties, he encountered the counterculture in Newcastle. He was sufficiently stimulated by it to recollect his own adolescence in *Briggflatts* (1966).[19] This poem plotted his own life course, from exploitative "innocence" to death's "endless night," against a powerful evocation of the history of Northumbria, and drew on various sources, from Anglo-Saxon and Persian epics to Wordsworth's *The Prelude*. The poem appealed to the Beat generation on both sides of the Atlantic, but then fell into obscurity, in spite of the critical efforts of Donald Davie in *Under Briggflatts* (1989).[20] For a poem emulating music and written to be read aloud, it is surprisingly disjointed alike in its rhythms and topics. Bunting's references to music are

17. Hulme, *Speculations*.
18. Spaide, "The Improbable Life."
19. Bunting, *Briggflatts*.
20. Davie, *Under Briggflatts*.

vague gestures with even less serious purchase than those in the *Four Quartets*. Bunting may have identified himself as a Quaker, but there is barely any trace of Quakerism in his poetry.

James Kirkup (1918–2009) was born in South Shields and attended Durham University. He became a conscientious objector in the Second World War and performed his national service in forestry. His objections had no religious element and turned around his contempt for male heroics. Later he became poetry Fellow at Leeds University. He was a prolific poet and translator in several languages, and his poems were marked by precise and deft observation. He worked at universities around the globe, including Kyoto University. He also wrote a major poem on the bombing of Hiroshima and Nagasaki. He was associated with the agnostic Ethical Society of Bayswater and with the Progressive League founded by H. G. Wells. James Kirkup was a flamboyant gay who was eventually embarrassed by all that followed on account of a blasphemy trial (the last in England) for his necrophiliac poem on the dead Christ after the crucifixion, "The Love that Dares to Speak its Name." Unfortunately this helped obscure a career of signal literary achievement, though it made Kirkup an icon of the gay movement.

It is worth mentioning here the career of Christopher Logue (1926–2011) because in different ways it parallels the talent for the bohemian and countercultural lifestyle obvious in both Bunting and Kirkup. Logue was born in a Catholic family in Portsmouth, but soon showed a talent for disruption and mayhem. He was best known as a translator (or "rewriter" in his own words) but he was a natural inhabitant of the half-world and of demonstrations and protests generally, especially against nuclear armaments. He was interested in parapsychology and wrote jazz poetry, pornography, and works of visceral violence. He has been described as a pacifist, which only indicates how the word can migrate to pick up looser meanings about opposition to "the establishment," symbolized in protest about "the bomb." I am reminded of the way I bemused my own conscientious objection tribunal in 1948 by combining Christian pacifism, classic liberal opposition to conscription, objections to fighting our erstwhile Russian comrades, and an artistic preference for creation over destruction.

Cliff Ashby (1919–2012) was brought up in the family of a peripatetic Methodist minister. He left school at fourteen without any qualifications to work as a window-dresser. Called up, he opted for agricultural work, which brought him into touch with artists, writers, and poets and a pacifist community in Essex cofounded by Max Plowman. After a period as a dairyman, he confirmed his poetic vocation and was encouraged in it by Charles Sisson of *Poetry Nation Review* (PNR). He published from time to time in PNR, beginning with "Latter Day Psalms" in 1976, and ending with two poems published in 2006. His swansong collection was published in 2008. Ashby's poems exemplify his alienation from modern life, his contempt for respectability, and his sense of our common isolation. In one of his poems he asks "Sweet Jesus" to cut him down with "the sickle of his mercy" because he is lonely and a stranger in the land.

The alternative radical response to pacifism is Marxism, and I follow my group of pacifists with a group of Marxists. Hugh MacDiarmid (1892–1978) was a pseudonym, or more properly a *nom de guerre*, for an intensely committed Scottish nationalist and communist who entertained almost every nostrum in the book, including fascism. He also rivaled R. S. Thomas in his Anglophobia, at times preferring the Germans, however politically threatening they might be, to the English and the French. He was born in Dumfriesshire, the son of a postman, and became a teacher. He began his writing career in Wales writing for a socialist journal founded by Keir Hardie. His views were formed, or maybe reinforced, by First World War service in the Royal Army Medical Corps, and it is interesting that his son, Michael, became a conscientious objector in the Second World War. From 1933 to 1942 he lived on a remote Shetland island.

It was by something analogous to religious conversion that he elected to write in "synthetic Scots" or Lallans, a decision that some Scots initially thought condemned him to marginality. His reputation probably turns on his early lyrics in which he moved from a fusion of feminine and masculine characteristics to a dour and wilful masculinity. In later years he conceived of a kind of objective poetry that might encompass a universal knowledge without God. He is today regarded as a key member of the Scottish Renaissance who stands in the genealogy of Dunbar and Burns. The sections of his poem "Lament for the Great Music" reluctantly and perhaps mischievously included by Larkin in his Oxford anthology, on the unselfish intellect and the Scottish role in its emergence, gives the flavor of a curiously prosaic and abstract delusion:

> There is no great problem in the world to-day
> Except disease and death men cannot end
> If no man tries to dominate another
> The struggle for existence is over. It has been won.
> The need for repressions and disciplines has passed.
> The struggle for truth and that indescribable necessity,
> Beauty, begins now, hampered by none of the lower needs.[21]

Edgell Rickword (1898–1982) was a war poet awarded the MC for gallantry in the First War. He separated himself from the Georgians and was

21. Larkin, *Oxford Book of Twentieth-Century Verse*, 274–77.

strongly influenced by Sassoon's "Counter-Attack" as well as by H. G. Wells and William Morris. He mixed with the leading figures of the left, including Sylvia Townsend Warner and the noted Marxist theorist Jack Lindsay. In his journalism he began with a vigorous critique of the sacred cows of the Edwardian era, such as Masefield and Chesterton. Affected by the depression, he became a communist in 1934 and became co-editor of the *Left Review*. He sought a clean break and a place for the "negative emotions" of satire in the tradition of Jonathan Swift. From that point on, his poetry became subordinate to political satire.

Sylvia Townsend Warner (1893–1978) was the daughter of a Harrow schoolmaster who homeschooled her. She showed considerable musical ability and started her career, working on Tudor church music, with (among others) her lover Percy Buck. Shifting to literature, in 1923 she began a long friendship with T. F. Powys at his home on the Dorset coast at Chaldon. Here she met and fell in love with Valentine Ackland and they lived together in their Dorset home in Frome Vauchurch until Ackland's death. She had become a communist, and visited Spain in the Spanish Civil War for the Red Cross. Her poetry expresses sympathy with the marginal, vulnerable, and exploited as well as erotic attraction and political commitment. Her characteristic themes were a repudiation of Christianity, a rejection of conventional gender categories, an understanding of the role of the unmarried spinster, lesbian love, and witchcraft. Witchcraft was seen as empowering women in the noble lineage of Sibyls and female saints.

Christopher Caudwell (1907–1937) was born into a Roman Catholic family in Putney, South-West London, and educated up to the age of fifteen at a Benedictine school. However, he then moved with his father, who was literary editor of the *Daily Express*, to Bradford in Yorkshire. Here he worked as a reporter on the *Yorkshire Observer* and made his way to Marxism. He now began to rethink everything from poetry to philosophy, and, in 1936, joined the Communist Party in Poplar, East London. He drove an ambulance in Spain during the Civil War, joined the International Brigade, and was killed in February 1937. His writings were published posthumously—*Illusion and Reality*, on poetry, in 1937, and *Studies in a Dying Culture* in 1938. These books were major contributions to Marxist understandings of culture.

I include Roy Campbell (1900–1957) here as an outlier, because he was a poet who rejected the pacifist and Marxist options. He was born in Durban, South Africa, and his reputation has suffered on account of his having sided with the nationalists in the Spanish Civil War, in spite of his opposition to racism and active service in support of the British war effort in the Second World War. He was one of the few intellectuals who opposed

Freudianism and Marxism in the thirties, and he became a Catholic in 1936. His poetry had remarkable qualities described by Roger Scruton (quoted in Campbell's Wikipedia article) as "vigorous rhyming pentameters, into which he infused the most prodigious array of images, and the most intoxicating draft of life."[22] Campbell also produced fine translations, for example of the poems of St. John of the Cross.

I conclude with three poets belonging to a later generation who responded to very different aspects of "the century of war" beginning in 1914: George Macbeth (1932–1992) as a poet framed in adolescence by the blitz, by the sound of bombs and the wail of sirens, as I was; Tony Harrison (1937–) framed by the dropping of the atom bomb and the Gulf wars; and James Fenton (1949–) framed by experiences which also overlap mine, at least in Germany, Lebanon, and Israel. His varied production included the wars of colonialism, especially in Asia.

George Macbeth was born in Scotland, where his father worked as a mining engineer, and brought up in Sheffield. In 1940 a bomb shattered the family home, and in the following year his father walked out into a raid and never returned. This is all recounted in his *A Child of the War* (1987) including the wartime sexual freedom and associated fumblings and male tussling. He recounts the (to me) familiar atmosphere of a church youth club and induction into politics, in his case into active anti-communism following the disorienting switch from Russia as ally to Russia as enemy. His medical exemption from compulsory military service horrified him as much as acceptance horrified me and stimulated my politico-religious conscientious objection. All this was the shared experience of wartime and of the immediate post-war period. He won a scholarship to New College, Oxford, and then became a BBC arts producer. His poetry, which extended to twenty books, was associated with the Group and initially sometimes violent and macabre. In the mid-sixties he became, along with people like Horowitz and Ginsberg, a performance poet in a style linked to popular music. He died in Ireland of motor neurone disease.

Some of his poems have a slanting and perhaps ambiguous reference to Christianity. One example might be "The God of Love." It appears to be an animal poem about a pack of wolves attacking oxen in a frozen landscape, but may also be about the war issue and the role of religion as a primitive and ritual response to danger. The oxen mobilize to protect the calf in the center of the ring they form around it. The calf may represent the sacred, or the God of love, but is already dead with its horns frozen in the ice, perhaps

---

22. "Roy Campbell (Poet)," https://en.wikipedia.org/wiki/Roy_Campbell_%28poet%29, accessed July 2016.

the slain God. Yet the adult oxen cradle it in the circle of their antlers formed in a defensive arc. The poem finishes with the statement that their God of love required their death. It appears to be directed against masculine defensive and aggressive stratagems: the bone-headed bull oxen are contrasted with the maternal concern of the owl flying above the scene.

Tony Harrison is the son of a baker in Leeds. He went to Leeds Grammar School and then to Leeds University where he became a classicist. He later pursued an interest in languages, for example learning Czech. He is deeply concerned by issues of the working class, working class language, culture, and class conflict, for example, in his poem "V" (1985) written about the miners' strike and the desecration of his parents' grave. Among his many realizations of classic texts, his reworking of the medieval mystery plays was particularly successful. He uses Greek myths to articulate strong views on contemporary conflicts, for example in Bosnia and in Iraq. He wrote of the charred body of an Iraqi soldier in the first Gulf War. In the poem "Shrapnel," he linked the bombing of Leeds in the Second World War with the atrocities of the attacks on London on July 7th, 2005.

For Tony Harrison the "ritualized beauty" of poetry best conveys a profound unease with war and violence dating back to newsreels of concentration camps in 1945 and the celebration of victory over Japan against the background of Hiroshima and Nagasaki when he was still a child. The celebratory street fires obscenely mimicked the firestorm of atomic warfare. Harrison's pacifism is not so much a worked-out political principle—else it would encounter the standard paradoxes of principled non-violence allowing free rein to unprincipled violence—as it is a visceral horror of all that war entails. It is a manifesto in favor of all the everyday good things of earth, including human and humane coarseness. That celebration of the gifts of the senses comes out very clearly in his excoriating and funny take on the doomsday imaginings of the visionary of Patmos in "The Pomegranates of Patmos."[23] Like any Greek rejoicing in the rich fruits of the good earth, he'll defiantly eat pomegranates and figs to give joy to his days. The riot of metaphor that sets up an extremely unattractive and bejewelled heavenly city is not for him.

James Fenton is the son of a theologian, biblical scholar, and student of mystical spirituality, and was himself a Durham cathedral chorister. He attended Repton independent school, followed by Magdalen College, Oxford, where he switched from English to Philosophy, Politics, and Economics, the discipline that nurses the intelligence of future politicians. His poetry

---

23. Tony Harrison, *The Gaze of the Gorgon* (Newcastle: Bloodaxe Books, 1992), 28–35.

in every sense took him very far from home while bearing clear marks in its themes and points of reference of his middle-class clerical origins, beginning with a knockabout and abusive undergraduate poem, written with John Fuller, his tutor, about hating Catholics and their Catholic God. Fenton joined the *New Statesman* in 1971 and also became a revolutionary Trotskyite socialist, along with his close Oxford friend Christopher Hitchens. The mutation from religious righteousness to revolutionary political righteousness, but shorn of humility, is familiar from German university experience, as I personally discovered from my own acquaintance with universities in Germany in the seventies, notably Berlin. Equally familiar to anyone who has lived long with the radical left is the transfer of tribal loyalty to colonial people in violent struggles with western imperial powers, especially America. In Fenton's case that meant sympathizing with the old imperial power of Japan in its first brush with the new imperial power of America, actively siding with the insurgents as they entered Saigon, and, initially, even with the Pol Pot regime in Cambodia, until he recognized the barbarism they represented. Fenton's *Children in Exile* (1997) evokes migrants to Italy from Cambodia, "graduates of famine" condemned to war "by geography."

James Fenton has been celebrated as a writer who deploys the unexpected poetry of science to refresh traditional resources, as in *Terminal Moraine* (1972), and as a poet of war and violence who combines poetry with the eye of a journalist, simultaneously very engaged and oddly at a distance. His models here are the popular poetry of Kipling redeployed in the anti-imperial cause, and above all Auden. His *The Memory of War* appeared in 1982. One of his best poems is his "German Requiem" about the victims and survivors of war, and the necessity of forgetting.[24] His more recent writing, which includes nonsense poetry in the Lear/Carroll tradition and love poetry, perhaps moves away from his earlier commitments. His partner is the writer Darryl Pinckney.

His remarkable poem "Jerusalem," which draws in part on the imagery of the Bible, is particularly interesting because of the questions it raises about the sharply-angled "truthfulness," or rather untruthfulness of poetic rhetoric from the point of view of a social-scientific analysis of the endemic divisions of Us and Them and the implicit or overt violence that must follow. I discussed this aspect of poetic rhetoric at the very beginning of this book because what might be called the numinous surprise of poetry can be deployed simply to point towards a phenomenon as having a self-evident valence without any support from empirical understanding. Science of any kind is a laborious and prosaic source of understanding, often at odds with

---

24. Schmidt, *The Great Modern Poets*, 220–21.

the standard devices of poetic rhetoric when that rhetoric is deployed from a great height to underscore political righteousness. That is especially the case when an author gestures negatively towards the role of religion as a referent we wrongly think we know perfectly well and falsely imagine we can make generalizations about. I earlier cited the atypically banal sentiments of Thomas Hardy about two thousand years of celebrating Mass climaxing in the use of poison gas. The truth value here is vapid to vanishing point but rhetorically it excites acceptance just as Arnold's historically false statements about the "sea of faith" excite acceptance.

Fenton's poem adopts various voices, all of them familiar to anyone who has spent time in Jerusalem, including the insistent questions posed by Israeli security. Implicitly the writer stands above all the sources of human identity and survival that flow into the "cisterns" of conflict. He only gestures towards the overt and presenting surfaces of conflict and of mutual exclusion to the detriment of the long and complex history of nations and empires that makes them explicable. Of course, it is worth saying again that poetry does not and cannot deliver sustained argument or causal analysis or historical narrative, even though Wordsworth tried in his "philosophic song." It is thus at the service of illumination and of falsehood and (again as I said in my initial comments) is not controlled by intellectual responsibility. The rhetoric of poetry provides concentrated and impacted imagery serving moral purposes and passions, but these can depend for their force on keeping serious understanding at bay. You are invited to stay with, and luxuriate morally in, the presenting "insight." The invitation is all the more seductive when the images serve to reflect and reinforce the pleasures of shared and taken for granted attitudes in a self-confirming circle. Perhaps Plato's concerns about the dubious relation of art to truth, including poetry, receive support for reasons he could not then imagine.

Chapter 8

Eliot and Auden

I was of the generation in the nineteen-forties for whom Eliot had changed everything both as critic and as poet. The change had occurred some two decades before, but my generation of sixth-formers were just picking it up as a novelty, both with regard to the reinstatement (say) of the Metaphysicals, and intimations of radical modernism. For us the syllabus of "recent" literature had been, and still was, dominated by the Romantics. But, maybe because we had an exceptional teacher, W. H. Gardner,[1] who was the modern editor of Hopkins, we were introduced to Donne and to "The Love Song of J. Alfred Prufrock" (as well as to Hopkins). From there we went on in due course to absorb some of Eliot's critical writings directly, and pretty much the whole of the emerging canon of Eliot's poetry, including the *Four Quartets* and the plays. We read Helen Gardner on Eliot, and knew the poetry as well as we knew *Hamlet*. Of course, the "we" quickly fragmented. What I encountered in a teachers' training college was a little more than a Georgian anthology. Perhaps these experiences are specific to particular student generations. In the contemporary climate one might need to ask how far back historically courses in English go, what role is assigned to poetry, especially pre-Romantic poetry, and how far poetry is partly assimilated to the inculcation of acceptable social and political attitudes: a decorative version of civics.

Eliot and Auden have to be dealt with at extended length, given their dominance and influence, and above all given their special relevance to the concerns of this essay. I take Eliot's criticism first because it sets the scene for the poetry. Eliot's criticism matters partly on account of its intrinsic

---

1. Gardner, *Gerard Manley Hopkins*.

historical importance, but partly because that criticism is infused with issues related to Christianity. The same is true of Auden, though Auden's concern with Christianity came much later than Eliot's and has been much less influential, for reasons that will need to be explored. Regarding criticism in general, Eliot's essay on "Tradition and the Individual Talent" (1919–1920) was extremely important, while, with specific regard to religion, there is his discussion of the relation of literature to ethics and theology.[2]

I begin with a brief discussion of Eliot's "Tradition and the Individual Talent" as part of his considered view of poetry and culture. For Eliot, tradition is a sense of the past in the widest sense of what is handed on of a whole cultural inheritance across time, cultures, and languages. Tradition is the presence of the past in the present. We live with the past, and what is new subtly alters the past and our sense of it, so that tradition actively shapes the future as well as bringing the past into the present. Eliot also argues that poetry is not Wordsworth's "spontaneous overflow of powerful feelings," but the result of an ability to receive and fashion anew images, phrases, and feelings into the artwork. Poetry should be distinct from the personality of individual poets, so that they sacrifice themselves for it. Here Eliot is perhaps stating a norm for himself as well as putting forward a norm for poetry generally. Eliot's exacting desiderata for the poet are worth comparing with exacting desiderata put forward on by Auden in *The Dyer's Hand and Other Essays* (1962):[3] one ancient language, two modern languages, thousands of lines by heart, no literary criticism, courses in prosody, rhetoric, and philology, as well as desirable options including mythology and liturgics.

When it comes to literature and faith, a key essay, "Religion and Literature," is in Eliot's collection *Essays Ancient and Modern* (1932–1936),[4] though in that same collection there are also important ancillary essays on Baudelaire and Pascal. I mention these other essays because, particularly in the case of Baudelaire, they gesture towards the increasingly international dimension of English literature. In Eliot's case there are influences at work both from the United States and France. With regard to the United States, there is the Unitarian and moralistic background of Eliot himself (with its surprising latent tendencies to Catholicism), and also the modernist influence of Ezra Pound. With regard to France, there is a background in Jules Laforgue and in the influence of Baudelaire, whom Eliot regards as essentially Christian in his apprehension of the world.[5]

2. "Tradition and the Individual Talent," in Eliot, *The Sacred Wood*, 39–49.
3. Auden, *The Dyer's Hand and Other Essays*, 77.
4. Eliot, *Essays Ancient and Modern*, 93–112.
5. Crawford, *Young Eliot*.

It is worth noticing here the massive literary critical influence in the United States of Cleanth Brooks, an Anglican Christian whose approach complemented the approach of Eliot. (My acquaintance with Brooks turned on our shared concern for the historic English Prayer Book.) The canon presented by Eliot in his earlier criticism was re-presented by Brooks in his classic *The Well Wrought Urn*.[6] For some people, tradition, understood as established norms handed on, and modernity, understood as the contemporary, experimental, and even the obscure, are antithetical. On the contrary, they are complementary. Indeed, the argument of this essay is that tradition, including ritual and liturgy, is conspicuously recovered by modernism.

Brooks believed, with Eliot, that literature was not a surrogate for religion, nor was literary criticism about the emotional response of the critic. The universal was realized in the particular rather than in abstraction, and the religious was realized by suggestion, indirection, analogy, ambiguity, and paradox. The meaning of a poem can only be entered by close reading of its inner structure (something not opposed to historical and contextual understanding), and the poem cannot be reduced to its prosaic message. This Brooks called the heresy of paraphrase: a heresy regularly committed in this book.

In discussing religion and literature, Eliot deals specifically with what he sees as the secularization of literature, and with the stages of secularization through which literature has passed. He believes that an approach solely from the viewpoint of literary criticism is inadequate. There are also ethical and theological criteria which are the more necessary given the extent of contemporary ignorance and confusion. Eliot makes it clear that he is not dealing with specifically religious literature, meaning literature like the Bible, which has aesthetic qualities, or devotional poetry or poetry with a confessional purpose. Secularization of the novel has proceeded by stages: faith taken for granted but remaining in the background, faith doubted and contested, as in George Eliot and Hardy, and faith as entirely irrelevant given that the pursuit of literature includes any and every kind of experience and aesthetic pleasure irrespective of the consequences. The end point of secularization comes when experience is its own justification. Eliot regards contemporary literature as written by people with no sense or knowledge of the transcendent realm beyond nature, or even awareness that there are people who believe in such a realm. It is widely believed that ills can be dealt with by economic or social change and revolution: the secular political solution. It is the duty of Christians to bring other criteria to bear that are moral and theological.

6. Brooks, *The Well Wrought Urn*.

When we turn to Eliot's poetry, it is important to emphasize that his most famous poem, "The Waste Land" (1922), understood as the modernist manifesto by arguably the century's preeminent poet, both precedes his conversion (if that is the right word for some kind of inner resolution) and presages it.[7] The context is the horror of his marriage, the crisis in his career, and, above all, the crisis of his "spirituality." The inner substance of the poem is a kind of secular prophecy emerging from the heart of the contemporary world in the phantasmagoria of the great cities such as London. In that wasted land there is a deathly and deadening encounter with alienation and absence that cries out for redemption and is hinted at obliquely in the poem's mythic structure. That is perhaps conveyed most eloquently in the figure of Tiresias, the old man who has seen and foreshadowed all that is to transpire. It is also conveyed in the mythic Fisher King who is also the King who was fisher of men. Yet juxtaposed to the polluted Thames sweating oil and tar, there are always intimations that reflect Eliot's intimate pilgrimages into the interiors of the city churches. There is the "inexplicable Ionian white and gold" in St. Magnus Martyr, signifying the liturgical colors of the resurrection, and the dead sound on the stroke of nine in St. Mary Woolnoth, signifying the ninth hour when the Savior died and redemption was consummated.

The first poem written after Eliot's religious "resolution" was "The Journey of the Magi" (1927), drawing extensively on Andrewes's 1622 sermon on the incarnation: in Eliot's words, the sermon was composed of "flashing phrases which never desert the memory."[8] The poem moves from the marvelous birth to the desire for spiritual death: "I would be glad of another death."

But if "The Journey of the Magi" is "mere Christianity," to use a phrase of C. S. Lewis's, "Ash Wednesday" (1930) is Anglo-Catholic Christianity.[9] It represents "the beauty of incantation" as part of a wider liturgical union of image, rhythm, impacted allusion and meaning, enactment, and embodiment. Barry Spurr, in *'Anglo-Catholic in Religion': T. S. Eliot and Christianity* (2010), writes as an analyst of *poesis*, and he characterizes it as looking forward to the *Four Quartets* and Eliot's literary dramas, *Murder in the Cathedral* and *The Family Reunion*.[10] For Barry Spurr, the poem is presided over by the implicit presence of the Virgin Mary, even though she is only mentioned once. The "three white leopards" represent the powerful sensual drives of

---

7. Eliot, *Collected Poems, 1909–1962*, 61–86.
8. Eliot, *Collected Poems, 1909–1962*, 109–10.
9. Eliot, *Collected Poems, 1909–1962*, 93–106.
10. Barry Spurr, *'Anglo-Catholic in Religion.'*

the world, the flesh, and the devil, while the Virgin represents purity and the winding ascent of the Dantean stair. It is by this ascent that the pilgrim may attain beatitude and may spit out of his mouth the "withered apple seed" of sin. For Eliot, prescribed Catholic practices of penance and absolution take precedence over the Protestant reliance on grace and trust alone.

In *Four Quartets,* first published as a series in New York in 1943 and London in 1944, the themes of pilgrimage are again pursued, bringing together both *via* and *vita,* the way and the life. Pilgrimage is towards the life of love as taught by Dame Julian of Norwich, and her faith that "all manner of things shall be well."[11] For Eliot, pilgrimage is made through place and images of place within time, like East Coker and Little Gidding. Places are made holy by constant prayer and allow a momentary revelation of the eternal and timeless. They permit an intersection of light with quotidian experience, the impossible union of spheres of existence realized in incarnation. There is always for him a search for the spiritual truth at "the still point of the turning world," through the disabling fragilities of language, but also through the play of light and the playing of music where "you are the music while the music lasts." In this way we can be returned to the *hortus conclusus* of innocence and the Garden of Eden. The one sure path is the wisdom of endless humility. Only by wayfaring on that path can we hope for the descent of the dove at Pentecost and a redemption "from fire by fire."

W. H. Auden (1907–1973) came from an Anglo-Catholic family background, lost his faith at age fifteen, adopted a *marxisant* and Freudian approach to the crises of the thirties, and returned to the Anglican Church in 1940. That brief summary provides a frame in which to explore the poetry and the thinking of a major poetic presence. If Eliot was arguably the preeminent poet of the century, Auden was arguably the most marvelously gifted. The underlying difficulty for our understanding of him, at least according to the commentators, is that someone who was feted as the leading intellectual force and poetic presence on the left should, under the pressure of the same crises that drove his sympathy with Marxism, have returned to a Christianity very different from the ritualism that once so delighted him. The parallels with Eliot are obvious in that Eliot was received into the church *in camera* while Auden returned secretively. Eliot and Auden were both critically and personally attacked for their falling away from the true path. At the same time, there was a signal difference between the two poets. Eliot left behind a familial ethical Protestantism to adopt an unambiguous Anglo-Catholicism, whereas Auden left behind a familial Anglo-Catholicism eventually to embrace a form of Anglicanism with marked Protestant

---

11. Eliot, *Collected Poems,* 187–224.

characteristics. To embrace his faith again was, for him, very different from receiving it as a donation. It meant that he voyaged and quested among the theologians, like Niebuhr and Kierkegaard, seeking what made persuasive sense for him and subjecting teaching, for example on petitionary prayer and hell, to moral judgment. If Eliot's quest was towards supernal light, Auden journeyed towards a God who endured the cross and the shame within the grim realities of the everyday world. Prayer was to pay attention to the "other" in many guises, of which the "limestone landscape" evoked in one of his most beautiful poems is just one example. The "other" was at the heart of Christianity as expressed in the commandment to love your neighbor as yourself. For Auden, Christianity had a primary horizontal reference as well as a vertical reference.

If Auden's lapse from the true secular faith lost him one audience, his embrace of Christianity did not gain him a new one, and this loss without compensatory gain has meant the occlusion of much of the poetry he wrote in the latter part of his life. The introduction of my sixth form cohort to Eliot and Donne (and Hopkins) did not include a whisper about Auden. When I eventually read Auden's poetry I had no frame within which to grasp it, and my first intimations of its greatness came through performing the extraordinary realizations of his poetry by Britten, such as *On This Island*, and through listening to the Saint Cecilia Ode. Perhaps Auden's lifestyle worried Christians, or maybe they were diverted away from him by an approach that relied on indirection, given that "no man hath seen God at any time."

In an article in *First Things* (August 2012), Alan Jacobs has tried to remedy this neglect and incomprehension.[12] Jacobs points out that Auden, as a Protestant Christian, was dealing with questions that resisted answers and with doubts not easily assuaged. He cites some of the key writings of Auden's later development, such as "For the Time Being: a Christmas Oratorio," "The Sea and the Mirror: A Commentary on The Tempest," and "The Age of Anxiety: A Baroque Eclogue." Auden had hoped that these extraordinarily ambitious works might minister to a sick society, even though (as he put it in his poem for Yeats) poetry "makes nothing happen." Maybe the very extent of our failure pointed to a Christian understanding, or maybe, as he put it in "The Sea and the Mirror," "the way of truth / Was the way of silence." Auden was also obsessed with the necessity that inheres in nature and the freedom that inheres in humanity. We are compound beings subject to necessity but also capable of choices with consequences, in a morally saturated world where promises may be kept or broken, where we assume responsibility for time and also live in the foreknowledge of mortality. In

12. Jacobs, "Auden and the Limits of Poetry."

Auden's poems about the body there is a profound feeling of gratitude for the "Precious Five" senses, and, in his masterly "Horae Canonicae," the unrepeatable events of judgment, crucifixion, and deposition are reenacted in the canonical hours and rhythms of the liturgical calendar.[13] If one wants further understanding of Auden's theological position, profoundly Protestant within a Catholic liturgical frame, then it is strikingly evident in three essays in *Forewords and Afterwords*.[14] Auden has faith in the suffering God who does not compel recognition but chooses to be a victim of man's self-love.[15] Auden is also very Anglican in his appreciation of liturgical and institutional integrity, while being "reticent" about doctrinal matters and "enthusiasm."[16]

Much of what is suggested here about Auden's faith is derived from Edward Mendelson's review in the *New York Review of Books* (December 7th, 2007) of Arthur Kirsch's *Auden and Christianity* (2007). Mendelson says that when Auden originally lost his faith, he also realized his vocation to be a poet as an alternative. He now believed that religion had been superseded by solutions derived from Marxism and Freudianism and that salvation lay in psychotherapy and economics. He was also influenced by D. H. Lawrence and by esoteric speculations, for example, the writings of the mystical polymath Gerald Heard. And yet he still reverted to the language of Christianity. Just as Shelley despaired of fully relieving Byron of Christianity, so Christopher Isherwood feared that if left to himself Auden would gravitate to a fusion of grand opera and high mass.

But there were other dangers undermining Auden's secular faith, especially its foundations in the liberal humanist idea of human goodness. These minatory dangers came from the dual horrors of communism and fascism. When visiting Barcelona in the course of the Spanish Civil War, he was horrified by the persecution of Catholics and the closure of churches. To deploy hatred and violence in the name of an eventual fraternity was to ruin and undermine a good end by bad means. As for fascism and Nazism, he sought an unconditional standpoint from which to pronounce their ideals, objectives, and methods unequivocally wrong. Human beings were all equal and were all ends in themselves, because they were created in the image of God. And beyond that, Auden had a vision of divine love, or *agape*, not unlike the vision of happiness experienced by W. B. Yeats. Sitting with friends one day, he had a sense of being invaded by a power beyond himself

---

13. Auden, *Collected Poems*, 475–86.
14. Auden, *Forewords and Afterwords*, 33–78.
15. Auden, *Forewords and Afterwords*, 37.
16. Auden, *Forewords and Afterwords*, 71.

that enfolded all his companions. This was expressed in his poem "A Summer Night."[17] Yet—and here he was influenced by the realist theologian Reinhold Niebuhr—there was always an insidious corruption that visited the most exalted projects and was revealed in the terrible irony of where these projects ended up in practice. Corruption was ubiquitous, and he expressed his awareness of it by writing of loving your crooked neighbor with all your crooked heart. In all your affections, for example for his lover Chester Kallman, you were using others as symbolic stand-ins: therapy and Christian penitence could be complementary.

For Auden, the theology of the incarnation meant that the social body and the physical body were sacred: you must not deny the body. It also meant that the divine was realized in the suffering body of Christ on the cross, and Auden believed, as one or two medieval paintings suggest, that the Father participated in the suffering of the Son as he cried out in pain at his abandonment in a cruel and indifferent world. In the famous poem on the Brueghel painting of the fall of Icarus in the Musée des Beaux Arts, Brussels, Auden finds the shadow and analogue of the unnoticed suffering of God in the universal indifference that greets the fall of Icarus.[18] Auden also had a doctrine of creation that further expressed the stamp of the divine image on each human, by the giving to each unique individual a proper name. The God who numbers all by name does not deal in statistical aggregates.

Although Auden had traveled far from the ritualism of his childhood, he retained a strong sense of the rite and its proper language. This is important for the perspective of this book to the effect that the horrors of the twentieth century brought modernist poets and musicians to a renewed understanding of the rites of ruin leading to restoration. When it came to language, he felt that the ritual union of the unborn with the dead required its proper language. Like Eliot (and Waugh for that matter) he was shocked by the impoverishment of language in revised liturgical texts. When the revised liturgies came to his local church of St. Mark-in-the-Bowery he slipped away to the Russian Orthodox Church to hear the liturgy in Church Slavonic.

Auden is often grouped with other poets prominent in the thirties: Stephen Spender (1909-1995), Louis MacNiece (1907-1963), and C. Day-Lewis (1904-1972). I am not here concerned with the complex sexual relations of the poets in this group, for example, those concerning Christopher Isherwood, though Isherwood's attraction to Vedanta might have its

17. Auden, *Collected Poems*, 103-4.
18. Auden, *Collected Poems*, 146-47.

incidental interest. The focus has to be on the poetry of Spender, MacNiece, and Day-Lewis, and its left-wing political focus. These poets, with Auden, might be seen as successors to the Bloomsbury Group in the twenties, even though they did not share its aesthetic doctrines and distanced themselves from it as insufficiently radical. They have been described as obsessed by the First World War, which they blamed on capitalism. For Spender, MacNiece, and Day-Lewis the answer to the social question lay in politics, and perhaps it might be worth suggesting that the reliance on politics is a characteristic ideological trait. They knew their enemy, and their reliance on politics and social reorganization defined a mode of understanding so comprehensive that it obviated any need for charity. It even stigmatized the "most excellent gift of charity" as a barrier to progress in its recourse to temporary palliatives. There is a crisis and there is a political solution. Eliot summarized this approach as one where we dream of systems so perfect that no one need be good. Of course, the result was often disillusion, for some sooner, for others later. The disillusion can be charted from the Molotov-Ribbentrop pact onwards. Spender, for example, cooperated with intellectuals like Arthur Koestler in the 1949 publication *The God that Failed*.[19] It is worth taking Spender, MacNeice, and Day-Lewis separately.

Stephen Spender was born in Kensington, West London, and, after the death of his mother, attended University College School, Hampstead. He went up to University College, Oxford, but left without a degree: he was later to be made an honorary fellow of the college. Spender went to Hamburg after university and was then invited to Berlin by Christopher Isherwood: the final years of the Weimar Republic were seen as a haven for those seeking freedom, including freedom for homosexuals. Spender was acquainted with the Auden circle, and in 1936 joined the Communist Party, with some marginal involvement in the Spanish Civil War. He later became disillusioned and was for a period editor of *Encounter*, unaware that its publisher, the "Congress for Cultural Freedom," was covertly subsidized by the C.I.A. He taught in the USA and held a chair in English at University College, London, from 1970–77. One critical opinion is that he was better as an autobiographer, examining the dilemmas of his life, than as a poet.

Louis MacNiece was born in Belfast, Northern Ireland, the son of a Church of Ireland priest. His mother died in 1914, and in 1917 his father remarried and MacNiece was sent with his sister to school in Sherborne. From there he won a classics scholarship to Marlborough College, followed by an award to Merton College, Oxford, reading classics. Thereafter his life was one of marriages and complex heterosexual relationships, periods

---

19. Koestler et al., *The God That Failed*.

of teaching at various universities, and frequent collections of poems, for which Faber became the main publisher after 1935. Auden became his lifelong friend at Oxford, and on occasion they collaborated, for example on *Letters from Iceland*, published in 1937. From 1941 on he worked for the BBC.

MacNeice's approach to life was vaguely aesthetic and Epicurean, and latterly bibulous. He sympathized with the left of the thirties, but was dubious about its Marxist doctrines. He believed in particularities and ephemeral things rather than pitiless abstractions. Doctrines must be disciplined by personal observation. Political beliefs do not provide overarching imperatives. He has been described as a liberal individualist in a polarized age. His most famous poem "Bagpipe Music" expresses the despair following the Great Depression.[20] It was "no go" practically all the trivia of life "as the glass is falling hour by hour." One of his late poems, "Didymus," concerned St. Thomas, whose doubts he found congenial.

C. Day-Lewis was born in what was then an Irish county in the United Kingdom, the son of a Church of Ireland clergyman. After the death of his mother he was brought up mainly in England and educated at Sherborne School, before going to Wadham College, Oxford. There he had an undistinguished career, but came under the influence of Auden. He became an active communist and wrote on political themes, holding that the "Promethean fire of Enlightenment" should be for human benefit not private profit. During the Second World War, he worked for the Ministry of Information, and then taught in elite universities: Oxford, Cambridge, and Harvard. He had by then long realized that he found political commitment incompatible with the poetic vocation: his faith was now poetry itself and the world of nature. Although his later poetry has not attracted much critical attention, he had his rewards, and, in 1968, became poet laureate.

---

20. Larkin, *Oxford Book of Twentieth-Century Verse*, 395–96.

Chapter 9

Faith and Place

Faith has often been located: the numinous manifests itself in the holy place. But that place is not always in the temple as in the vision where Isaiah encounters the holiness of God and knows himself a "man of unclean lips." It can also manifest itself in a particular spot of the natural world, which by the act of naming becomes the "house and gate of heaven." So Jacob named a particular place Bethel, making it synonymous with the traffic of angels between earthly and heavenly.

Wordsworth, as a preeminent poet of place, was aware of the power of language and of naming to defeat the depredations of time and mortality long after his body and the bodies of those he loved had become as evanescent as "the grass of the field." In her essay on "Wordsworth and the Sacralization of Place," Deeanne Westbrook points out that in his five "Poems on the Naming of Places" (1799–1800) Wordsworth adapted the biblical etymological tale, as in Jacob's dream of Bethel, to produce poems wherein "language can rescue humans from silence and oblivion, smudging the boundaries between death and immortality, oblivion and fame."[1] The place and the name "live for evermore."

Deeanne Westbrook suggests that a recurring idea of this period concerns the power of language realized in speaking, naming, and composing. In a poem for his future bride, Mary Hutchinson, Wordsworth names a garden spot "among the ancient trees" to which, as in Milton's *Paradise Lost*, the privileged speaker and companion are "brought." This unknown but beautiful spot is a place to which no wayward angels might find their way. The "hidden garden" is Mary herself as in the biblical Song of Songs.

1. "Wordsworth and the Sacralization of Place," in Woodhead, *Reinventing Christianity*, 127–38, 131.

Deeanne Westbrook concludes her essay by citing Wordsworth's "Home at Grasmere," in which he acknowledges himself as a type of Adam but more favored than he, asking

> What Being, therefore, since the birth of Man
> Had ever more abundant cause to speak
> Thanks . . . ?
> [. . .]
> Surpassing grace
> To me has been vouchsafed: among the bowers
> Of Blissful Eden this was neither given,
> Nor could be given, possession of the good
> Which had been sighed for. . .[2]

In this chapter I concentrate on poets of place, many of them religious. I begin with George Mackay Brown (1921–1996) in the Orkney Islands, and Jack Clemo (1916–1994) at the other extreme of Britain in Cornwall. Mackay Brown was acquainted with poverty, depression, and mental distress, and left Orkney very rarely. He was encouraged by another Orcadian poet, Edwin Muir, and much influenced by Gerard Manley Hopkins. He became a Catholic in 1961, and even considered the seclusion of monastic life. One of his main collections of poems, *The Year of the Whale*, was published in 1965.[3] He deprecated the spiritual hollowness of urban civilization and the loss of myth and ritual, and saw himself as "interrogating silence." Like Yeats, he thought in terms of cyclical time. He also contemplated the timelessness of the themes of birth, death, salvation, and love, rather than time as a progressive forward march. Christianity superseded the old and bloody rituals of priestly sacrifice with the sacrifice of bread and wine in which God himself was at once deity, priest, and victim. These themes recurred in his novel about Magnus, an Orkney chieftain who died sacrificially rather than defend himself and his patrimony with violence.[4] The opera, *The Martyrdom of St. Magnus*, written in 1976 by Peter Maxwell Davies, another resident of Orkney, set a libretto adapted from Mackay Brown's novel, *Magnus*. As in the novel, Magnus was paired with Dietrich Bonhoeffer, who sacrificed himself and endured a shocking death under Hitler for the good of his people.

Jack Clemo (1916–1994) very early lost his father in the First World War and was brought up by his devout evangelical mother in the rural-industrial

---

2. "Home at Grasmere," ll. 117–26, quoted in Westbrook's essay, "Wordsworth and the Sacralization of Place," in Woodhead, *Reinventing Christianity*, 131.

3. Brown, *The Year of the Whale*.

4. Brown, *Magnus*.

landscape of St. Austell, Cornwall. This brings us to the other extreme of the country from the Orkneys. Troubled by increasing deafness and blindness, Clemo worked in the bleak and resistant environment of the Cornish clay pits. These pits provided him with a pervasive metaphorical resource. They generated the austere beauty of his poetry and his sense of hard-won grace and being "deep in the Word." His Calvinist sense of providence set him apart from the temperate religion of most chapel- and church-goers and also directed him to seek a "creed embedded" marriage. This search was animated by a mystical erotic strain of feeling satisfied by his marriage to Ruth Peaty, a laundry woman from Weymouth in Dorset. Moving to Dorset (with occasional visits to southern Europe) softened his apprehension of the world, and imbued him with a deep sense of gratitude. This softened apprehension of a life renewed in "broad Autumn" brought out a series of poems about Dorset that have some affinity with the work of the Dorset mystical writer T. F. Powys. At the same time, Clemo could still recall his early sense of "freak and chaos" as he stood on the "fragmented crust" of Chesil Beach. But then he gratefully recognized the solace of "she who gaily slithers by me," and who enables him finally to "taste human love's vivacity."[5]

The next two poets also provide a north-south contrast. Norman Nicholson (1914–1987) illustrates the role of physical and industrial ecology in the formation of poetic imagination. There are so many kinds of ecological space, so-called Celtic fringes, highland and lowland, highlands and islands, and such places as the coastal margin of small industrial and port towns west of the Lake District like Whitehaven, Bootle, and Millom. Nicholson lived most of his life in the industrial town of Millom, with its quarries, iron works, and maybe dangerous proximity to the nuclear plant of Windscale. He can be thought of as a poet of the western littoral.

He was born in Millom in a Victorian terraced house and saw the changes that occurred as the area became a rust belt. He wrote:

> they shovelled my childhood
> Onto a rubbish heap.[6]

He also rejoiced in the resilience of earth that is made for the farmer rather than for industrial exploitation:

> the lovely resistance
> Of blackberry, blackthorn, heather and willow . . .[7]

---

5. Jack Clemo, *Selected Poems*, 148.
6. "On the Dismantling of Millom Ironworks," in Nicholson, *Collected Poems*, 297.
7. "The Bloody Cranesbill," in Nicholson, *Collected Poems*, 361.

Nicholson was influenced by a community associated with a Wesleyan chapel, and, in 1940, was confirmed in the Church of England. His life of William Cowper is one testimony to a conversion. His poems sometimes set western Cumbria in a biblical setting. One poem was about the apocalyptic possibilities of nuclear disaster:

> The toadstool towers infest the shore
> Stink-horns that propagate and spore
> Wherever the wind blows.[8]

Charles Causley (1917–2003) was also a poet of the western littoral, far to the south in Cornwall. He was born in Launceston and educated at a teacher training college in Peterborough, eventually becoming a schoolmaster. Because of the early death of his father in 1924 due to war injuries, he had initially to earn money as an office boy before enlisting in the Royal Navy and serving as a coder in the Second World War. His experiences in the Navy and at war emerged in his poetry. Like Norman Nicholson's, his poetry was direct, rooted in the life of ordinary people and in his Christian faith. His reputation has gradually grown as someone working away from the mainstream, and in the view of Ted Hughes he was one of the most impressive writers of the twentieth century.

R. S. Thomas (1913–2000) was born in Cardiff, the son of a sailor, and spent much of his childhood in British port towns until his father eventually settled down in Wales. He read Latin and played rugby at Bangor University. He then sought ordination and became a priest-poet fiercely engaged by the people and landscape of Wales. This Wales was a creature of his imagination, and he remained more than ambivalent about the reality. Wales presented him with a culture that allotted the priest a carefully delimited space of operation but resisted attempts to go beyond that space and implement the wider implications of Christianity as Thomas understood it. Sometimes that delimited space made demands he felt unable to fulfill, as when he attended the bedsides of the dying and hopelessly recognized the inadequacy of his ministrations.

He cherished the Welsh language as the tongue of a conquered people still invaded by English tourists. Like many Welsh people alienated from England and its wars, he was a pacifist who supported the Campaign for Nuclear Disarmament. His last parish was located on the tip of the sacred Llyn Peninsula, as far away as possible from contamination. He detested modern civilization and its gadgets, though his congregation of hill farmers longed for them as ways of softening their harsh existence. He was also

---

8. "Windscale," in Nicholson, *Collected Poems*, 282.

a traditionalist in church practice, preferring the 1662 Book of Common Prayer and the symbolism of facing east. His duty was to preach the teaching of his church rather than to indulge his own opinions and the doubts which often beset him, though he was not entirely uninterested in the questionings of non-realist theology. For him, language was both the medium of divinity and a barrier to the occasional sunlight that broke through the harshness and darkness. Like Kierkegaard, he recognized that faith was a leap in that dark. He was a difficult character, devoted nevertheless to his often uncomprehending flock. His main poetic protagonist, Iago Prytherch, was a farmer without culture or refinement who represented an elemental force, and perhaps also the human predicament.[9]

John Betjeman (1906–1984) attended Marlborough public school before going to Oxford, where he had an undistinguished career and was notably at odds with C. S. Lewis. This part of his career is covered by his autobiographical poem, *Summoned by Bells* (1966).[10] His real education was probably completed during his time with the *Architectural Review*. He became a champion of Victorian architecture, seeing it as the visible realization of a period's spiritual life and, through the "Victorian Society," seeking to preserve as much as possible from the depredations of developers. He also helped edit Shell Guides on Cornwall (1943) and Devon (1936). Betjeman was probably bisexual but he nevertheless married the Hon. Penelope Chetwode, and, when they drifted apart, had a long partnership with Lady Elizabeth Cavendish.

Betjeman is the poet of place or rather of places: Auden labeled it topophilia. One of those places is Cornwall, the county of rugged cliffs tumbling into the Atlantic and of odd and forgotten saints. The other is the totally different world of suburbia. He is also a poet of culture, or rather cultures: one of those cultures is class, another is Anglo-Catholic Christianity, and with that the atmospherics of Anglicanism and the wider spectrum of English Christian atmospherics. His poem "Undenominational" shows his wide sympathies in his picture of a Noncomformist preacher adjuring simple folk in his chapel.[11] Betjeman has a unique power and knack of evoking cultural and ecclesiastical worlds through significant particulars and indicative minutiae. The evocations appear to be amused and lighthearted but they also encompass darkness, death, and tragedy, as when the "first class brains" of the higher civil servant spilled out on the road in an accident.[12] We are all subject to what the liturgy calls the "changes and chances" of a fleeting

9. Thomas, *Collected Poems, 1945–1990*.
10. Betjeman, *Collected Poems*, 399–481.
11. Betjeman, *Collected Poems*, 28.
12. "Mortality," in Betjeman, *Collected Poems*, 288.

world. His poems were rarely devotional. It has been suggested that whereas Thomas Hardy evoked the Christmas story "hoping it might be true," Betjeman evoked the story fearing it might be false, as in the repeated phrase "and is it true . . . ?"[13]

Unexpectedly, the internationalist Charles Tomlinson (1927–2015) belongs here.[14] He was first introduced to a wide-ranging experience of literature by two exceptionally stimulating teachers. After such an induction to rigor and depth he deeply regretted the contempt for language and grammar that turned everything before the Romantics into remote and alien country. He had his second induction at Cambridge from Donald Davie, with whom he formed a close intellectual relationship. From Davie he learnt the kind of poetic- and self-restraint that made confessional poets like Sylvia Plath and Ann Stevens seem solipsistic. Like Davie he was very influenced by American poetry as well as other literatures, for example Spanish and the poet Machado. He belonged to the great company of poet-translators like John Dryden.

He was also an unusually wide-ranging poet of place, from his home town of Stoke to the mining districts of Cararra. He found his equivalents of "Limestone Country" in such places of the American Southwest, where you discover that America too is a country with ruins. He could sound like a secular humanist, except that he was deeply affected by Catholic culture, Giotto, and Dante, and clearly reticent about naming what resists nomenclature. He was against extremes, whether the lust for a personal end to it all or for a political ending: Danton or Trotsky.

William Butler Yeats (1865–1939) was, of course, one of the major figures of the century and was also a poet of place, in his case Ireland. Like Browning's "Home Thoughts from Abroad," Yeats's "Lake Isle of Innisfree" is the quintessential poem of place based on nostalgia, as the initial hint of the parable of the prodigal son returning home suggests: "I will arise and go . . ." Yeats was of Anglo-Irish background and related to the Anglo-Irish Ascendancy. He is perhaps best known for his passionate reflections on the movement for Irish independence and its tragedies, especially the Easter Rising of 1916. We are here moving outside the ambit of Christianity into a personal and idiosyncratic occultism. There is no particular point in repeating analysis of a group of famous poems expressing his view of the world, such as those anthologized in Philip Larkin's *Oxford Book of Twentieth-Century Verse* (1973), itself the successor to Yeats's own *Oxford Book of Modern Verse, 1892–1935*.[15] I am

---

13. "Christmas," in Betjeman, *Collected Poems*, 155.

14. Material partly drawn from interview with Julian Stannard, "Charles Tomlinson at Brook Cottage."

15. Larkin, *Oxford Book of Twentieth-Century Verse*; Yeats, *Oxford Book of Modern Verse*.

thinking of that relatively small group of poems that are widely known, such as "The Lake Isle of Innisfree," "When You Are Old," "Easter 1916," "Sailing to Byzantium," "Byzantium," "The Second Coming," "A Prayer for my Daughter," "Under Ben Bulben's Head," "Among Schoolchildren," and "Crazy Jane on God." His early lyrics owed a debt to the Pre-Raphaelites.

What we need to notice, particularly in relation to the two women most important in his life, Maud Gonne and Georgie Hyde-Lees, is that he was interested at various times in theosophy, reincarnation, Rosicrucianism and the "Golden Dawn," spiritualism, and automatic writing, as well as committed to a religious rejection of materialism that owed little to Christianity. In his last years he also had some sympathies with political totalitarianism, Italian-style, fostered by his acquaintance with Ezra Pound. His resources were Irish myth, landscape, and folklore, he drew his symbolism from everyday Irish life, and some of his key associations were with the work of the Abbey Theatre, Dublin. He was horrified by decrepitude and fascinated by cyclical views of time. This view of time comes out in his most famous and prescient poem, "The Second Coming," where he asks:

> And what rough beast, its hour come round at last,
> Slouches towards Bethlehem to be born?[16]

A careful discussion of Yeats's relation to Christianity was provided by Cleanth Brooks in *The Hidden God: Studies in Hemingway, Faulkner, Yeats, Eliot, and Warren* (1963) in a chapter titled "W. B. Yeats: Search for a New Myth."[17] Earlier in the book, Brooks makes a comment that links Faulkner and Yeats. Both are universal in touching on themes drawn from their environment which are intrinsic alike to Christianity and the human condition, such as trial by affliction, the radical nature of corruption, and its redemption by sacrifice. And both represent a provincial culture where to be behind is to retain resources elsewhere massively depleted. It is these resources that enable Yeats to criticize advanced urban and industrial society by turning to Irish history and tradition. For Yeats, the enemies are science, or perhaps a particular interpretation of science, and Whiggery, by which he means a leveling and rancorous rationalism:

> That never looked out of the eye of a saint
> Or out of a drunkard's eye.[18]

---

16. Larkin, *Oxford Book of Twentieth-Century Verse*, 79.
17. Brooks, *The Hidden God*, 44–67.
18. "The Seven Sages," in Yeats, *Collected Poems*, 271–73.

For Yeats it is not so much that Christianity is under attack as it is his personal sense of being robbed of an ancestral faith by science. The only alternative for him is to create a mythology and an infallible church of poetic practice passed from generation to generation beyond the possibility of the kind of refutation that besets philosophy. Blake belongs to an earlier generation of this poetic church, and Blake and Yeats alike create their own mythology. This mythology is both traditional and an intensely private creation (as we shall see again in Ted Hughes). It is rooted in a primitive wisdom tradition larger and older than Christianity, which, unlike Christianity, unfolds and turns back on itself in cycles that are almost Spenglerian. Like Spengler, it has a sense of an imminent ending.

And yet the vocabulary of this tradition can be explicitly Christian, as in a poem by Yeats on prayer. Moreover, the world of the thirties is touched by eschatology as in the poem "The Gyres." "Irrational streams of blood are staining earth . . .We that look on but laugh with strenuous joy."[19] In this perspective, Christianity is very far from the timid or respectable pieties of the Victorian era, but rather infused with awe and dread. In this form it is able to represent perennial problems. Yeats is here as difficult to fathom as Shakespeare because he first gives himself over to one dramatization and then gives himself over to an opposed dramatization. In "A Prayer for My Son," he seems to take the incarnation very seriously before suggesting that Wisdom will correct what the peasant gospeler got awry. So Yeats simultaneously commits himself and is tentative and vacillating: Hegel at one moment, Madame Blavatsky at another. In his poem "Vacillation," addressed in its closing lines to the Catholic thinker Baron von Hügel, Yeats seems both to be sympathetic to his faith, yet reluctantly committed to a different party of poets. The members of this party take over from the saints and immerse themselves in the world rather than renouncing it. Any surrender to the burning vision of Isaiah in which the prophet knows himself "a man of unclean lips in a people of unclean lips" might even cauterize the poet's witness to the freedom of the spirit and its burden of responsibility. The most poignant moment in the poem comes in the fourth section, where he describes himself in a crowded London cafe and assailed by such an access and excess of happiness that he feels blessed and able in his turn to offer blessing to others.

I include Seamus Heaney (1939–2013) here as a poet of a place and culture—the place and the culture of County Derry. Of course, that culture includes a religious aspect, though usually implicit in the background. Certainly he is identified with the nationalist cause as that is embedded in

---

19. Yeats, *Collected Poems*, 337.

the culture of Catholicism. He is the major poetic presence in Ireland after Yeats, and he has also recognized a genealogy in the poetry of locality in the writing of fellow Irishman Pat Kavanagh (1904–1967). Heaney evokes all the varied dimensions of the Northern Irish world, both the customs and crafts of its cattle-herding Gaelic past and Ulster's industrial revolution. Though he has celebrated the heroes of Irish independence, he has always tried to place "the Troubles" in a wider historical and human context, and for the discerning reader there is a backwash of bleak ironies. Quoting Joyce, he speaks of seeking "the rote words in the rite order."[20] Heaney accepts the primary vocation of poetry as the keeper and finder of the inner life. That inner life is realized locally, so that he describes the springs of his imagination as off-center. At the heart of that "parish" is the family farmhouse of Mossbawm as evoked in a part of a poem dedicated to Mary Heaney called "Sunlight." The poem was written in memory of his mother soon after her death in 1975. It is an affectionate and unsentimental portrait of the hard-working rural woman as he remembered her, standing by the stove in the kitchen, hot and floury from baking, with sunlight through the window lighting her "scuffed hands."[21]

There is, of course, also a rich Protestant culture in Northern Ireland, often obscured. One example, might be Tom Paulin, a poet who was initially a Trotskyite, and sought to recover the radical republican Protestant tradition of the eighteenth century as it carried on the genealogy of John Milton.

Dylan Thomas (1914–1953) is a poet associated with Wales, especially the southern coastal village of Laugharne. Whether there are serious religious echoes in his poetry has to be a matter of judgment. His father was a teacher in Swansea Grammar School, totally anglicized and violently opposed to all religion. Yet the Welsh environment up to the mid-century had been divided between Puritan Noncomformity and a culture of drink and sport. Certainly the habits of Dylan Thomas and the luxuriant mythology growing up around them did not commend him to Welsh Puritans. Thomas was also deviant in being apolitical in a fiercely politicized culture. He came nearest to politics when considering filing as a conscientious objector at the outset of the Second World War, but was in any case saved from coming to a decision by rejection on medical grounds.

According to Rowan Williams, writing in the *New Statesman* (August 1, 2014), himself a Welshman and poet, as well as prelate, Dylan Thomas was crucially formed in the Kardomah Cafe in Swansea, in the company of fellow artists and poets like Vernon Watkins. Williams refers to the world

---

20. Rahim, "Interview with Seamus Heaney."
21. Heaney, *New Selected Poems*.

of Carmarthenshire evoked by Thomas as having more in common with Southern American Gothic than English rural fictions. For Williams, the Romanticism of Thomas can feel embarrassing in a post-Romantic era, but he strongly appreciates Thomas's formal inventiveness and tight verbal patterning. He also detects a deep unease and uncertainty underneath the feverish assonances. Dylan was supported by Edith Sitwell but he was uncertain of the quality of his work and conscious that some dismissed it as the highest form of fakery.

As to any religious aspect to Thomas's poetry, it was clearly outside any orthodox form of faith. Perhaps his collection *Twenty-five Poems* can be taken as indicative.[22] These poems include a sonnet sequence, "Altarwise by owl-light," where Thomas moves from a pre-Christian primitivism to a Christian mythology of love, in which crucifixion and resurrection are sites of spiritual conflict. In these poems, and in "And death shall have no dominion" (with its Pauline reference), Dylan Thomas can be seen as a celebrator and performer of a rite of primal creation and the human condition.

Vernon Watkins (1902–1967) was a poet of place, in his case the Gower peninsula on the southern littoral of Wales, and someone who wrote of his own sense of the revelation brought by the incarnate Christ. His religious experience emerged from a breakdown that can also be seen as a breakthrough. Revelation came not in the abstract universalisms of reason but in the minute particulars of our shared environment, whether bird, beast, or flower or beach and sea. Like the Welsh poet of the Brecon area, Henry Vaughan, he was visited by "bright shoots of everlastingness," emanating from beyond time, but foreshadowed and represented by temporal experience. In the view of Rowan Williams, he went to the heart of Christianity in a poem on a christening where he wrote of kissing our own losses.[23] He also was a kind of shaman or bard of the various embodiments of the visible world who could discern in ancient mythologies anticipations of the coming of the redeemer.

He was born in Maesteg on the southern edge of the mining valleys but brought up in Swansea where his father worked in a bank. From very early on his sole ambition was to be a poet. But his school and university experiences were hardly happy and he returned to Wales to follow his father into a bank simply in order to earn a living. In 1941 he joined the RAF, working at Bletchley Park until 1946. His writing was for long overshadowed by the myth of Dylan Thomas, but he has been gradually recognized

22. Thomas, *Twenty-Five Poems*.

23. http://aoc2013.brix.fatbeehive.com/articles.php/2459/archbishop-on-bbc-radio-3-vernon-watkins-swanseas-other-poet, accessed August 2016.

as a sophisticated major poet. He himself despised "the bubble reputation," whereby fame either alights or eludes. Any interest in reputation could easily inhibit a Romantic in a post-Romantic world and a Christian in a secular one. For him it was enough to be faithful to his vision.

Chapter 10

Larkin to Hughes; Plath to Duffy

Philip Larkin (1922–1985) was, for much of his working life, the very successful librarian of the University of Hull. He was born in Coventry, and his father was a self-made man who had risen to become Coventry City Treasurer. His father combined a love of literature, which he passed on to his son, especially Pound, Eliot, Joyce, and Lawrence, with Nazi sympathies. He certainly passed on the former to his son, but there is debate among critics about how firmly Nazi sympathies were implanted in Philip.

After some homeschooling, Philip Larkin attended the local primary school and then the local senior school. In spite of not doing well at the School Certificate, he stayed on in the sixth form and won a scholarship to St. John's College, Oxford, to read English in 1940. Poor eyesight meant that he was rejected for the army, and he emerged with a first in 1943. During his time at Oxford, he formed important relationships with other students interested in poetry, as well as drink and jazz, above all Kingsley Amis (1922–1985). He and Amis became lifelong friends. Both had very complex sexual liaisons, but whereas Amis was influenced by the virtually compulsory Marxism of the university and then moved (with several other intellectuals) strongly to the right, Larkin's views often seemed to reflect popular prejudices. Both were attached to "The Movement." Larkin's poetic models were Hardy and Yeats and his approach has been described as one of Romantic fatalism in which he observed commonplace experiences with a wry detachment. His evocation of the commonplace made him the most popular poet of his time.

Larkin was brought up a skeptic and remained a skeptic, without interest in religion or theology. His writing mirrored a time in the sixties when unbelief emerged as unproblematic, and he felt no need to defend it. Some commentators have seen his position as providing a starting point for exploring sociological accounts of secularization and religion as diminished and obscure. In his poem "Church Going," he is aware of the church as a repository of historic meaning, and feels an awkward reverence for "a serious place on serious earth," but he has no sense of anything beyond that.[1]

His dismissal of religion as a "moth-eaten brocade" suggests scant knowledge of contemporary religious life. In a similar way, his notorious remarks about the damage wrought by the family and about the recent invention of sex tell you more about him than about either the family or sexuality, though, of course, both institutions were in obvious transition. His poem on "Water" is interesting partly because he begins by saying what he would do if asked to *construct* a religion.[2] But it also interesting because he envisages a version of baptism by water that is all-encompassing, and elicits a genuine *metanoia*. He seeks a "sousing" and a "devout drench." Maybe he harbored a deep sense of contamination that demanded what the psalmist also demanded when he asked to be washed "throughly" from all his sins.

At this point, I simply select a couple of poets, Paul Muldoon and Thom Gunn, who illustrate important themes. Paul Muldoon was born in 1951 in a nationalist enclave in County Armagh, Northern Ireland. There were few books at home except for Catholic pamphlets and an encyclopedia, which Muldoon voraciously devoured. After a period reading English in a desultory way at Queen's University, Belfast, he became an arts producer for BBC Belfast. Thereafter he taught creative writing in various universities in England and also in the USA to which he emigrated in 1987. His poems were regarded as difficult, sly, and allusive and were brought together in four collections. Paul Muldoon also wrote libretti for operas and lyrics for his rock band.

Bernard O'Donoghue discusses his work in an undated essay, "Language and the Transcendent in Modern Irish Poetry."[3] He mentions that some have felt that when the Troubles were raging around him, Muldoon ducked political issues with metaphors and poetic analogies. O'Donoghue suggests that post-faith philosophies address the same existential problems as religion. In some of Muldoon's work we have the secular equivalent of the pilgrimage. In others, he has drawn on Christian spiritual structures, and, like Tom Paulin, has deployed Christian titles, for example (following Donne) "Vespers, Good Friday 1971: Riding Westward."[4] Whereas Yeats

---

1. Larkin, *Collected Poems*, 97.
2. Larkin, *Collected Poems*, 93.
3. O'Donoghue, "Language and the Transcendent."
4. Muldoon, *Selected Poems 1968-2014*, 6.

tried to go beyond the quotidian through the occult, Muldoon set out on the same journey through drugs and the shamanistic exercises of Native Americans.

Thom Gunn (1929–2004) was born in Gravesend to parents who were both journalists. They divorced when he was ten, but his mother awakened in him an interest in poetry, before she committed suicide in his teenage years. After attending University College School, Hampstead, Thom Gunn did national service before reading English at Trinity College, Cambridge. His poetry was associated with The Movement in his concern for spare language, and was then influenced by Ted Hughes. In 1954, he migrated to the USA, teaching at Stanford and Berkeley, partly to be with his partner, Mike Kitay.

Commentary on Thom Gunn focuses on the shift in lifestyle and the shift to freer forms that accompanied the move from Cambridge to the bohemian world of California. In the sixties and seventies he was increasingly interested in homosexuality and drugs, and he has been described as the last of the commune dwellers. Perhaps his best known volume was *The Man with Night Sweats*. It was published in America 1992 and dominated by the tragedies of death and life and by elegiac recollection of the many around him whose lives were destroyed by AIDS.[5] He died of substance abuse at his home in Haight-Ashbury.

Ted Hughes (1930–1998) is considered one of the towering figures of the second half of the twentieth century. He stands alongside Larkin and Heaney. He was born in Yorkshire, and was deeply affected by the landscape and wildlife of the Yorkshire moors. He was also affected by his time at Cambridge, where he was inducted into the bardic tradition of English poetry. This bardic tradition was for him filtered and fostered by myth, esoteric traditions, and Jungianism, as well as Buddhism. Hughes is here in alignment with Yeats. He believed these esoteric traditions could fuel the imagination in a way that might help heal the terrors of the "dark subconscious" and the deep divisions in the human psyche. One aspect of experience he particularly explored was the "innocent" and incessant struggle for survival in Nature and its human analogues. His collection *Crow* (1976) is anguished, bitter, and apocalyptic.[6] Hughes was also acutely aware of epiphanic potentialities in the natural world, for example his response to a huge shoal of fish described in "That Morning."[7]

5. Gunn, *The Man with Night Sweats*.
6. Hughes, *Crow*.
7. Hughes and Keene, *River*.

Hughes's marriage to Sylvia Plath (1932–1963) has even been compared to the relationship between the Brownings, though in their case it was disastrous rather than fruitful and fulfilling. Hughes's role in Sylvia Plath's depression and suicide has been endlessly debated, and is beyond the scope of this enquiry: Hughes's *Birthday Letters* (1998) offer one account.[8] Plath's poetry has been described as confessional, though she also wrote landscape poetry about her own vision of the Pennines. Her confessional poetry took its material from her everyday experience. Her collection *The Colossus* (1960) focused on death, redemption, and resurrection, and her final poems charted her grief and despair.[9]

Kathleen Raine (1908–2003) lies firmly in the esoteric tradition of which Ted Hughes was also an exemplar. Her acknowledged masters were Blake and Yeats, and, for Raine, poetry and religion were one and the same. She attempted to bring together science, eastern mysticism, and Neoplatonism. She was also a perceptive admirer of David Jones.

Her father was a miner's son in Northumberland who went to Durham University and became a schoolmaster and Methodist lay preacher. On moving to Ilford, where a hated suburbia was already encroaching, Northumberland became her paradise lost. She won a scholarship to Girton, Cambridge, to study sciences, and, over time, tried both atheism and Catholicism. She was the type of the seeker. She had other major losses as well as Northumberland. She was apparently very attractive, but her personal relationships were disastrous, and included the poet Charles Madge, as well as an impossible passion for Gavin Maxwell, who was gay. She particularly detested Margaret Thatcher, and her individualistic notion that there was no such thing as "Society."

She became (with her close friend the mystical batik artist Thetis Blacker) a moving spirit in the "Temenos Academy of Integral Studies" which, as the name suggests, sought a unified and holistic religious vision. There she had friendships with other poets and writers. Apart from Vernon Watkins, these included David Gasgoyne (1916–2001) and Peter Redgrove (1932–2003). David Gasgoyne, who began life on the Isle of Wight and singing as a choirboy at Salisbury cathedral, was a man of fragile sexuality, apocalyptic, politically very radical, addicted, surrealist, and engaged by a faith which was also faithless. Peter Redgrove shared Kathleen Raine's scientific background and was a kind of meditative and almost shamanistic poet engaged by the wonder of the everyday. Kathleen Raine also wrote a group of poems for Charles Causley.

---

8. Hughes, *Birthday Letters*.
9. Plath, *The Colossus*.

Elizabeth Jennings (1926–2009) was born in Boston, England, but the family early moved to Oxford where she stayed for the rest of her life. She was the only woman identified with The Movement of poets like Amis, Larkin, and Davie, and its ideal of restraint. Her poetry was lyrical, and traditional rather than innovative. She was a devout Roman Catholic, and reflected carefully on the relation of poetry to faith and to priesthood. In "Every Changing Shape" (1961), she saw both priest and poet as committed to self-mastery.[10] They had a shared ordination to communicate shared meanings, and to utter words of transformation and reconciliation on the model of the Eucharist. Elizabeth Jennings also intimately understood R. S. Thomas's discipline of waiting though times of emotional drought, darkness, and meaninglessness: at one point she suffered a serious breakdown.

Ruth Pitter (1897–1992) was born in Ilford, Essex, to primary school teachers who encouraged her in writing poetry. She made her living in the furniture business where she exercised her gifts as a painter, and, at the same time, regularly published new and collected volumes of poetry. Like Elizabeth Jennings, she was traditional in style and content, which may account for the extent to which she was overlooked. At the same, she appeared in major anthologies and was admired by David Cecil and C. S. Lewis. Lewis became a friend and influenced her to the point where she gave up what had been her Bohemian lifestyle and was confirmed as a prayer-book Anglican.

Stevie Smith (1902–1971) was born in Hull, but her father was a shipping agent who went to sea and disappeared from her life. When she was three she moved, with her mother and sister, to Palmers Green in North London where she attended Palmers Green High School and North London Collegiate School. There were perhaps three formative experiences in her life. One was life in a household without men, under the eye of a very difficult aunt. "The lion aunt" brought the sisters up as their mother became more and more seriously ill, dying when Stevie was sixteen. This experience fostered a sense of independence in her and her sister, very different from the kind of home where father knows best. Another formative experience was a period between the ages of five and eight with TB in a Broadstairs sanatorium. This fostered a dark side of her, much concerned with grief, fear, and death. Throughout her life she was subject to depression, and welcomed death as a natural alternative to suicide. In her later years, her wry, intensely shy, and sensitive humor turned more to suffering, faith, and the end of life. Her most anthologized poem was "Not Waving but Drowning." It is a laconic description of a man dying on a beach, muttering to those standing

---

10. Jennings, *Every Changing Shape*, (Manchester: Carcanet Press, 1996).

around who watched, unconcerned, thinking he was waving cheerily as he floundered out there in the water, drowning.[11]

A third formative experience came with her employment with publishers, where she was brought into contact with left-wing artists and writers. This milieu contrasted with her conservative and devout Anglican background, a world where she appreciated the decent communal goodness of Christians, the psalms and hymns, and the choreography of the church. The contrast could have contributed to the oscillating ambivalence of her attitude to faith, so that she constantly interrogated the god in whom she did and did not believe. At one point she described herself as "a lapsed atheist."

In an internet essay, Anne Bryan discusses Stevie Smith and God.[12] She quotes a key text from the poem "God the Eater." This is a description of her compacted faith and doubt. The God in whom she "does not believe" nevertheless consumes her whole life; he is all to her as she is to him.[13] The final quotation from the declaration of love in the Song of Songs is powerful and unmistakeable. It should be placed against her expression of the classic dilemmas of belief in a poem called "The Reason." She reflects again in the characteristic, half-amused, half-despairing tone of many of these dark but oddly insouciant poems, that her life is "vile," she hates it, and perhaps she will "leave it." But then hope springs again and maybe she might after all "thrive." The problem, she concludes, is that she simply can't decide whether God is "good, impotent or unkind."[14]

She doubted the divinity of Christ, because the paradox of the incarnation made no sense to her. It was a contradiction rather than a paradox. As another poet, Kingsley Amis, commented, Christ did not even endure the ultimate test of marriage. Yet she acknowledged "The Airy Christ" who only wanted people to listen to his song rather than love him because he died for them.[15] For Stevie Smith the world had tired of human gods, and of following my leader, whether the leader was the Pope in Rome, or Lenin in his mausoleum, or the name of Christ "exalted above every name." But then, in a poem rightly called "Egocentric," she confesses that she can't respond to a God who shows no sign of being especially responsive to her. Better say goodbye to him, without trailing prolonged regrets. That is the grown-up thing to do. Or is it?[16]

11. Smith, *Selected Poems*, 167; Smith, *All the Poems*.
12. Bryan, "Smith and God."
13. Smith, *Selected Poems*, 196.
14. Smith, *Selected Poems*, 40.
15. Smith, *Selected Poems*, 200.
16. Smith, *Selected Poems*, 23.

Her poem "Edmonton, thy cemetery . . ." swings between the dreary face of death and a belief that the rational calculations of this world do not apply in "the heavenly kingdom-come." Here her ambivalence about faith reaches the most positive point in its oscillation when contemplating the graves of the dead.[17]

Carol Ann Duffy (1955–) became Poet Laureate in 2009, following Andrew Motion, and was the first Scot and LGBT woman to hold the office. She was born in the Gorbals, Glasgow, and her father was an electrical fitter with a strong Labour Party attachment. When she was six, her family moved to Stafford and she received a Catholic education. But when she was fifteen, her convent school became an old people's home, and she said goodbye to Catholicism without regrets. She had wanted to write from early adolescence, and at Stafford Girl's High School her teachers turned the light full on.

Carol Ann Duffy describes herself as an atheist, and it is interesting to explore what she makes of religion. In an interview for *The Guardian*, 3rd December, 2005, she says she believes "Poetry and prayer are very similar. I write a lot of sonnets and I think of them almost as prayer."[18] Her poem "Prayer" (1984) typically draws on memory, and ritual language, whether religious or secular:

> Pray for us now. Grade 1 piano scales
> console the lodger looking out across
> a Midlands town. Then dusk, and someone calls
> A child's name as though they named their loss.
> Darkness outside. Inside the radio's prayer -
> Rockall, Malin, Dogger, Finisterre.[19]

Myth, solidified metaphor, and fairy tale are omnipresent in all human discourse, whether religious or secular. Her poem, "Ash Wednesday 1984," about the practice of confession, brings out the frightening aspects of metaphor used as more than metaphor and of stories which, like Hansel and Gretel, harness fear and inquisition in the service of love.[20] It was just this use of wrong means for good ends that scandalized Stevie Smith. At the same time, the powerful and resonant language retained in the religious framework by rite and rote remains a rich resource for the poet. For Carol Ann Duffy, poetry almost takes the place of religion in a secular society. This is perhaps one reason why she seeks to disseminate poetry, and, in her

17. Larkin, *Oxford Book of Twentieth-Century Verse*, 343–44.
18. Anderson, "Christmas Carol."
19. Schmidt, *Harvill Book of Twentieth-Century Poetry in English*, 678.
20. Duffy, *Collected Poems*, 12.

own work, writes on current themes like ecology that provide appealing material to those who construct educational syllabi. Carol Ann Duffy recognizes and exploits the public space opened up for poetry by new technology.

Chapter 11

Donald Davie, Charles Sisson, and Geoffrey Hill; Denise Levertov, Andrew Motion, and Michael Symmonds Roberts

I come finally to a group of poets with a major if complex relation to Christianity. They are Charles Sisson, Donald Davie, Geoffrey Hill, Denise Levertov, Andrew Motion, and Michael Symmons Roberts. The first four were mainly of the twentieth century, though Geoffrey Hill lived until 2016. I knew Sisson, Davie, and Hill personally, so my treatment is affected by that knowledge. Davie I encountered initially following his friendly response to a review I wrote in the *Times Higher Education Supplement* of his work on the hymnody of eighteenth-century Dissent. Through his kindness, that review led to my association with the highly innovative *Poetry Nation Review* (PNR) published by Carcanet Press. It also led to friendships with Michael Schmidt, the moving spirit at Carcanet and PNR, and with Charles Sisson, also closely connected with PNR. Davie, Schmidt, and Sisson all supported the 1970s campaign in which I was deeply involved to save the Book of Common Prayer and the Authorized Version of the Bible, in church, and society and in education at large. I sought to save both from being relegated to the status of museum pieces or just forgotten to the point where understanding of English literature and Christianity was seriously disabled. Another powerful literary ally was the poet Brian Morris for whom I wrote an introductory essay (quoting Auden for my title, "Why

Spit on your Luck?"), in his edited book, *Ritual Murder* (1980).[1] I was guest editor for a complete issue of PNR to pursue the cause of the BCP and the AV.[2] Arguably, without denying the need for fresh biblical translations or for liturgical reform, the deposition of these central reference points was part of "the Break" remarked on by David Jones, coming in either the early or the mid-twentieth century. Maybe the deposition was consequent on "the Break." As for Geoffrey Hill, I knew him and his Jewish wife, the librettist, poet, and (later) Anglican priest Alice Goodman, at a rather later date when he and I (and Christopher Ricks) were associated with Boston University. That relationship was renewed intermittently when Geoffrey Hill and Alice Goodman returned to England.

Dealing with Sisson, Davie, and Hill is difficult, partly because they were all also major literary critics, though not perhaps as pivotal in criticism and revised views or revivals of major poets as Eliot. I begin with Charles Sisson (1914–2003) in some modest detail partly because his political and social criticism is relevant to my specific interests here. He was, for example, overtly anti-Catholic in times when this traditional prejudice was increasingly covert. In a period spent in France he became interested in Charles Maurras and in "Action Française," a movement both monarchist and Catholic, though Maurras was an agnostic. One of Sisson's major essays is on Charles Péguy, radical socialist, nationalist, and Catholic, who died in the war "face down among the beetroots."[3] It is interesting that Geoffrey Hill wrote one of his finest poems on Péguy.

Patrick McGuiness and Charles Louth, in their "Introduction" to *A C. H. Sisson Reader* (2014),[4] comment that Sisson, like Donald Davie, was unusual in adopting a modernism, through Pound, seemingly at odds with the British cultural inheritance. He was, perhaps, the heir of Hulme with his belief in order and community and in his support for democracy, fully conscious of its imperfections. He was like Hulme also in his espousal of the "religious attitude" that could sometimes be independent of belief and for which Christianity might even be just a historical given. Sisson had a deep sense of the imperative demands of political realism and of the insidious corruptions of sin in the body politic, though he did not follow Hulme in supposing humankind beyond redemption. He was strongly against vague mystics dabbling in politics regardless of consequences, and believed in the power of rigorous ideas and the importance of observing limits. In spite of

---

1. Morris, *Ritual Murder*.
2. Martin, "Crisis for Cranmer and King James."
3. Sisson, *Avoidance of Literature*, 47.
4. Louth and McGuiness, *A C. H. Sisson Reader*.

his English accent, the breadth of his scholarship, shown in many translations, was European.

Charles Sisson was born in Bristol, a West Country stronghold of Noncomformity, in a Methodist family. He read English and Philosophy at Bristol University and he reacted negatively to the left-liberal consensus against nationalism and for pacifism, in a way consonant with the acerbic essays of T. S. Eliot. He had a career as a civil servant, retiring with the rank of under-secretary. As part of his role he engaged in a wide-ranging cross-cultural survey of administration that also looked to five centuries of English history. He was a vigorous critic of Bagehot as someone whose economistic attitude neglected the vital role of the "ornamental" and ritual aspects of the constitution. Ritual lay at the heart of political action and mediated the realities of power. In politics as in religion, Sisson was a constitutionalist with an admiration for Richard Hooker on ecclesiastical polity. He also had grave doubts about the very existence of the individual, in a way resembling Eliot's comments on subjectivity and personality. That doubt came out in his novel *Christopher Homm*, published in 1955,[5] and in the poem "The Usk," in which the second section begins "Nothing is in my own voice because I have not / Any."[6]

Sisson's collections of poetry made little impact until the publication of *In the Trojan Ditch* in 1974. Much of his approach to life, death, and precarious faith comes out in "The Usk":

> So among tombs
> Truth may be sought, and found, if we rejoice
> With Ham and Shem and Japhet in the dark
> The ark rolls onward over a wide sea.
> Come sleep, come lightning, comes the dove at last."[7]

In the same collection his poem "What a piece of work is Man" raised a central issue for this discussion:

> How does it happen that the table leg
> Has this curve in one age, that in another?
> [...]
> Conception rules the art,
> How then can one man speak to another?[8]

---

5. Sisson, *Christopher Homm*.
6. Sisson, *In the Trojan Ditch*, 33.
7. Sisson, *In the Trojan Ditch*, 34.
8. "What a piece of work is Man," in Louth and McGuiness, *C. H. Sisson Reader*, 35–36.

He was also a poet of place: Somerset streams and trees seen from his Langport window. No one since Webster and Donne so often "saw the skull beneath the skin."

Donald Davie (1922–1995) was born in a Baptist family in Barnsley, living in the "ravaged landscape" of the West Riding of Yorkshire. He attended a local grammar school and was early taken by poetry, for example Palgrave's *Golden Treasury*, and acquired an intense interest in architecture. He won a scholarship to St. Catherine's College, Cambridge, but in 1941 joined the navy and went to northern Russia. These bare biographical facts tell us a great deal about his abiding affections, though not about his strong attachment to his wife, Doreen, whom he several times addressed in his poetry. Apart from poetry itself, these affections were English Dissent, buildings, chapels and churches, and the literature of Russia, above all Pasternak, but also the literature of Poland and of Eastern Europe generally during the Cold War. Like Charles Sisson he was immensely learned and a major critic, and his Christianity was hard won. The rest of his biography is best summarized in terms of the academic posts and places he worked in after his period as undergraduate and postgraduate at Cambridge. He held academic posts in Ireland and California: Ireland he left shocked by the indiscriminate murders of the IRA, in California he enjoyed a fruitful association with the poet Yvor Winters. He also taught at Essex University and Vanderbilt University and spent time in Italy.

Donald Davie was associated with "The Movement" of poets who valued purity of diction, like Kingsley Amis, Philip Larkin, and Robert Conquest, and was perhaps its principal theorist. His *Purity of Diction in English Verse* came out in 1952 and in 1955 *Articulate Energy: an Enquiry into the Syntax of English Poetry*, both of which were seriously influential—and contested. He recommended a return to the rationality of the eighteenth century and to the respect for genre that he believed had been lost with Wordsworth. He said, for example, that Gerard Manley Hopkins had no respect for language, and produced hideous, muscle-bound monstrosities. He was also critical of the symbolist tradition which he identified in Eliot's "Ash Wednesday" and *Four Quartets*, believing that Eliot conceded too much to the logic of music. Davie's *Collected Poems, 1950–1970* brought together selected poems from several previous collections and was published in 1972.[9]

Here I draw out aspects of Donald Davie's critical work and poetry of interest to the concerns of this enquiry. His religious loyalties to what he saw as the rational and enlightened tradition of conservative and orthodox Dissent inspired his interest in its literature, poetry, and hymnology. The

---

9. Davie, *Collected Poems*.

Dissent of Robert Browning did not attract his admiration. In his loyalty to Dissent he was influenced, as I was, by the writings of Bernard Manning, of Jesus College, Cambridge, defending and elucidating the dissenting tradition. Donald Davie was also a poet of place, for example in poems on all forty shires of England in his collection *The Shires* (1974),[10] as well as poems about Essex and East Anglia, and about England, Ireland, and Italy. He was thoroughly skeptical about the predominant influence of what he saw as the sentimentalities of the left, and horrified by the "insane" irrationalities of the sixties. He was also appalled by the immoral sensualities of Dylan Thomas, and a defender of the moral content of poetry.

Donald Davie eventually became an Anglican and a fierce defender of the Book of Common Prayer and the Authorized Version of the Bible (the King James Bible), both of which he saw as exemplifying the pithy "plain style" he himself embraced. He was one the few poets to write specifically about secularization, and through his daughter-in-law, the sociologist Grace Davie, he wrote a poem called "Ordinary God," based on the reply to a survey question about whether the respondent believed in a God who actively intervened in human affairs. The response was "No, just the ordinary one." It appeared in his most revealing collection of poems, with wry references to, and adaptations of, the psalms, *To Scorch or to Freeze: Poems about the Sacred* (1988). His "The Thirty-ninth Psalm, Adapted," following the psalm used at the Book of Common Prayer service "At the burial of the dead," ends:

> Hear my prayer, O Lord,
> And please to consider my calling
> It commits me to squawking
> And running off at the mouth.[11]

His last book involved translations of the psalms from the Countess of Pembroke to the present, in which he characteristically challenged the Romantic concern with originality.[12]

Sir Geoffrey Hill (1932–2016) was born in Bromsgrove, Worcestershire, the son of a policeman, and he attended a local county high school before winning a scholarship to Keble College, Oxford. The bare facts of his distinguished scholarly career give few clues to the estimate of him as the greatest poet of his generation and successor to Eliot as both poet and critic, or to his commitment to morality and Christian faith. They say nothing

---

10. Davie, *The Shires*.
11. Davie, *To Scorch or Freeze*, 2.
12. Davie, *The Psalms in English*.

about his times of chronic anxiety and depression, or his belief that the supposed difficulty of his writing was at one with the sheer difficulty and mystery of other people and everyday living. Perhaps he was a difficult man because of his intense commitment to integrity and honesty.

Geoffrey Hill taught at Leeds University from 1954–1980, and was a teaching fellow at Emmanuel College, Cambridge, from 1981–1988 before taking up a post as professor of literature and religion at Boston University from 1989–2006. He then returned to England and was professor of poetry at Oxford from 2010–2015. He was knighted in 2012, and lived his final years in England in Fulbourn Rectory, where his wife was parish priest. His first volume of poetry, *For the Unfallen*, was written in 1952 but not published until 1959, when it made a massive impact.[13] Something of its thematic repertoire comes through the lines that form the sixth day of the first poem, "Genesis":

> By blood we live, the hot, the cold
> To ravage and redeem the world
> There is no bloodless myth will hold.[14]

This thematic repertoire linked the violent horrors of the early modern period with the totalitarian horrors of modernity. Geoffrey Hill sought to mediate the witness of martyrdom. There followed a fallow period and then *King Log* (1968) and *Mercian Hymns* (1971). In 1985 his *Collected Poems* were published by Penguin.

Towards the end of the nineties there was a late flowering of six volumes in ten years: *Canaan* (1997), *The Triumph of Love* (1998), *Speech! Speech!* (2000), *The Orchards of Sion* (2002), *Without Title* (2006), and *A Treatise of Civil Power* (2007). Much of this writing has been seen as a contemporary pilgrim's progress, bringing together autobiography, theology, and history in defiantly modernist style. Geoffrey Hill's work has been characterized as marked by sobriety, moral passion, civic engagement, and a focus on the themes of faith, innocence, redemption, and the struggle with evil. His writing is allusive and recondite, for example in its etymological reference, multi-layered and multilingual. He pushes the resources of English to the limit. Perhaps the poem "The Pentecost Castle," from *Tenebrae* (1978),[15] on what is, in a literal sense, the most profound moment in the liturgical year when all the lights are put out, may give some indication of the compressed power of Geoffrey Hill. The third section begins:

---

13. Hill, *For the Unfallen*.
14. Hill, *Collected Poems*, 16.
15. Hill, *Tenebrae*.

> You watchers on the wall
> [. . .]
> tell us what you saw
> the lord I sought to serve
> Caught in the thorn grove
> his blood on his brow.

It continues in a fourth section:

> At dawn the Mass
> burgeons from the stone
> A Jesse tree
> Of resurrection.[16]

Denise Levertov (1923–1997) merits inclusion not simply on the quality of her poetry but because she united in herself several ethnicities and languages as well as Judaism and Christianity. She was Welsh on her mother's side, and through her absorbed a tradition of Welsh dissenting opposition to war as well as of radicalism generally. There was also an anti-war tradition and a broad radicalism on her father's side. He was an Anglican priest who came from a Jewish Hassidic tradition. He originally taught at Leipzig University, but was interned as a Russian alien in the First World War. He came to England as a priest, working in Ilford, Essex, where Denise Levertov was born. Denise's parents gave her a rich multilingual home education, including the poetry of Tennyson, and Denise became very early aware of a vocation to be a writer and poet. This transition from Judaism may seem very unusual but it is not that infrequent.

Denise Levertov was a nurse during the London Blitz, and began by writing traditional neo-Romantic verse tinged with almost Brahmsian melancholy. But in 1947 she met Mitchell Goodman, American son of Jewish migrants, and in 1948 the couple moved permanently to the USA. Later both she and Mitchell Goodman became intensely involved in movements against the Vietnam War, though they were by now divorced. After the initial move to America, Denise Levertov assimilated the American intellectual scene and was influenced by William Carlos Williams and the Black Mountain poets, "projectivists" who worked on the immediate improvised breath or utterance within the line.

In her later years, she moved slowly from agnosticism to Christianity and (in 1989) to Catholicism, though she maintained her anti-war radicalism. In the earlier stages of this journey she explored the relation between faith and doubt, darkness, death, and light, and she perhaps shifted to a

---

16. Hill, *Collected Poems*, 138–39.

sacramental sense of God in the natural world and in the inward self. She found the sacred in the everyday. Her directly religious poems are collected in *The Stream and the Sapphire*, published in 1997.[17] These poems, complementing a volume on nature and ecology, seek (in her own words in her "Foreword") to imagine historical personages like Caedmon and St. Peter. They also try to enter, in the manner of Ignatian spirituality, into the events in the New Testament, such as the liberation of Peter from prison. They include significant references to Rilke, Thomas Merton, Lady Julian of Norwich—and to Schnittke, a Russian Jewish composer who also moved to Catholicism. The poem, "Psalm Fragments (Schnittke String Trio)," explored every form of negation before holding on to precarious twigs that should break and yet remain firm.[18] Her poem "The Servant-Girl at Emmaus," when the resurrected Jesus was known "in the breaking of bread," is based on a painting by Velasquez.[19]

Andrew Motion was born in 1952 into a family with no interest in books, but when he attended Radley College, an inspiring teacher turned the light on, especially for poetry, and he went on to read English at University College, Oxford. Since then, he has been associated with attempts to make poetry accessible. This was helped by his role as poet laureate from 1999–2009, and through the astonishing technical means now available. He believes more people are now reading poetry than ever before. Andrew Motion was also very active in opposition to the Iraq War.

At one stage, Andrew Motion was criticized for recommending the Bible be read as literature: echoing a criticism once made by Auden when he wrote we should not "speak with such / As read the Bible for its prose."[20] But since that time, Motion has been drawn, with his wife, into the church as a supportive community, and finds satisfaction in the experience of liturgy, as well as reasons for reading the Bible beyond its literary qualities. He finds parts of the Bible exceedingly strange, and also finds saying the creed hard work, given what he sees as its resistance to a metaphorical reading. He also now reads Herbert more appreciatively than was once the case, having previously preferred Donne as more dramatic than Herbert and more often secular. (He is deeply moved by Britten's settings of Donne's *Holy Sonnets*, because they simultaneously give potent reinforcement to the affirmations of the poetry while in their spare economy allowing space for the poetry

---

17. Levertov, *The Stream and the Sapphire*.
18. Levertov, *The Stream and the Sapphire*, 21.
19. Levertov, *The Stream and the Sapphire*, 43.
20. "Under Which Lyre: A Reactionary Tract for the Times" (Phi Beta Kappa Poem, Harvard 1946), in Auden, *Collected Poems*, 259–63.

to make its own impact.) Herbert's devotional approach in *The Temple* has gained in appeal for Motion by the way it finds divinity in ordinary activities like sweeping a room or all the cumulative similitudes that build up in Herbert's poem "Prayer." The same simple approach to divinity in ordinary dress informs a poem, titled "Simple," which Motion himself wrote on the story of the great draught of fish at the end of St. John's Gospel.[21] Motion fastens on the significant details, like the number of fish caught or the brazier, because for him the transcendent emerges in the detail. The poem represents Motion's approach to faith. He fastens on the uncertainty about the figure on the shore, both definite and indefinite, and on the surprising plenitude of joy that may lie in wait. The approach bears comparison with the profound musical setting of the same passage by James MacMillan, "Since it was the Day of Preparation."

I might have concluded my comments with Simon Jarvis's extraordinarily ambitious (and unfinished) seven-thousand-line poem, *Night Office*, published in 2013,[22] but that is a major enterprise in itself. Instead, I turn to Michael Symmons Roberts. Roberts was born in 1963 in Preston, Lancashire, before his family moved to Newbury in Berkshire, where he attended a comprehensive school. He then went to Regent's Park College, Oxford, to study philosophy and theology, with the express purpose of converting Christian students to what he saw as the obvious commonsense of atheism. But then he gradually concluded that the obvious is only such with respect to the premises from which you start, and lapsed from his atheistic faith. After a time as a journalist, he joined the BBC and eventually became a full-time writer and professor of poetry at Manchester Metropolitan University.

Michael Symmons Roberts converted to Catholicism and collaborated with the Catholic composer James MacMillan on two commissions for the promenade concerts and on *The Sacrifice*, an opera performed by Welsh National Opera. His poetry is in a lyric tradition, but informed by science as well as philosophy and theology. He has been described by Jeanette Winterson, herself from a Pentecostal background, as "a religious poet in a secular age"[23] His six collections have attracted many prestigious awards, including the T. S. Eliot Prize in 2002 and 2004.

---

21. Andrew Motion, "Simple," 2004, a poem written for the BBC television program "What the World Thinks of God," broadcast on BBC Two on 16th February, 2004.

22. Jarvis, *Night Office*.

23. Jeanette Winterson was chair of judges of the Forward Prize for Poetry, 2013, awarded to Michael Symmons Roberts for his collection of poems *Drysalter*. Report at: https://www.theguardian.com/books/2013/oct/01/drysalter-wins-forward-poetry-prize. The quotation in the text is her commendation of Symmons Roberts for the Poetry Archive.

His collection *Drysalter* was published in 2013, and repays some scrutiny as picking up the tradition of writing on the themes of the psalms, for example in the work of Donald Davie already referred to.[24] The title of the collection refers to a trader in salts, dyes, and chemicals, and its hundred and fifty poems complement the hundred and fifty psalms in the Bible, to which there are frequent references. It has been rightly described as a series of meditations on spirit discerned in unlikely places and epiphanies in unlikely moments. Although I have read the whole collection, as well as the collection entitled *Corpus* (2004),[25] I take my cues from Victoria Mackenzie in a review of *Drysalter* for the *New Welsh Review*, which seems to me to catch the import of these poems very successfully.[26] She notices that many of the psalms are hymns in praise of the unloved objects of contemporary society, like photo booths, roller coasters, and car factories. His ability to find the spiritual in the material is epitomized in his hymns to sometimes unlovely objects where he recognizes that the way to the soul is through the body. Again, you must not deny the body. The poem "In Praise of the Present" affirms the here and now. Like so many of the psalms, the poem calls upon God, simply in the hope that he may be listening. Feelings of homesickness for the Wales of the past recall an older order. The line between normality and apocalypse is always fragile in the work of Michael Symmons Roberts, and the link between motorways and the garden of Eden more intimate than we have imagined.

---

24. Symmons Roberts, *Drysalter*.
25. Symmons Roberts, *Corpus*.
26. Mackenzie, "Review of Drysalter."

Chapter 12

Conclusion

As I said at the outset, this has not been a sociological survey or a literary-critical assessment of English poetry, but an enquiry into different ways of negotiating the great axes of human life from the adoption of Christianity in England to the present. It enquires into modes of understanding as they have been manifest in the highly sensitive lens of poetry at different periods. That lens has picked up other elements quite distinct from Christianity but partially fused with it, such as the pagan honor code, Renaissance humanism, and Enlightenment rationality. In the course of time, Christianity has altered and the non-Christian elements have also altered. I have suggested, in terms based in my work on secularization over the last half-century or so, first of all, that there is a constant secularization understood as adjustment to "the world." This found a paradoxical realization in the secular effects of the Reformation attempt to return Christianity to its original fountainhead: a desacralization of the natural world, a transfer of the sacred from the monastery and the privileged clergy to the *koinonia* of the family, a rejection of extra-biblical miracles and of mystical ecstasies. I have suggested, secondly, that the onset of secularization in institutional terms is not a one-directional movement *from* the religious *to* the secular. The point about a staggered movement can be underlined by contrasting the last quarter of the eighteenth century with both the seventeenth and the nineteenth centuries. There is also a marked change in tonality over the years between 1680 and 1715, along the lines argued by Paul Hazard in *The Crisis of the European Mind: 1680–1715*,[1] though a change in tonality is not to be straightforwardly equated with a decline in religion.

1. Hazard, *Crisis of the European Mind*.

At the same time, as I suggested in my introduction to this book, it seems to me that there is some kind of significant break either in the early or in the mid-twentieth century. This break can be identified most easily in the intelligentsia and it only partially correlates with the empirical state of what the French call religious *appartenance*. About religious practice and belief, sociologists lay different emphases on a slow secularization dating back to the nineteenth century and a more dramatic change signaled in the late sixties. Wherever and whenever the break occurred, I have been interested in three genealogies: a secular genealogy reaching back to Shelley, but more often identified as gaining momentum in the later decades of the nineteenth century; a non-Christian religious genealogy dating back to Byron and earlier, but gaining momentum in the late nineteenth century; and a surprisingly resilient Christian trajectory up to the present. That Christian trajectory has mutated over the decades in terms of the issues that trouble Christian poets: the nineteenth-century concern with scientific advance and biblical criticism becomes a concern with the nature of western civilization and then a concern with the depredations of industrial and urban society, in particular its debased culture and materialism. These mutations are important, but I do not think they represent cumulative reasons for disbelief piled one on top of another to make the skeptical case. They might be cumulative for some people, but my suspicion is that Geoffrey Hill was not much worried by Renan or Strauss or the implications of advancing scientific knowledge for the Christian narrative. What exercised Robert Browning is not what exercised Geoffrey Hill. For that matter, what exercised Robert Browning was not what exercised Elizabeth Barrett Browning. That raises the question about a difference between the poetry of men and women when it comes to religion, complementing the documented differences in practice and belief between men and women.

There are also mutations and massive variations in the expression of hostility towards religion. Shelley believed religion to be fundamentally implicated in the monstrous injustices of the social order. Blake was hostile to religion, the church, and the social order, but that was because he believed in a radical Christianity. The objections of Shelley and Blake were very different from Swinburne's objection to what he saw as Christianity's denial of life and its richness. When we come to the radicals of the thirties, they often took a religiose attitude to political belief, above all Marxism, but they mostly did not see religion at the heart of an unjust capitalist order. Sylvia Townsend Warner was perhaps unusual in seeing religion as an integral part of a *massa damnata*. Mostly, poets saw the root of injustice lying elsewhere, and religion as a marginal issue, or just an outer mask of a social order on the brink of destruction.

Conclusion 149

Marxism raises the standard question of so-called "secular religions." Notoriously, Marxism was "the God that failed," whereas Christianity is built on redemptive power of a God who "failed" on a cross. It takes failure as its starting point. The resilience of Christianity (and of liturgy) has something to do with a sense of the profound resistance of human affairs to optimistic estimates of human progress and perfectibility. That does not mean we should reject liberal values, but it does mean we should reject liberal anticipations of a future where history as we know it comes to a stop. The ancient snake of corruption stirs in the primeval mire, and the greater the ambition to achieve a secular New Jerusalem, the more terrible the Fall. *Corruptio optima pessima.* Marxism secularized the crises of eschatology before the expected *parousia* of the New Man, and what emerged was unmistakably the Old Adam of Christian theology.

The other great secular religion was nationalism, and here matters were more complex, because, on a wider North Atlantic map, religion was sometimes fused with nationalism and the Enlightenment, as in America, while religion was elsewhere opposed by a fusion of nationalism and Enlightenment, as in France. On the whole, in England nationalism and Enlightenment were more inclined to co-opt religion than to oppose it. England more resembled America than France, and after all England and America were culturally and historically affiliated. The question then becomes how nationalism in England was related to religion in its poetry.

Here we encounter one of the major fissures in the academic analysis of nationalism. There are those, like Ernest Gellner and John Breuilly, who see nationalism as an ideology of modern industrial society displacing religion while retaining some of its features like charisma, the elevation of saints or heroes, and founding fatherhood. I have certainly argued that nationalism retains those religious features. But I have also argued, following Anthony Smith and others, that nationalism has deeper roots in what Smith called ethno-symbolism such as we find in ancient Israel.[2] It seems to me that England early acquired a national consciousness, long before the modernity of the industrial revolution, and that it replicated very ancient features such as are identified in John Burrows's *A History of Histories.*[3]

In poetry, that is signaled by Shakespeare in *Henry V*, a play in which references to England and God (and St. George) are very prominent, and in John of Gaunt's deathbed speech about England as "demi-paradise" in *Richard II.* Shakespeare is, of course, projecting nationalism back nearly two hundred years, but it is worth remembering that Shaw and others have

2. Smith and Riley, *Nation and Classical Music.*
3. Burrows, *A History of Histories.*

located English (and French) national feeling as far back as the confrontations and mobilizations of the Hundred Years' War. Nationalism of a republican kind is very evident in Milton and in his references to a "puissant nation," but these references are found in *Areopagitica*, not in the poetry. In David Loewenstein and Paul Stevens's (eds.) *Early Modern Nationalism and Milton's England* (2008), it is argued that the nation is a powerful imaginative construct for understanding both Milton's prose and his verse: the divine Son in *Paradise Lost*, for example, can be understood as a republican hero.[4] The sense of England as a rising and powerful new Israel was, of course, donated to the nascent USA, and Milton was in time co-opted by American and British nationalists alike. Something of that sensibility can be found in Thomson's *The Seasons*, where England as new Israel is combined with England as new Greece and new Rome. The cultivation of myth is always an essential part of the construction of national identity, as became very obvious in the poems of MacPherson, in Scott's "Lay of the Last Minstrel" (1805), Tennyson's "Idylls of the King" (1885), and—later—Yeats's recourse to myth as a foundation for Irish identity.

In Christopher Smart, nationalism is combined with admiration for the native English Church rather than for the foreign Church of Rome, a sentiment that recurs regularly in English culture right up to Charles Sisson in the mid-twentieth century. Blake's vigorous sense of the nation is part of his complex mythology, but his "Jerusalem" has had an extraordinary twentieth-century history in becoming (as set to music by Hubert Parry in 1917) a second national anthem appealing to conservatives and socialists alike, though for very different reasons.

Perhaps it is worth noticing here the role of Unitarianism in the radical politics of the young Coleridge in the early nineteenth century, but Unitarianism seems usually to have manifested itself in prose: Martineau, Gaskell, and Dickens. Under the pressure of the French threat, Coleridge could write of England with passionate affection in his "Fears in Solitude" (1798). In a rather similar way, once Wordsworth had foresworn his early enthusiasm for radical change and for the French Revolution, he expressed affectionate thoughts about the nation, even in its failures, as in the sonnet apostrophizing Milton where he says (in 1802) "Milton! Thou shouldst be living at this hour, / England hath need of thee."[5]

Henry Newbolt and Rudyard Kipling were both poets of the imperial period in English history, though Kipling's sense of the nation had its elegiac strain, and was, in its way, surprisingly inclusive. Rupert Brooke perfectly

---

4. Loewenstein and Stevens, *Early Modern Nationalism and Milton's England*.
5. "London 1802, II," in Quiller-Couch, *Oxford Book of English Verse*, 1084.

caught the patriotism that swept young England in the early months of the First World War, but that was later overtaken by the sober and disillusioned reflections of poets like Owen and Sassoon, and by a pacifist sentiment animating several writers during the inter-war years. The climate had altered by the beginning of the Second World War, and Charles Sisson and Donald Davie had a decent commitment to the cause of the country in the struggle with totalitarianism rather than anything resembling the older nationalism. Both saw active service. Geoffrey Hill had a deep affection for England and its history, but dismissed with some contempt the accusation that he cherished a "chthonic nationalism."

What was much more prominent than overt nationalism in English poetry was a sentiment about particular places and landscapes in England. It was a sentiment that motivated the desire to defend it almost as sacred ground. It was mobilized in English propaganda and was often linked by poets to affection for churches as special places that stored the history of a people. Something of this emerges in Donald Davie's collection *The Shires* (1974) and in Eliot's line in "Little Gidding," "History is now and England."[6] As far back as the First World War, Siegfried Sassoon expressed this emotion about the Weald of his childhood, even though he was eventually disillusioned about the war. One has only to think of the intense feelings about Gloucestershire in poets and musicians alike.

It is here that we come to the essential issue broached in the introduction of the nature of conceptualization in poetry as that bears on its relationship to faith. Throughout this whole analysis, one of the principal themes in English poetry is the rejection of abstraction in favor of particularity. The universal is revealed in the particular, and that has a close affinity with the idea that the sacramental is realized in the material: eternity conveyed in a grain of sand or in a grain of bread. The poetic pursuit of the significant particular is linked to the perceived difficulty of pursuing philosophic arguments in poetry. Wordsworth may seem to have had aspirations towards "philosophic song" in *The Prelude*, but his argument is intermittent and diffuse and depends on the support of evocation to secure any kind of conviction. Poets in the eighteenth century, like Pope and Johnson, came closest to argument in their poetry, but perhaps it is better to see their writings as a form of sage and humane reflection or wise commentary. Coleridge's poem, "Religious Musings," is full of capitalized and portentous nouns like Folly, Life, Pity, Mind, Adoration, Fancy, and Oppression that disrupt the flow of images.[7] This is all very different from the surprisingly simple lines in "The

---

6. Eliot, *Collected Poems*, 222.
7. Coleridge, *Poetical Works*, 108–25.

Ancient Mariner" (1798), following on a "salvation history" of unjust killing and penance. "He prayeth best who loveth best / All things both great and small."[8]

Some of the Marxist philosophical reflections of Hugh MacDiarmid verge on the unreadable. Poetry can be philosophically or ideologically inflected, but once the logic of argument becomes dominant, poetic inspiration dies the death. No doubt this is why Yeats sought a mode of religious discourse cordoned off from philosophy, and therefore from all possibility of refutation. He was trying to gain access to a realm that escaped the tyranny of conceptual thinking.

The question of logical argument rather than suasion by the power of evocation is bound up with the proximity thought to exist between poetry and prophecy, or even poetry and prayer. Poets feel themselves possessed by a message for their times to be delivered with all the vatic power at their disposal. They come close to religious utterance in their ability to evoke and invoke. Poets call up and call upon. If you think of prayer as a form of attention, then a poem can become a form of prayer. The very idea of inspiration, understood as possession by the power of the Spirit, brings poetry very close to religious utterance. At the same time most poets believe we are only talking about pregnant similarities rather than near identities. I have earlier stressed the proper autonomy of expressions of faith and the importance of rejecting near identity while recognizing potent proximity. We have then to explore the differences. There are, for example, different kinds of metaphorical concentration in the two activities so that in poetry there are only shadowy equivalents of the interlocking genealogies of imagery that inform liturgy.

What do I mean about different kinds of concentration in poetry and liturgy? In a poem you find striking images that link seemingly disparate things metaphorically. Liturgical imagery and metaphorical linkages are never striking in that way. If they drew attention to themselves on account of individual originality they would intrude on the flow of governing images as these are organized in coherent families linked to a sacred narrative. In liturgy the chief governing idea is sacramental, in that the concept of body and blood is organically linked to bread and wine. Everything else is governed by a metaphor of body and blood, intimate to the point where the metaphor participates in what it stands for. That close participation is again linked in the most intimate way with the idea of gift, offered and received. The linkage is literally embodied in the sentence at the heart of the sacramental action: "This is my body." Take, for example, grain as a metaphor and

---

8. Coleridge, *Poetical Works*, 209.

its various metamorphoses. The metaphor of grain is linked with generic ideas of fruit, harvest, and sustenance, with the minute that carries the infinite, with the broken that makes whole, and with the unconditional gift of the body received to refresh the body with the medicine of immortality. The metaphor of grain and its various metamorphoses is cross-referenced against the metaphor of the shared table as that links the idea of fellowship, unity, and sharing with the idea of host and guest. The metaphor of table is in turn linked with a group of metaphors to do with innocent and sacrificial lambs, good shepherds, and safe folds. There are numerous families of this kind, each cross-referenced against all the rest, rather as icons on the iconostasis are organized according to an iconographic scheme. There are families grouped around the ideas of light, fire, and water, and a large topographical family involving deserts, wildernesses, streams, fountains, wells, pathways, and mountains as well as cities, gates, and temples. The meanings are relatively stable because they are the shared stock of a community engaged in repeated collective and choreographed expression: the images of lily, rose and thorn, for example, are deployed as part of an understood repertoire. Similarly a reference to a passage through a river of death or to a passage through the waters of cleansing, or to the inexhaustible fountains of life, is understood without recourse to hermeneutic scrutiny.

When poets quote liturgy, they do so precisely in order to call to mind this repertoire as a shared reference point. Sometimes the references are more glancing, and depend on the reader's having some background knowledge of, for example, the understood meanings of wilderness and city. The crucial difference remains that in poetry metaphor is not necessarily intimately linked with what it signifies, nor is it choreographed spatially and temporally. And its metaphors are not organized according to a governing scheme. Its comparisons can be very extended, as in Shakespeare's sonnet where the loved one is compared to a summer day, but they are not cross-referenced in multiple families.

At the same time, there are analogies between liturgy and poetry, in spite of the differences. Dylan Thomas, for example, can be understood as the maker, performer, and celebrant of a rite that deploys rich concatenations of religious imagery. The poet can act like a celebrant and can bring to bear images derived from the language of faith, without at all assenting to a particular religious perspective. In *In Parenthesis*, David Jones deploys liturgy as a shared frame deployed in cumulative historical depth for understanding the nature of sacrifice. There are also poems whose emotional freight is so potent that the poet has natural recourse to images drawn from religion. Two obvious examples are Keats's last sonnet, "Bright Star," and the "Anthem for Doomed Youth" by Wilfred Owen. Both poems deploy

Catholic imagery: the "sleepless Eremite" and "priestly absolution" in the case of Keats, and "hasty orisons," "passing bells," and "shrill demented choirs" in the case of Owen.[9]

There is a rather different kind of problem about the extent of the public reception of poetry and its influence. Obviously, the influence of poetry partly turns on technologies of reproduction, such as the explosion of print in the eighteenth century and the emergence of a sizeable literate public. But since that time, there have been mutations of taste and vagaries of print consumption that, for example, downgrade poetry in favor of the novel as a source of influence. The novel has the clear advantage over poetry of narrative and character. In any case, the variable appeal of different kinds of poetry vastly affects what influence it can hope to exercise: Kipling's fluent popular verse had far more impact on his large readership than the poetry of Bridges, and Betjeman enjoyed far more public recognition even than Auden. In recent times, it may well be that internet technology has once again made poetry widely available, and performance poetry may have attracted a different popular audience in the twenty-first century. But availability may not be the same thing as influence: Shelley's Romantic vision of the vocation of poets as "the unacknowledged legislators of the world" was delusory at the time and is even more so now. Auden embraced the vocation of commentary but was not deluded about its impact. This study assumes that the writings of poets tell us a great deal about the intellectual weather, but it also assumes they do not make the weather and have not done so since a common culture of the literate was shattered beyond repair. Even in the eighteenth century there were diverse publics, metropolitan and provincial.

There is a deeper question lurking behind these reflections, and it concerns the nature of poetry itself. The question suggests there has to be some acknowledged boundary between poetry and prose. It has already come into preliminary focus in the difference between the profound poetic content of the collective art of liturgy and the personal creations of individuals, apart that is from some kinds of folk creation and the ubiquitous contributions of anonymous writers in the Middle Ages. The issue also comes into focus in classifying the work of writers like Siegfried Sassoon and David Jones. Both writers evoke the same events in the First World War and, in spite of differences of experience as between an officer and a private soldier, both are examples of marvelously sustained and concentrated prose poetry. The difference lies in shifts in the depth of reference and in a heightening of

---

9. "Bright Star," in Keats, *Selected Poems*, 219; "Anthem for Doomed Youth," in Owen, *War Poems of Wilfred Owen*, 12.

language which, were they to occur in Sassoon, would be experienced as disruptive shifts of tone.

Perhaps the answer to the question "What is poetry?" as distinct from a question about "the poetic" lies in a certain regularity exercised within a more (or less) disciplined scheme. Rhyme is not necessary, nor is strict metrical discipline. That is evident the moment you include the psalms within your understanding of poetry. So perhaps it comes down to rhythmic shapeliness and artful repetition. Poetry is not primarily concerned to argue in abstract terms but to evoke and invoke, and that is precisely what brings it into close proximity to expressions of faith.

I conclude by referring to the viewpoints of two personal friends, Donald Davie and Michael Schmidt. Davie was someone whose life-course illustrated the thesis of this book about recourse to hard-won faith after the horrors of the twentieth century. For that purpose, I am using the "Introduction" by Clive Wilmer to his edited volume, *With the Grain: Essays on Thomas Hardy and Modern English Poetry* (1998).[10] Wilmer points to a tension in the critical work of Donald Davie between one who held reason, clarity, and formal order over against the dishevelments of 1940s neo-Romanticism, and the vigorous champion of Ezra Pound who contemplated the farthest reaches of modern experiment. It is Hardy who focuses the tension. Davie wrote about Hardy as the last great poet to be unequivocally part of the native English tradition, in a genealogy that came to include Edward Thomas and Philip Larkin. At the same time Davie regarded the change wrought by international modernism as irreversible, whereas, for Larkin, modernism had destroyed the connection between poetry and the reading public forged by Kipling, Housman, Brooke, and Omar Khayyam.

Hardy saw poetry as a modest art with limited expectations, and Davie sympathized with this precisely as a response to the horrors of the Second World War and the disastrously misjudged politics of the modernists, even though it warred somewhat against his sense of the poet's high calling. Then, in 1964, he accepted a chair in what was effectively a department of comparative literature at Essex and became pro-vice-chancellor of the university. This was a formative experience. In this unaccustomed administrative role he took the progressive Labour Party view about the necessary modernization of Britain, even though his northern dissenting background was Tory rather than Socialist.

Whatever Davie's commitment to patriotic responsibility and to stability, he was determined that the art he loved should inhabit the real world, and specifically not the post-modern dalliance with desire and fantasy. In

---

10. Davie, *With the Grain*.

any case it seemed to him paradoxical and absurd that the country of the industrial revolution should so often give itself over to pastoral dreams about a "green and pleasant land." But then he encountered the student rejection of all amelioration and the repudiation of liberal education as so much hypocrisy and "repressive tolerance." At Essex (and in my own case at LSE) a long endurance of abuse by irresponsible, self-righteous, and footloose students left an indelible scar. It stimulated a determination to defend academic freedom against latter-day millenarians for whom all necessary authority was dismissed as authoritarian. That was the point at which I invited him to contribute to the academic fight back through my edited book, *Anarchy and Culture: The Problem of the Contemporary University* (1969).[11]

After many years in the USA, in California and at Vanderbilt, Davie returned home to a house in rural Devon. Here he wrote some his best criticism and some of his best religious poems, culminating in the sequence "Our Father," poems concerned with England, a vexatious age, the sacred, and an uneasy faith.[12] He was therefore somebody who illustrated the thesis of this book about the recourse to religion after experience of the political disasters of the twentieth century, including the experience of an attack from within on the very idea of the university. He held fast to rationality, and to what Eliot referred to as the sacrifice of the self and the escape from personality, not because his emotional life was meager, but precisely because he was a man of intense emotions and consequent vulnerability.

I draw finally on Michael Schmidt's "Introduction" to his edited volume, *The Harvill Book of Twentieth Century Poetry in English* (1999),[13] partly because Schmidt's predilections overlap with my own. Schmidt points out that so many of the religious poets of the past were ignored at the time, and have only been rediscovered in the twentieth century. Schmidt also suggests that we cannot overestimate the importance of T. E. Hulme, killed in action in 1917. He affirmed discontinuity, in the sense that images not usually associated can be significantly juxtaposed. He argued for an accurate, intellectual, and pessimistic poetry (perhaps as part of his "religious attitude" and sense of the ubiquity of corruption) in an age when our view of the world is no longer underwritten by religious certitudes. He also argued against meter, given that meter facilitates, and "poetry is not a facile art." "Metre and the rhetorics that go with it can inflate a poem . . . If a poem is true it

---

11. Martin, *Anarchy and Culture*.

12. "Our Father," in Davie, *Poems and Melodramas*, 18. First published in *PN Review* 107, vol. 22 (1996).

13. Schmidt, *Harvill Book of Twentieth-Century Poetry*, xxvii–xxxviii.

must cut its own path through language."[14] Schmidt concludes that there are at least two kinds of poetry, and two kinds of audience. One seeks a collective response. Its aims are immediately political like those of the Beat Poets. It seeks solidarity and its origins are in the popular biblical tradition. The other also derives from Bible and Prayer Book, but seeks a communal response that is more akin to communion than solidarity.

---

14. Schmidt, *Harvill Book of Twentieth-Century Poetry*, xxx.

Chapter 13

Afterword

Here I return to my critique of secularization, insofar as it is a teleological assertion about a fundamental move *from* a religious *to* a secular condition. This assertion is rooted in a particular understanding of modernity, whereby modernity points forward to deliver an irreversible secular condition. My critique of secularization sought seriously to weaken this teleological assertion, and my analysis of English poetry tried to show that there was no such steady movement towards the secular. Instead it suggested that there were shifts back and forth between the relatively secular and the religious: for example, the move to the secular in the eighteenth century by comparison with the seventeenth century, with a reversal in the nineteenth century. However, the situation in the nineteenth century was ambiguous, to the extent that it could also be seen as a harbinger of the secular. It seemed to me that there was indeed some kind of break in the continuity of Christian establishment that might be dated in the late nineteenth century, or, alternatively, at various points in the twentieth, such as the nineteen-thirties or sixties. However, this break was remarkable for the resilience of the Christian tradition in poetry, particularly in relation to the decline of the ideology of progress and potential utopia as it came to terms with the exemplary horrors of the modern period. There is plenty of good authority, Gadamer for example, for the idea that "the Break," or the breakdown of Christian culture, can be attributed to the cumulative effects of the two World Wars. My argument has been that these effects are also responsible for the Christian response. The Christian resilience in poetry I called "the return of the liturgical," meaning a recognition of the relation between corruption and ruin, and between redemption and restoration. It seemed to me that the great masters of modernity embodied this return.

The return involved two strands, the explicitly Christian, as in Eliot, and the generically spiritual, for example in Yeats.

Perhaps I may bring together some of the kinds of secularization noticed in the course of my argument. First we have the various metamorphoses and mutations that came as Christianity assimilated and was assimilated by paganism, Renaissance humanism, and Enlightenment, for example, such alien materials as alchemy and astrology, as well as the more complex case of Neoplatonism. There are other types of secularization, for example, an important group of forms of secularization that emerged in the late seventeenth century. Amongst these were the partial separation of Christianity from a preponderant role in the exercise and legitimation of power, and its emergence as the exercise of personal virtue. The recognition by Hobbes, following a Machiavellian model, that power is its own legitimation, is a cognate secularization. There are other secularizations in the 1700s and around 1800, first towards a rational religion, and then towards a subjectively appropriated and individualized religion aside from belief and the institution of the church. The nineteenth century was marked by the rise of secular religions in nationalism and political ideology linked to the historicization of experience. Two principal waves of scientific advance have been identified as inimical to religious understandings, in the late seventeenth and early nineteenth centuries, the latter including the impact of scientific history on the approach to the Bible, and the adoption of a philosophical utilitarianism whereby calculation displaces principle, or of the adoption of the para-scientific philosophy of positivism whereby mind, and with it art, poetry, and the humanities generally, are rejected as sources of understanding. Here my position approximates Marilynne Robinson's, especially in her *Absence of Mind* (2010), where she defends the "felt life" of the mind and takes issue both with versions of the hermeneutic of suspicion concerning our inward mental life and with the systematic reductionism of Richard Dawkins.[1] I have myself taken issue with Dawkins on account of his egregious ignorance of the sociological understanding of the social reality of religion.[2]

In the course of my analysis, I also identified a fragmentation of religion to include various spiritualities and non-Christian mysticism, and what might be seen as an increasingly horizontal understanding of transcendence. There were changes in vocabulary, whereby Christian notions like sin were partly displaced by therapeutic concepts, or a notion like faith

---

1. Robinson, *Absence of Mind: The Dispelling of Inwardness*.
2. Martin, *Religion and Power: No Logos without Mythos*.

was attenuated. I pointed out that, in the vocabulary of Donne, faith was a much more dense term than it was in Tennyson.

That raises the ultimate issue, which is whether the break in the cultural establishment of Christianity in the twentieth century was accompanied by a straightforwardly non-Christian culture of gratification. We can ask whether the turn to the self was a mutation of Christianity, or whether it inaugurated an orientation that went beyond Christianity.[3] We can ask whether, in the wake of the fragmentations set in motion by the Reformation, we have arrived by unintended happenstance at a condition of moral chaos.[4] We can query whether moral judgment has been undermined by what Philip Rieff called *The Triumph of the Therapeutic*.[5] I should emphasize that my view is the reverse: we are chronically inclined to accept views off the shelf on the say-so of others, to be suborned by secular myth, to work with binary oppositions falsely identifying *the* source of all our woes, and to be morally judgmental to the point of deploying pathology as a mode of condemnation. Rieff's somber analysis may be just a period-piece emanating from the sixties.

In just the same way, the questions raised by David Riesman et al. in *The Lonely Crowd* (1951), about shifts from tradition to the scrutiny of inward conscience and then to the scrutiny of significant others, may be another mid-century period piece.[6] The speed of cultural change generates a whole genre of analyses of *the* modern condition, especially the North American condition treated as a synecdoche for humanity in general, to the exclusion of alternative routes to modernity. These, then, are just some of the questions lurking behind my examination of the vicissitudes of faith and doubt in the perspectives of English poetry.

One analysis is peculiarly apt for my intellectual purposes: the sociologist Christian Smith's *Moral, Believing Animals: Human Personhood and Culture* (2003).[7] Christian Smith argues that humans are animals that believe, and, through all the manifest ambiguities of experience, discern good from evil. In what matters most there are no scientific criteria to guide: we can do no more than guard our norms by telling and forthtelling our narratives. Every mode of life is embedded in a moral order, whether it is the marketplace or science, and these are manifested in the stories we tell.

---

3. Taylor, *Sources of the Self*.

4. MacIntyre, *Ethics in the Conflicts of Modernity*; Gregory, *The Unintended Reformation*.

5. Rieff, *The Triumph of the Therapeutic*.

6. Riesman et al., *The Lonely Crowd*.

7. Smith, *Moral, Believing Animals*.

Sociology is the critical scrutiny of those moral orders, and in that endeavor it is not so much positive science as it is close kin to literary criticism. This book rests on precisely that assumption.

That is not the only assumption on which it rests. It may seem surprising in someone who initially formulated the critique of secularization as a teleological narrative, that in the course of this book I note one secularization after another, not excluding the consequences of the Reformation as a movement to recover the primal sources of faith. That is because those sources were so rapidly secularized by the structures of power on which they depended for their survival and propagation. The same was true of the initial establishment of Christianity, when it simultaneously suborned the structures of power with an alternative vision and was suborned by those structures to act as a primary mode of political legitimation. Christianity subverts the orders of wealth and violence and is subverted by them. That was where I began, with the discussion of *Beowulf* and "The Dream of the Rood" as an initial instance of a prolonged negotiation between the pagan codes of honor and feud that provide the default position of political life and the Christian imperatives of love, forgiveness, redemption, and reconciliation. The secularization of an unworldly religion is endemic and that engenders a paradox. As the Christian religion is eased out of the structures of power by other sources of legimation, say, in the late seventeenth century, that too counts as secularization. This book recounts both processes.

Something very important follows from the subversion by power and wealth of a faith that in its initial thrust subverts power and wealth. It is one of the assumptions of established Christianity, say, in the time of John Donne, that notwithstanding the depredations of sin, the imperatives of Christianity are capable of being realized here and now. This assumption remains pervasive up to the modern era so that Matthew Arnold, for example, imagined he could extract a viable moral core from historic Christianity. Christianity was so familiar to him that he could read its scriptures without any notion of their strangeness, of their eschatological promise, and the radical subversion they embodied. It did not occur to him that the problem he encountered on reading them was not that they contravened scientific norms but that they challenged and contravened precisely the social norms he took for granted. These norms were rooted in Protestant secularization and Protestant religious aspiration, and supposed that Christian imperatives were straightforwardly realizable in the everyday world, for example in the patriarchal family. The impact of biblical criticism was only in part the revelation of the sources of the normative scriptures. After Schweitzer's classic 1906 study of eschatological anticipation in the Gospels, biblical criticism made plain to the naked eye the radical anticipatory promise of the scriptures.[8] It also became clear that liberal theological attempts to reduce the Gospels to contemporary moral aspirations and programs of amelioration did not face what Reinhold Niebuhr called the "impossible possibility" of their demands.[9] They presented another world, where violence and wealth were not the supreme arbiters, which is why Christian vocabulary split into two realms. Christian vocabulary exemplified a double entendre between real temples and real cities and a heavenly temple and a heavenly city "not made with hands," between real exiles and our personal inward exiles, between actual wildernesses and our encounter with the wilderness within and its exemplary temptations to illegitimate power.

Precisely the recognition of the impossible possibility underlay "unworldly" monasticism, its disciplines and its rhythms, except of course that "the meek" in the monasteries literally inherited the earth and needed constantly to be subject to the principle of *semper reformanda*. The same recognition underlay the enactments of liturgy, because liturgy is the collective poetry of the Christian promise of a different order and of what the New Testament calls *metanoia*. It is the "kingdom" that burgeons as a secret seed made momentarily visible in continued enactments of praise and a sacrificial gift of grace beyond price. It really is the "transvaluation of values" around a shared table. I am acutely aware of course that there is from the outset, even prior to the New Testament, an oscillation between adamant peaceability and taking the kingdom by storm that replicates itself throughout Christian history, even though resolved by entering Jerusalem on a donkey and proclaiming a kingdom "not of this world" before Pilate, prior to ascending the hill of Golgotha.

Here I come to a particularly profound secularization that I signaled by a reference to the musicologist Daniel Chua, when it was thought that the Christian *telos* and *kairos*, the vision of a better world, were capable of realization in the world by revolutionary force and all the bloodshed that entailed. Here my concluding observations recoup my initial critique at the beginning of this book. Of course, the new world of 1789 encountered perpetual postponement and, in Chua's view, the disappointment was only partly assuaged by the longings embodied in the aesthetic. When secularized eschatology had worked itself out in violent political messianisms of various kinds, the limits and appalling dangers of trying to institute the perfect became clear as never before.[10] Browning, in "Abt Vogler" and in

---

8. I do not accept later attempts to reverse the analysis of Schweitzer, in particular what seem to me the absurd attempts of the Jesus Seminar to present Jesus as a sage influenced by Greek skepticism.

9. Niebuhr, *Interpretation of Christian Ethics*, especially chapter 2.

10. Talmon, *Political Messianism: The Romantic Phase*.

"Christmas Eve," more than once expressed how hard it is to be consistently Christian, even at the personal level. He recognized the paradox of Christianity because it was too hard for the merely earthbound but also set up a demanding aspiration that looked heavenward. Law stands over against us as well as acting as the bulwark of all effective social action. Without it morality is meaningless and with it we are "under condemnation." That is precisely why law encounters grace "pressed down and running over." The waters of life are imbibed "without money and without price" because divine generosity freely offered has absorbed the price in the body of Christ.

The transfer of a religious template forged in the Hebrew Scriptures, and in the hopes of an oppressed people for release from exile, either to Romantic nationalism or to Marxist ideology, is plentifully illustrated in the writings of the poets studied here, especially in the nineteen-thirties. Hugh McDiarmid illustrated Romantic nationalism and revolutionary Marxism simultaneously. I am not saying that the values of those who sought after changes for the better were mistaken in their objectives but, as Thomas Hardy presciently commented in "In Tenebris II," they certainly "exact a full look at the Worst." I am criticizing the belief that decent hopes of amelioration are underwritten by history through the operations of a secularized Providence. We should not be so surprised, and even enraged, that history proves so recalcitrant and resistant to our expectations. Eliot was right in "Gerontion" when he pointed to history's "many cunning passages."

Wordsworth provides an exemplary instance of a response for which real and lasting transformation was a simple possibility here and now in the world where alone true happiness is to be achieved or not at all: "Bliss was it in that dawn to be alive."[11] When he realized what had been unleashed, he attributed failure to unfortunate and malignant circumstances, not the operations of a more profound and insidious corruption. That is why the central elements in the Christian narrative of ruin and redemption made no sense to him, even though he constantly invoked what he thought of as religious imperatives, for example in his "Ode to Duty," "Stern daughter of the voice of God."

Secularized Providence expresses itself in many ways and there are very important way-stations before the outbreak of exemplary revolutionary violence in the late eighteenth century and its first messianic and world-conquering realization in the early nineteenth. One key manifestation can be located in James Thomson, and it complements the massive changes chronicled by Paul Hazard in his classic study, *The Crisis of the European*

---

11. "French Revolution as it Appeared to Enthusiasts at its Commencement," in Wordsworth, *Selected Poems*, 131–32.

Mind: 1680–1715.[12] Thomson moved from Christianity to a religion drawing on the Newtonian revolution, and this religion was the last viable example of the idea that a secure ontological root could be located in the operations of the cosmos.

So we already have several secularizing revolutions: the Reformation, the advent of the Newtonian cosmos, and the rise of a secular Providence rooted in history. But in the course of my argument, I placed considerable emphasis on what David Jones called "the Break," when both Eliot and Auden recognized the extent of the change and its implications, and questions were raised as to whether Christianity was giving way to a culture of the self, and/or the transcendent diminished to little more than a horizontal reference. Some of the poets of the later twentieth century illustrate the primacy of the self, whereas others, like (say) D. H. Lawrence in an earlier generation, illustrate a mutation of the word "God" to refer to an immanent principle.

Here I want to say something about the gap that causes with regard to understanding the religious past in its own terms rather than as subserving some other approved end, such as the advent of progress or the arrival of the new. Alison Shell has raised these questions in an acute form in her discussion of the problems attending our understanding of early modern Catholicism in England.[13] She notes the extent to which prejudice marginalizes Catholic poets from the canon and excludes them from the roll call of victims as followers of an outdated, potentially oppressive faith and therefore getting what they deserved. Although she does not say so, the central Christian category of the innocent victim is now reused to validate any cause of which an author approves. Indeed, there is competition for the status of most abused and victimized group in order for its members to pass judgments from a privileged moral high ground: righteousness is imputed in proportion to degree of suffering, claimed or real.

An example of recontextualization that most easily comes to mind is the rediscovery of Blake, who was in his idiosyncratic way a Bible-believing Christian, as a prophet of nineteen-sixties antinomianism. People are both forgotten and rediscovered because they do or do not fit. Christina Rossetti has been rediscovered and recontextualized by feminism at the expense of what was most important to her. The feminist theme is, of course, necessary and important, but not so as to occlude the central role of Rossetti's faith. Karen Dieleman, in her study of the influence of the experience of liturgy on three female poets, Rossetti among them, had to work hard to establish

12. Hazard, *Crisis of the European Mind*.
13. Shell, *Catholicism, Controversy, and the English Literary Imagination*, 1–20.

the primacy of that experience when its role ought to be as obvious to us now as it was to them then.[14] In the case of John Henry Newman, I was peculiarly conscious of what recontextualization tells us about the "enormous condescension" of the present towards the past and the urge to assimilate it to contemporary understandings. Taken seriously, Newman's poem "The Dream of Gerontius" is an emphatic expression of dogmatic Catholic faith, but to contemporary commentary on (say) its most eloquent realization by the Catholic composer, Edward Elgar, it is about the fear of death in general. How we read the past and tailor it to our own preoccupations tells us about our present. There could be no surer index of what the historian E. P. Thompson excoriated as the "enormous condescension of posterity."[15] Not just religion, but other cultural forms are pared down to the requirements of what Charles Taylor called "the immanent frame." One of the major aims of this book has been not only to challenge the delusions of secular Providence, but to recover the past on its own terms. I assume, with von Ranke in his critique of all-encompassing philosophies of history, that "every age is immediate to God."

14. Dieleman, *Religious Imaginaries*.
15. Thompson, *Making of the English Working Class*, 12.

Appendix

Hymnody

Hymnody provides a major indicator of the state of English (and Welsh) religion over three centuries, and it is one which needs to be set against the massive backdrop of the choral tradition, especially in the nineteenth century. Hymnody and the choral tradition taken together tell us so much that we need to know about English and Welsh religion, in the same way that Lutheran hymnody and the German choral tradition tell us so much of what we need to know about German religion at the same period. That would be almost as true of the United States. American culture, at least among white Protestants, shared an appropriation of the Authorized Version of the Bible, actively shaped by the choral tradition of *Messiah* and to a lesser extent by *Elijah*. In what follows I shall suggest that the anti-deist theology of *Messiah*, as formulated by Charles Jennens, was as influential as the language in which it was expressed. But that is to leap forward comparatively, when the primary task is to establish the specific role played by hymnody in England over the period from 1700 to the present.

Let me suggest different ways in which this very complicated issue might be approached. The first way invokes two very similar Victorian religious cultures, one in Huddersfield, a Yorkshire mill town, and another in Maesteg, Glamorgan, on the southern edge of the south Wales mining area. At the height of rapid and early industrialization, these closely knit religious cultures, which we might loosely call Evangelical and Methodist, sang a shared repertoire of hymns and a repertoire of the three choral masterpieces central to the (broadly) British musical tradition: *Messiah*, *The Creation*, and *Elijah*. That is some indication both of the weakness of the indigenous tradition after Purcell and its remarkable receptivity to European influences. Now, it might easily be supposed that, sociologically, nothing much turns on collective singing and a shared repertoire. In fact this ignores one of the most eloquent indicators of cultural presence available to us, one which tells you how people announce that presence and how they literally raise their voices to declare they are there and who they are. You need think only of the role of soul music, gospel, and jazz for African Americans to realize the dimensions elided by this self-imposed limitation.

Let me expand this a little. In modern phraseology this particular religious culture in Yorkshire or Wales was hard-working, aspiring, and, in its everyday practice, disciplined and controlled: by contrast the hymn and oratorio singing, along with the revival meeting and powerful sermonizing, was its direct experience of the divine. This is how they encountered God. Members of this culture also knew that they were looked down upon by the social elite and disliked for their vigorous assertion of their presence, and they countered this with their superior righteousness. They might be slighted by their social superiors, Matthew Arnold for example, but at least they were right with God. So we are not just talking about a widely pervasive national culture of hymnody and oratorio but a widely pervasive and self-conscious class culture. People in this culture also became aware that, by the twentieth century, the great works providing their access to the divine were denigrated, just as they themselves were denigrated The metropolis saw them and their music as provincial. Their enthusiastic amateur approach to performance based on mass participation was overtaken by much smaller metropolitan professional groups espousing a quite different aesthetic deriving from a revolution in performance. This aesthetic transformed the performance of *Messiah* in particular, and left the older style stranded in a cultural cul-de-sac.

This is not at all a mainly musicological issue: it provides vital clues about the cultural decline of Methodism in what had been its northern English and its Welsh strongholds. The musical clues take us to the heart of one of the most salient religious declines of the twentieth century. The assignment of a powerful musical tradition to a cultural backwater provides a synecdoche of what happened to Methodism. Methodism became divided by the different traditions that had flowed into the uniting church of 1933 and left their mark on its 1933 hymnal to be discussed immediately below: these were a Wesleyan tradition pointing towards liturgy and Anglicanism, and a very different revivalist tradition that might eventually find a home in the charismatic movement, except that denominations like the Baptists might seem more easily adapted and welcoming to the charismatic style and its new hymnody. The older style of Noncomformity, quintessentially represented by a large Methodist church, morphed into a quite different Noncomformity of free churches run by pastors with a rather different hymn repertoire. At the same time, this new repertoire, such as Graham Kendrick's "Shine, Jesus, shine" or Collin Raye's "Here I am, Lord," remains outnumbered in lists of contemporary favorite hymns by older favorites. It is surprising that a hymn like "The old rugged cross," associated with the American evangelist Billy Sunday at a time in the early twentieth century when his type of revivalism had maximum influence, should be such a contemporary favorite, alongside the classics of Wesley and Watts.

One of the problems in this area is the specific agendas cherished by worship leaders. Another is the individualistic character of new hymns, so that favorites, for example from the charismatic Australian church "Hillsong," very often center round the first person singular. It is also worth remembering that as Methodism spread through its hymns and its music so Pentecostalism, as an immensely expansive Evangelical tradition derived in major ways from Methodism, has been spread through its music. That happens to include the choral tradition, so that in Campinas, Brazil, I attended a "Two Choirs" choral festival and it ended with the "Thanks be to God" and the "Hallelujah" chorus from *Messiah*. Even in such a remote cultural context—the nexus of Evangelicalism—a distinctive popular music, a choral tradition including Handel, manifested itself. This association of Evangelicalism with a quite limited religious sector of Handel's vast output quite plausibly damaged Handel's reputation.

The Methodist Hymnbook of 1933 represents a classic and wide-ranging compilation, able to tell us most of what we need to know about the varied sources of the hymn-singing tradition. It was the last of its kind and merits close examination by way of the principles on which it was based, as set out by David Rumsey in "The Three Doctrines of the 1933 Methodist Hymnbook."[1] The writers in this hymn book and its compilers faithfully reflected the social preoccupations, doctrines, and theology of the Methodist Church going back to the eighteenth century (as well as an Anglican heritage in its inclusion of canticles and chants for psalms). Eighteenth-century Methodism looked back to a Lutheran tradition that achieved its culmination in the sacred music of the eighteenth century, above all in the cantatas of Johann Sebastian Bach and their often Pietist texts. Luther passionately espoused music as the gift of God and a source of peace and joy, and he believed that a minister who could not sing was not properly up to his calling. However, the Lutheran tradition behind Methodism differed from it in preferring unison singing with organ accompaniment. Methodism, by contrast, preferred part-singing without organ accompaniment. Where

---

1. "The Three Doctrines of the 1933 Methodist Hymnbook," in Sharpe and Sharma, *The Sum of Our Choices*, 309–56.

Lutheranism and Methodism were at one was in giving *equal* importance to the Bible and to the chorale—or, in the Methodist case, to the hymn book. The hymn book was the sung word of God as distinct from the said word of God, and that word was above all else the Pauline theology of faith and grace alone. Hitherto, the main sources for musicians had been the Gospels, or Old Testament/Hebrew Bible subjects (as in most of Handel's oratorios) or the book of Revelation. Now it was Paul, either in the sacred music of Bach (much inflected as it was by constant anxiety about whether you were really right with God and by flight from the fleeting and evil world), or it was in the Anglo-Saxon Evangelical tradition where George Frederic Handel was a major influence. In both traditions the dominant theory was the Baroque understanding of "the affections" as conveyed in potent musical figures. John Wesley and Handel were contemporaries, and Handel was a musical messiah for Methodism. Of course, Handel represented many modes other than this, but for Methodism he provided a musical sense of the church militant and triumphant, such as you find in the hymn specially written for Methodists to words by Charles Wesley, "Rejoice the Lord is king," with tune titled "Gopsal," the country seat of Jennens. For that matter you find the same positive musical sense in "Thine be the glory" with Handel's tune "Maccabeus," though here there is a French Protestant rather than a Methodist connection. Given this positive Handelian tonality it is entirely appropriate that the first hymn in the MHB is "O for a thousand tongues to sing," for which one of the tunes, "Lyngham," offered typical opportunity for lively part singing.

At the same time the MHB provided a conspectus of different kinds of hymnody as well as a numerous selection of Anglican chants. These were Scottish and Genevan metrical psalmody, Lutheran chorales, like "Now all the woods are sleeping" (Gerhardt), including magnificent translations from the German by John Wesley such as "Now have I found the ground wherein," and choruses from American sources that illustrated the Methodist principle (later adopted by the Salvation Army as a another Methodist derivative) of converting secular tunes to sacred use. Methodists adopted innovative principles well beyond the standard common meter, long meter, etc., and did so with lively rhythms and faster tempi in major keys. As Rumsey puts it, Anglicans sang quietly, and Catholics (at that time) not at all, whereas Methodists sang robustly. And, as indicated above, the foundation was the Pauline doctrine of salvation by faith and trust, not the Anglican tendency to revert to promoting good conduct. Like the Lutheran state church, the Anglican state church did not dare to trust in faith and grace alone, and in the Anglican case too easily reverted to "people, be good!"

Even if the hymn was Pauline, the Anglican sermon skirted Paul uneasily, sniffing antinomian chaos.

Something further needs to be said about the themes embraced in the 1933 hymn book because they hint at future directions that had a potential to weaken the specific character of Methodism on which maybe it depended for survival: not the kind of thing one can securely know. One theme expressed a Methodist sense of being solid citizens that was not at all at odds with the character of the dominant traditions in Methodism. For example, the hymn book included Robert Bridges's hymn "Rejoice, O land in God thy might," Cecil Spring-Rice's "I vow to thee, my country," as well as Kipling's "Land of our birth, we pledge to thee" and his famous "Recessional" beginning "God of our fathers." Apart maybe from the "Recessional," the general tenor of these might make contemporary congregations uneasy, but at that time the sentiments probably remained acceptable. At the same time other themes were being accommodated that were no part of the Methodist ethos, for example John Addington Symonds's

> These things shall be: a loftier race
> Than e'er the world has known shall rise . . .

These were sentiments clean contrary to the Methodist, and indeed the general Christian, understanding of sin and redemption. Yet they were accommodated, and you can trace the seepage of this kind of sentiment into Methodism, placed under the head of the spread of the light of Christ and his rule in "this dark world of sin." Elements in Methodism could be adapted to it without too much critical scrutiny. As for the eloquent hymns and poems by the American Quaker John Greenleaf Whittier, there was no disjunction, even though Whittier represented a seriously different Christian tradition. These hymns tapped into a contemporary sense of the "Brotherhood of Man and the Fatherhood of God." For this, Methodists and most Christians felt natural sympathy, as represented, for example, by "O brother man, fold to thy heart thy brother," and "Dear Lord and father of mankind, forgive our foolish ways." Today these hymns are normally sung to magnificent tunes by Parry.

But what of the future for Methodism and the place of that very large body of hymns by Charles Wesley that anchored Methodist emphases even more than the forty-four normative sermons of John Wesley? My supposition is that those emphases did not remain secure. Nevertheless, Methodism did become increasingly open to the broad reforms and changes in hymnody associated with Ralph Vaughan Williams. What had totally disappeared were some of the governing categories of John Wesley's original book of 1780, such as the progress of the soul to salvation, which Wesley described in a remarkable "Preface" as a body of "experimental and practical divinity" conformable to the shape of Christian *experience*. This preface was an intimation of Romanticism from an unexpected quarter. It was also a statement of the Evangelical understanding of the relation of faith to poetry expressed with remarkable felicity in enlightened prose. Indeed, the same enlightened prose was deployed in Wesley's Oxford sermons, such as one on the Catholic spirit, whereby we might love each other alike even if we did not think and believe alike.

Openness to change and to contemporary reform becomes very clear from the "Preface" to *The School Hymn Book of the Methodist Church* of 1950. The preface welcomes those changes associated with schools and the BBC that, working in tandem, excluded the sentimental. Gone were such morbid offerings as the sometime popular hymn by Albert Midlane (tune by Stainer)

> There's a home for little children
> Above the bright blue sky;

and the once ubiquitous "Hear the pennies dropping . . . every one for Jesus." Yet some old favorites of junior Sunday School were retained, such as "Jesus bids us shine" and "Jesus wants me for a sunbeam." These overlapped a genre associated with the "Children's Special Service Mission" (an organization often preaching on summer beaches) like "A little talk with Jesus makes it right, all right," "I am H.A.P.P.Y" and "Wide, wide as the ocean." Generations of Christian children, the author included, were socialized by these jingles, drew pictures with crayons, and played with sand, often overseen by devoted and often Evangelical unmarried women as well as sometimes by Evangelical male superintendents, and that happened in churches otherwise not markedly Evangelical.

As for the hymn book itself, the editors worked with categories like "God in Nature," "Service," "Adventure," "Work and Workers," "Spring," and "The Human Family." Given that this was a production especially for children, it would be worth looking at the special services provided, particularly its revised creed ("Responsive Services," No. 25). The provision of choral readings of psalms and collects could be seen as reinforcing the Anglican tendencies in Methodism. More than that, whereas the 1933 book barely approached carols at Christmas, the Methodist school book of 1950 included a whole section of them, for example "Ding Dong! merrily on high," indicating that the parallel reform associated with the *Oxford Book of Carols* had succeeded. Here it might be worth looking at American Baptist Christmas hymns, where that reform has plainly not taken place. The old order did not change everywhere.

It is appropriate now to broaden the discussion by reintroducing distinctions I made in 1967[2] to delineate the very different musical cultures in English religion: carol, hymn, and chorus—the first emanating from upper status groups and associated with elite choirs, especially in Anglican cathedrals and college chapels; the second emanating from the aspiring middling classes and Noncomformist chapels; the third emanating from popular revivalist religion and under considerable American influence. Of course, all three groups of people sang hymns, but with different preferences. To make an informed stab at these different preferences, the Anglican tradition might lean more to "Praise my soul the king of heaven" (good for weddings and state occasions), the aspiring tradition of Charles Wesley might lean more to "O for a thousand tongues to sing" (marvelous for mass gatherings, especially with brass added), and the populist, American-influenced tradition might lean more to "Rescue the perishing, care for the dying" and "To God be the glory." These were hymns by the American Baptist writer Fanny Crosby, who was a major influence on the popular revivalists Moody and Sankey. Fanny Crosby revived a tradition of Christian intimacy found in many female writers of the period, for example, Charlotte Elliot, in "Just as I am, without one plea / But that thy blood was shed for me." Prolific and very popular hymn writers like Fanny Crosby and hymns by Moody and Sankey created a widespread musical culture rooted in revivalist choruses, like "Blessed assurance, Jesus is mine" and "Draw me nearer, nearer, blessed Lord, / To the cross where thou hast died," that practically comprised an American cultural colony in England. This was a kind of folk music with significant roots in the American Sunday School, and its theme was very much blessed assurance. People were assured that, apart from "the ninety and nine that in safety lay in the shelter of the fold," as the famous hymn had it, with tune by Sankey, the Lord would seek after the one lost lamb, though at a terrible cost in blood. Often, the older Wesleyan tradition was displaced, as that had once displaced psalm-singing. In many Methodist churches, the main hymnal on the harmonium was Ira D. Sankey's *Sacred Songs and Solos*.

It goes without saying that these preferences very much overlapped. Anglicans sang Charles Wesley's "Love divine, all loves excelling," and Wesley was after all an Anglican. Moreover, these three categories need to be supplemented by traditions of psalm-singing looking back to the foundation of all sung poetry of praise in the Jewish hymn book of the psalms, though usually reframed in Christocentric terms. Of psalm-singing there have been two versions, one performed in plainsong and reaching back to the earliest forms of Christian music, and the other performed metrically,

2. Martin, *Sociology of English Religion*, 85–90.

dating from the Calvinist Reformation and arguably antithetical to the first. The Reformed tradition was so exclusively devoted to biblical models in its practice of psalm-singing that a Christocenric reading was rendered impossible, and it took a major innovation in eighteenth-century hymn-writing to enable congregations in that tradition to praise Christ through psalm-based hymnody. It is worth remembering here that Americans were initially resistant to the free devotional hymn-writing introduced by Methodism and to the kinds of personal feeling expressed in Wesley's "Where shall my wond'ring soul begin?" It was only with the influence of the Great Awakening, round about the mid-eighteenth century, that hymns took over from metrical psalmody.

That is my first approach, and it represents varieties *within* the Christian tradition. My second approach concerns the changes in the salience of hymn-singing as something very close to a Christian popular culture, and its highly significant eclipse in the second half of the twentieth century, interestingly enough at a time when hymns have become accepted as serious poetry.[3] As Methodism fragmented, so did hymnody, and the eclipse of the hymn as a form of Christian popular culture speaks loudly of the end of Christian cultural dominance in the second half of the twentieth century. But there are several metamorphoses to be traced before we arrive at the eclipse of the hymn, some of which actually aimed to revivify hymn singing and succeeded. If, for example, as a teacher you had sat in on morning assembly, now in the classroom not "the hall," you would, whether an active Christian or otherwise, have been delighted to have the tone of the day set by a BBC broadcast, embodying the reformed hymnody of the time as embraced by English education. There was no hint whatever of a crisis to come after the 1960s.

To understand this, it is best to begin with very important changes in the organization of schools and the teaching profession. Up to the 1960s, there was an extensive network of denominational colleges. Those who attended these, particularly in the primary sector, were principal agents for the dissemination of a diffuse Christianity based on knowing the key biblical stories and joining together at morning assembly in singing hymns. As a pupil in a church school in the thirties, I recollect singing "Now the day is over" at the end of every day in infant school and also singing such hymns as Mrs. Cecil Alexander's "There is a green hill far away," and her "All things bright and beautiful" in primary school at daily morning assembly. For

---

3. This shift was inaugurated by Donald Davie and given further scholarly expression in J. R. Watson's *The English Hymn: A Critical and Historical Study* (Oxford: Clarendon, 1999). Watson's comprehensive study is an extraordinary fusion of the literary, the historical, and the theological.

many English people today the latter hymn is their one remaining recollection of hymnody, so it is frequently chosen for funerals, however irrelevant to the occasion.

One major key to the widespread acceptance of a diffuse Christianity was, in my view, a female primary schoolteacher, not necessarily an active church-goer or especially favorable to clergy. But then, from that decade on, the network of denominational colleges was subsumed in major reorganization by the state which was part of the professionalization of school-teaching. Church influence was replaced by the often Marxist-influenced Institutes of Education, propagating theories about the class sources of curricula. At the same time the morning assembly was progressively de-Christianized to become little more than a moral pep-talk or simply organizational announcements such as were held to be suitable for a multi-cultural school intake; and in some schools the very idea of corporate assembly was made difficult by the architecture of new schools. There is another story to be told here of the farcical deterioration of religious education into decontextualized gobbets of information about world religions until diffuse Christianity in the state schools was replaced by widespread ignorance of everything and anything to do with Christianity. This change, which I vigorously criticized, was propelled by a sophisticated theology, often modernist in its understanding of symbols (for example, the experience of Resurrection), that was just too sophisticated for teachers, let alone pupils: hence the collapse. That led in turn to a disjunction between what was taught in the state schools and the many independent schools with varied Christian foundations, such as the "Woodard Corporation" set up in 1848 for the middle classes.

We now come to changes in hymnody that, in their intention, sought to widen and extend its appeal, moving on from the "sentimental" Victorian hymn, exemplified in the compositions of (say) Dykes, Monk, and Barnby that had exercised such astonishing and increasing influence for tens of millions during the course of the nineteenth century. Of course, these hymns survive in general use in spite of criticism by writers like Eric Routley—criticism which is now itself subject to criticism—and they are some of the best known hymns still in the repertoire, like "Holy, holy, holy" (tune: "Nicaea"), "Eternal Father, strong to save, whose arm doth bind the restless wave" (tune: "Melita"), which was especially popular among sailors "in peril on the sea," "The God of love my shepherd is" (tune: "Dominus regit me"), and "Praise to the holiest in the height" (tune: "Gerontius"). Monk is best remembered as the editor of the vastly popular *Hymns Ancient and Modern* (1861, with subsequent revisions) and for "Abide with me" (tune: "Eventide"). These Victorian composers were also disposed to champion the high church party, conformity to the liturgy, and the Book of Common Prayer within Anglicanism; Monk even introduced plainchant.

Before proceeding to twentieth-century developments we need to summarize the emergence of a distinctively Anglican musical tradition from the early nineteenth century on. At the beginning of the nineteenth century, the English parish church still fed on the metrical psalm and aspired to install an organ. At the same time, the spontaneity of Methodist worship was opposed to the central role of the choir. This was one major tradition in which the emphasis was on congregational participation and emotional immediacy. In its fuguing version, it required considerable musical versatility. However, this was rejected by High Churchmen. High Churchmen sought to improve music as an aesthetic experience with paid choirs singing from the chancel emulating the cathedral tradition, even though this was in a state of advanced decay and did not recover until the later decades of the nineteenth century. Tractarians sought to restore order to the liturgy, especially the centrality of the Eucharist and the adoption of plainsong melodies in which the congregation participated, along with the rediscovery of the music of the sixteenth and seventeenth centuries. This music, together with a repertoire of composers all the way from the Victorians and Stanford to Vaughan Williams and Britten, along with Haydn, Mozart, and Schubert, continues to provide standard fare, in concert with an organ repertoire based on Bach supplemented by the French organ school.

However, neo-medievalism failed to catch on with most Anglicans, and a middle ground emerged, following the cathedral model, with professional surpliced choir and qualified organist. With Stainer's appointment in 1872, St. Paul's cathedral now provided the model rather than Leeds parish church, and the publication of *Hymns Ancient and Modern* confirmed the centrality of the hymn, with the accent on the "ancient." Here, as already indicated, Dykes was a major influence and contributor. In tandem with the introduction of plainsong, German chorales, and old English tunes, there was a new recognition of the carol, particularly as a vehicle for presenting the doctrine of the incarnation. This recognition, which included composed as well traditional carols, was greatly enhanced by the Festival of Nine Lessons and Carols at Truro in 1880, and at King's College, Cambridge, in 1918. From all these varied influences there emerged the unique middle way of Anglican choral worship, distinguished by order, beauty, mystery, and contemplation.

The first of the books seeking to widen the scope of hymnody and reform it was *The Yattendon Hymnal*, published in 1899. It was intended for choirs by its editor Robert Bridges, who wrote an important "Practical Discourse." The hymnal provides the link between Victorian and modern hymnody and is notable for recommending an impersonal rather than an emotional or "pathetic" approach. Actually the format made the book rather inaccessible, and it would probably have fallen into obscurity apart from the work of Vaughan Williams and others associated with *The English Hymnal* (1906) and *Songs of Praise* (1925). It also favored a modal model that influenced the *Oxford Book of Carols* (1928). Bridges noted several main categories: plainsong unbarred in free rhythm; English, French, and German Reformation hymns; Restoration hymns—for example by William Croft, the composer of "St. Anne" as the tune for "O God our help" and "Hanover" as the tune for "O worship the King"—and modern hymns. Of Bridges's translations, several remain in contemporary use, for example "O sacred head," "O gladsome light," and "All my hope on God is founded."

The English Hymnal was edited by Percy Dearmer and Vaughan Williams, and Vaughan Williams was responsible for its musical quality, himself contributing some new tunes, such as "Sine Nomine" for the hymn "For all the saints," and "Down Ampney" for the translation of the fourteenth-century Pentecost hymn "Come down, O love divine." The book was designed for congregational use rather than for choirs, and was associated with the Anglo-Catholic wing of Anglicanism. Its preface by Vaughan Williams explained that much that had become popular in Victorian times was unworthy, and had to be dropped. The approved model was the simplicity of "All people that on earth do dwell" (tune: "Old Hundredth") and, another psalm paraphrase, "O God our help in ages past" (tune: "St. Anne").

The next significant publication in the reform of hymnody was *Songs of Praise* (1925), also edited by Percy Dearmer and Vaughan Williams, sharing the work with Martin Shaw. Percy Dearmer was a socialist who fostered traditional and medieval English music alongside his advocacy of good Anglo-Catholic liturgical practice, and Martin Shaw was composer of a popular folk mass. Since *The English Hymnal* had been regarded as too Anglo-Catholic, *Songs of Praise* sought a broader appeal, including an appeal to children, which commended it to schools and the schools programs of the BBC. Given this appeal to key educational and broadcasting institutions, an enlarged edition was published in 1931. Something of its character can be grasped by its inclusion of a hymn composed in that year by the children's author Eleanor Farjeon. Her "Morning has broken, like the first morning" became an immediate favorite, together with its Gaelic tune, "Bunessan." Another hymn-song in *Songs of Praise* in the same genre was "Glad that I live am I," with tune by Geoffrey Shaw. The tune "Bunessan" alerts us to the growing importance of "Celtic" melodies and sources, for example "Be thou my vision" (tune: "Slane") and also the hymn known as "St. Patrick's

Breastplate," beginning "I bind unto myself this day / The strong name of the Trinity," (with two Irish tunes, "St.Patrick" and "Deirdrie").

Something needs to be said about the influence of the *Oxford Book of Carols*, noted earlier, on the *School Hymn Book of the Methodist Church*. The editors were Percy Dearmer, Martin Shaw, and Vaughan Williams. Vaughan Williams was influenced by traditional folk song, and the *Oxford Book of Carols* favored folk melodies and arrangements of carols. The three editors did not reject "synthetic" or composed carols, but favored traditional ones, even though their work appeared too early to do full justice to medieval carols. That waited until the reset of the book in 1964. Moves to arrange carols for choirs tended to make them music for listening, though the outdoor element of carol singing remained very popular.

Carols are Christian folk music in a way that would conform to the understanding of the term by (say) the folklorist Cecil Sharp, and that is very different from what one means by describing hymns as folk music. In some ways, carols have not shared in the popular eclipse of the hymn. Apart from their outdoor performance in the Christmas season, that is because they are embedded in extremely popular carol services, including very numerous occasions in Advent for schools. There are also large numbers of people who come to church round about Christmas time. These people have conservative tastes and expectations, both as regards standard readings in traditional language, and with regard to the mix of Christmas carols and Christmas hymns. These include some of the most attractive works of devotion, whether hymns, composed carols, or traditional carols. For example, Christina Rossetti's poem "In the bleak midwinter" has been beautifully set by Gustav Holst, and also has a luminous setting by Harold Darke that is for many the climactic musical moment of Christmas and summation of its meaning. Those who attend these services will expect a much loved group of hymns as well as carols, always beginning with Mrs. Alexander's "Once in royal David's city," including such hymns as "See amid the winter's snow," "O little town of Bethlehem," "While shepherds watched," and "Silent night." The sequence always concludes with two hymns summarizing the doctrine of the incarnation: Charles Wesley's "Hark the herald angels sing" (with tune adapted from Mendelssohn) and "O come, all ye faithful," which is in part a sung version of the creed. There are kinds of popular music outside the church context, such as "Good king Wenceslas," as well as the very vaguely Christian or non-Christian selections of seasonal music played in shopping malls.

I have already indicated some changes in understanding and thematic repertoire, as they have manifested themselves in hymns, and, so doing, have provided evidence of the changing condition of Christianity in England.

They are prime evidence for the "condition of Christianity" question considered from inside. I now approach these significant changes directly and with some serious sense of their complexity. Various themes are clearly of major importance, but just as clearly problematic. I mean, for example, that there have been important changes and controversies in Christology, and therefore of the doctrine of the Trinity as defining orthodoxy, but the intellectual background of these may be expressed quite indirectly in hymnody, if at all. Or again, it is clear that the doctrine of hell has disappeared from hymnody, though some would date that to the nineteenth century and others to the twentieth. Any idea that illness was related to moral fault also disappeared, and now appears completely intolerable. It seems to me that, for England at any rate, hell definitely disappeared in the course of the nineteenth century: the controversy over the views of F. D. Maurice in the mid-century signaled the coming change. Considered as a brute fact, the disappearance of hell may seem unproblematic, but arguably it trails broad ranging consequences that demand exploration. By contrast, the doctrine of Christ's coming again in glory continues to be expressed in hymnody and liturgy—for example, the acclamation "Christ will come again"—but it has disappeared from everyday mainstream consciousness and is not expounded in sermons. One area where I discern no change at all concerns the belief in divine providence, which presumably reflects a consensus in its favor. It was, for example, passionately embraced by F. D. Maurice, whatever his other hesitations. Indeed, it was embraced even by deists such as the founders of the American Republic.

If we begin with Christology (and the Trinity) then the changes that Unitarians regarded as inevitable in editing and revising their collections of hymns (collections whose sheer number reflected their individualism) are highly instructive. They show very clearly both how hymnody is the embodiment of the group sense of the sacred, and how it reveals the theology and ecclesiology of a church at a given time. Of course, Unitarians are very much a special case: for them revision is imperative. Two points stand out. The first point is that Unitarian theology demanded that the principles undergirding those changes be made explicit. Controversy settled around linguistic expressions in hymns based on supplication to and through Christ, or which implied doctrines of sin and salvation unacceptable and incredible to Unitarians. An emphasis on ethics might in itself be compatible with some kinds of orthodox Christianity. But emphases on the cosmic good yet to be, implying liberal notions of progress such as were noticed above in relation to James Addington Symonds, and the tendency to abstraction derived from the influence of Romantic pantheism (God in Nature and the self), were much more problematic from the viewpoint of orthodoxy. The tendency to abstraction was further reinforced by the feminist demand for inclusive language. Expressions involving king, father, and lord were to be excised in favor (say) of generic creative love—a process which, if carried out consistently, would have left Bible and hymnody in tatters.

The second point is in tension with the first. It is that, in practice, hymns by Unitarians are not all that easily identified as such. Christians in orthodox churches sing them without a qualm. Conspicuous examples can be cited from among the many hymns of the political radical Sir John Bowring, who was economist, linguist, and governor of Hong Kong. His hymn "God is love, his mercy lightens" causes no problem. As for his "In the cross of Christ I glory," it sounds Evangelical, and could only be regarded otherwise by careful scrutiny of what it does not say.

That underlines my comments about the complexity of the task, and about the difficulty of locating quite indirect indications of theological change in matters of Christology and Trinitarian orthodoxy. A suggestion that I might write about theological change by tracing emerging shifts in the understanding of the person of Christ was made to me by the theologian Ninian Smart, but not followed up, perhaps because he doubted its viability. After prolonged inspection I am inclined to agree. Whether the hymns are medieval or Lutheran or Reformed or by classic writers like Wesley, Cowper, and Watts or by later authors, there is a shared christological orthodoxy. Among academics and theologians there were major debates from the seventeenth century on, but they did not seep through to hymns, just as other academic and theological concerns did not and do not seep through to congregations. This is no conspiracy to keep congregations ignorant of such debates. It is merely that, supposing local priests actually know them, they are hardly material for a devotional and exegetical address, and presuppose sophisticated prior acquaintance with academic discourse. A sermon is not a lecture.

There is another point worth considering here, and it is that if you look at hymns specifically under the heads of worship, praise, and creation they rarely raise questions of Christology, although there are sometimes references to the Trinity rounding off a hymn in a concluding verse. You simply encounter a vocabulary drawn from those generic titles of God in the Hebrew Scriptures, like King, Lord, and Father that have ruffled feminists. Isaac Watts, the father of hymnody, wrote such hymns, as did William Cowper (for example, "God moves in a mysterious way"), and these are often drawn from the psalms without Christocentric framing. A specifically Jewish doxological hymn like "The God of Abraham praise" appears quite naturally in a Christian hymn book as intrinsic to revelation. This reinforces the observation that Christianity depends profoundly on Jewish vocabulary and modes of address.

The one point where you might expect a pressure point in Christology to emerge would be through a fresh concern with the whole ministry of Jesus rather than the stark shift of orthodoxy from Christ's birth to his redemptive death. Examples of this exist, of course, but they turn around a small group of incidents selected for a homiletic purpose, like Jesus' remaining calm in the storm ("With Christ in the vessel I smile at the storm"), or calling disciples to be "laborers" in the harvest of souls, or (as in the hymn "When mothers of Salem their children brought to Jesus") upbraiding the "stern disciples" for turning children away when "of such is the kingdom of heaven." That particular saying seems strongly to support the understanding of the kingdom as burgeoning within rather than arriving from without by God's sovereign power.

Of course, as already indicated, most hymns in hymn books and regularly sung in churches are based on an orthodox Christology, especially so given that the vast majority are drawn from a treasury of many centuries. Congregations take this for granted. At the same time, hymns about the creation can celebrate a straightforward monotheism, and there is a visible strain of hymns that are life-affirming in the context of an evocation of the joys of the created world. "Glad that I live am I" is an obvious fairly recent example but older hymns like "For the beauty of the earth" or Mrs. Alexander's "All things bright and beautiful" or St. Francis's "All creatures of our God and King" convey the same affirmative sentiment about the wonders of Nature, eliding its unattractive and predatory aspects. That is how these hymns work, even though their authors may be completely orthodox.

What then of the disappearance of death and of hell? The disappearance of death from hymn books is due to the fact that its age-old omnipresence has disappeared from human consciousness for the first time in history. The disappearance of hell over roughly the same time period might seem unproblematic, given the dominance of moral objections to the idea of a God who inflicts eternal punishment on his creatures. Christians accept an implicit universalism, for which there is in any case some warrant in numerous Christian traditions, including ancient ones. Hell is no more than a form of stubborn alienation from God, and heaven is the expected destination of the soul for the vast majority. I am not sure how this might be compatible with a Christianity looking for "the resurrection of the dead and the life of the world to come," such as John Donne would have taken for granted. Among ordinary Christians, we are presumably dealing with a sentimental belief in immortality going back to Plato. Arguably, the effect is to make questions of sin and salvation less urgent. Of course, Christians still sing of heaven as the place of God's abode and the place of eternal joy, for example in Bernard of Cluny's "Jerusalem the golden" or Abelard's "How mighty are thy Sabbaths."

The contemporary handling of funerals is another area where hymns have been eclipsed, partly because there is an increase in non-religious funerals and also because of the influence of popular celebrities. Frank Sinatra's "I did it my way" plays the role of a secular anthem, and to some extent displaces such standard choices as "Abide with me," "The day thou gavest Lord, is ended" (with its imagery of darkness giving way to light), and "The Lord is my shepherd." In religious as in non-religious funerals, there is a shift to the commemoration of a life, so that a funeral that fails to recall the personality of the deceased is experienced as trangressive. A religious funeral is more likely to include a hymn, but the time constraints of crematoria and the displacement of singing by recordings still make hymns less likely. A recording of religious music is an acceptable alternative, (say) Mendelssohn's "Lift thine eyes, O lift thine eyes unto the mountains, whence cometh thy help."

When it comes to eschatology the New Testament, liturgy, and hymns bear impressive witness to Christian expectation along the lines of the book of Revelation: "Even so, come, Lord Jesus." But the doctrine is not expounded at all in its literal form, apart from what would be fringe churches in the English context. Eschatology is expounded only by way of the text "The kingdom of God is within you." Some fine hymns express it very clearly, such as "Rejoice the Lord is king," or "Thy kingdom come, O God" with its poignant cry "when comes the promised time when war shall be no more . . . ?" Milton's "The Lord will come and not be slow," written in 1648, is magnificent in its diction, and provides a paraphrase of Psalms 85 and 86. The anticipation of God coming to our land is part of the hope of the Puritans for a new England in every sense of the word, but today it is sung simply as a meditation on the petition in the Lord's Prayer "Thy kingdom come, thy will be done / On earth as it is in heaven." The political context has disappeared, and the eschatology has become an anticipation of a better world shared with many secular people likewise seeking betterment.

There is a final area of change in hymnody affected by political considerations. The problem of nationalistic hymns has already been touched upon, but there are also hymns that use military imagery, and missionary hymns whose tone about "heathen lands afar" is unacceptable. When it comes to military imagery, its use is metaphorical, as in the Pauline phrase "the helmet of salvation," but there are some Christians who feel uneasy about military metaphors. Typical hymns in this category are "Stand up, stand up for Jesus," "Soldiers of Christ arise," and "Fight the good fight." At the same time, apparent military language may belong to a very different setting. Wesley's magnificent "Captain of Israel's host and guide of all who seek the land above" is a typical Christian resetting of the Israelites' march to the conquest of the Promised Land as a metaphor of the progress of the soul to salvation through Christ. The archetypical missionary hymn, now obsolete, is Bishop Heber's early nineteenth century hymn "From Greenland's icy mountains," with phrases like "the heathen in his blindness bows down to wood and stone." The sentiment may be justified by Scripture, but not by contemporary opinion. The best kind of missionary hymn comes back from the mission field itself, for example the translation from the Urdu, "Jesus the Lord said 'I am the Bread, the Bread of Life for mankind am I.'"

The aim of this argument has been to use music as a synecdoche of the state of religion in England (and Wales), over time and particularly with regard to the condition of Methodism as the largest Noncomformist church, and with regard to Unitarianism as a faith tradition where theological positions have to be made explicit. I have tried to trace such evidence as there may be in hymnody, both in words and music, for shifts in Christology, eschatology, and ideas of a future state, as well as conceptions of the value of living, the self, and Nature. Finally I have suggested reasons for the popular eclipse of the hymn and why these have not led to the eclipse of the carol.

Bibliography

Anderson, Hephzibah. "Christmas Carol." *The Guardian*. https://www.theguardian.com/books/2005/dec/04/poetry.features.
Armitage, Simon, trans. *Pearl*. London: Faber, 2016.
Arnold, Matthew. *Matthew Arnold: A Selection of His Poems*. Edited by Kenneth Allott. Harmondsworth: Penguin, 1954.
Auden, W. H. *Collected Poems*. Edited by Edward Mendelson. London: Faber, 1976.
———. *The Dyer's Hand and Other Essays*. New York: Random House, 1962.
———. *Forewords and Afterwords*. London: Faber, 1973.
Beckwith, Sarah. *Christ's Body: Identity, Culture and Society in Late Medieval Writings*. London: Routledge, 1993.
———. *Shakespeare and the Grammar of Forgiveness*. Ithaca: Cornell University Press, 2011.
Betjeman, John. *Collected Poems*. London: John Murray, 2006.
Blair, Kirstie. *Form and Faith in Victorian Poetry*. Oxford: Oxford University Press, 2012.
Blake, William. *Poems and Prophecies*. Edited by Max Plowman. London: Dent, 1945.
Bosworth, Clifford E. "James Elroy Flecker: Poet, Diplomat, Orientalist." *Bulletin of the John Rylands University Library, Manchester* 69 (1987) 359–378.
Brigden, Susan. *Thomas Wyatt: The Heart's Forest*. London: Faber, 2012.
Brooks, Cleanth. *The Hidden God: Studies in Hemingway, Faulkner, Yeats, Eliot, and Warren*. New Haven: Yale University Press, 1963.
———. *The Well Wrought Urn: Studies in the Structure of Poetry*. New York: Harcourt Brace, 1947.
Brown, George Mackay. *Magnus*. London: Hogarth, 1973.
———. *The Year of the Whale*. London: Hogarth, 1965.
Browning, Elizabeth Barrett. *The Poetical Works of Elizabeth Barrett Browning*. Edinburgh: W. P. Nimmo, Hay and Mitchell, [1895?].
Browning, Robert. *Poems of Robert Browning: Containing Dramatic Lyrics, Dramatic Romances, Men and Women, Dramas, Pauline, Paracelsus, Christmas Eve and Easter-Day, Sordello and Dramatic Personae*. London: Oxford University Press, 1910.
Bryan, Anne. "Smith and God." http://www.strange-attractor.co.uk/stevie-smith/smith-and-god.html.
Bunting, Basil. *Briggflatts*. Tarset: Bloodaxe, 2016.

Burrows, John. *A History of Histories: Epics, Chronicles, Romances and Inquiries from Herodotus and Thucydides to the Twentieth Century*. London: Allen Lane, 2007.

Butler, Marilyn. *Mapping Mythologies: Countercurrents in Eighteenth-Century British Poetry and Cultural History*. Cambridge: Cambridge University Press, 2015.

Cecil, David, ed. *The Oxford Book of Christian Verse*. Oxford: Oxford University Press, 1940.

Chadwick, Owen. *The Secularisation of the European Mind in the Nineteenth Century*. Cambridge: Cambridge University Press, 1976.

Chalker, John. *The English Georgic: A Study in the Development of a Form*. London: Routledge, 1969.

Chaucer, Geoffrey. *The Riverside Chaucer*. Edited by Larry D. Benson. New York: Houghton Mifflin, 1987.

Chua, Daniel. *Absolute Music and the Construction of Meaning*. Cambridge: Cambridge University Press, 1999.

Clemo, Jack. *Selected Poems*. Newcastle-upon-Tyne: Bloodaxe, 1988.

Clough, Arthur Hugh. *Poems of Arthur Hugh Clough*. London: Macmillan, 1862.

Cockshut, A. O. J. *The Unbelievers: English Agnostic Thought, 1840–1890*. London: Collins, 1964.

Cohen, Mordecai Z., and Adele Berlin, eds. *Interpreting Scripture in Judaism, Christianity and Islam: Overlapping Inquiries*. Cambridge: Cambridge University Press, 2016.

Coleridge, Samuel Taylor. *Poetical Works*. Oxford: Oxford University Press, 1992.

Corcoran, Neil, ed. *The Cambridge Companion to Twentieth-Century English Poetry*. Cambridge: Cambridge University Press, 2007.

Crawford, Robert. *Young Eliot: From St Louis to "The Waste Land."* London: Jonathan Cape, 2016.

Dahlhaus, Carl. *Between Romanticism and Modernism: Four Studies in the Music of the Later Nineteenth Century*. Berkeley: University of California Press, 1980.

Davie, Donald. *Collected Poems, 1950–1970*. Manchester: Carcanet, 1972.

———. *The Eighteenth-Century Hymn in England*. Cambridge: Cambridge University Press, 1993.

———, ed. *The New Oxford Book of Christian Verse*. Oxford: Oxford University Press, 1981.

———. *Poems and Melodramas*. Manchester: Carcanet, 1996.

———, ed. *The Psalms in English*. Harmondsworth: Penguin, 1996.

———. *To Scorch or Freeze: Poems about the Sacred*. Chicago: University of Chicago Press, 1988.

———. *The Shires*. London: Routledge, 1974.

———. *Under Briggflatts: A History of Poetry in Great Britain, 1960–1988*. Manchester: Carcanet, 1989.

———. *With the Grain: Essays on Thomas Hardy and Modern British Poetry*. Edited and with an introduction by Clive Wilmer. Manchester: Carcanet, 1998.

Dieleman, Karen. *Religious Imaginaries: The Liturgical and Poetic Practices of Elizabeth Barrett Browning, Christina Rossetti, and Adelaide Proctor*. Athens, GA: Ohio University Press, 2013.

Drury, John. *Music at Midnight: The Life and Poetry of George Herbert*. London: Allen Lane, 2013.

Duffy, Carol Ann. *Collected Poems*. London: Picador, 2016.

Duffy, Eamon. *Reformation Divided: Catholics, Protestants and the Conversion of England*. London: Bloomsbury, 2017.
———. *The Stripping of the Altars: Traditional Religion in England c. 1400–c. 1580*. New Haven: Yale University Press, 1992.
Eliot, T. S. *Collected Poems*. London: Faber, 1934.
———. *Collected Poems, 1909–1962*. London: Faber, 1963.
———. *Essays Ancient and Modern*. London: Faber, 1936.
———. *The Sacred Wood: Essays on Poetry and Criticism*. London: Methuen, 1920.
———. *The Use of Poetry and the Use of Criticism*. London: Faber, 1933.
Ford, Mark. *Thomas Hardy: Half a Londoner*. Cambridge, MA: Harvard University Press, 2016.
Gadamer, Hans-Georg. *Truth and Method*. New York: Sheed and Ward, 1975.
Gardner, Helen, ed. *The Faber Book of Religious Verse*. London: Faber, 1972.
Gardner, W. H. *Gerard Manley Hopins: A Study of Poetic Idiosyncrasy in Relation to Poetic Tradition*. 2 vols. Oxford: Oxford University Press, 1961.
Gerth, Hans H., and C. Wright Mills, eds. *From Max Weber: Essays in Sociology*. London: Routledge, 1948.
Graves, Robert. *Fairies and Fusiliers*. UK: Createspace, 2014.
———. *The White Goddess: A Historical Grammar of Poetic Myth*. London: Faber, 1948.
Gray, F. Elizabeth. *Christian and Lyric Tradition in Victorian Women's Poetry*. New York: Routledge, 2009.
Gregory, Brad. *Salvation at Stake: Christian Martyrdom in Early Modern Europe*. Cambridge, MA: Harvard University Press, 2001.
———. *The Unintended Reformation: How a Religious Revolution Secularized Society*. Cambridge, MA: Harvard University Press, 2012.
Gunn, Thom. *The Man with Night Sweats*. London: Faber, 2002.
Hardy, Thomas. *The Complete Poems of Thomas Hardy*. London: Macmillan, 1976.
———. *The Poetical Works of Thomas Hardy*. Vol. 2. London: Macmillan, 1931.
Harris, Daniel A. *Inspirations Unbidden: The "Terrible Sonnets" of Gerard Manley Hopkins*. Berkeley: University of California Press, 1982.
Harrison, Tony. *The Gaze of the Gorgon*. Newcastle: Bloodaxe, 1992.
Hatt, Cecilia A. *God and the Gawain-Poet*. Cambridge: Boydell and Brewer, 2016.
Hazard, Paul. *The Crisis of the European Mind: 1680–1715*. New York: Fordham University Press, 1990.
Heaney, Seamus, trans. *Beowulf*. London: Faber, 1999.
———. *New Selected Poems, 1966–1987*. London: Faber, 2002.
Herbert, George. *George Herbert: The Complete English Poems*. Edited by John Tobin. London: Penguin, 1991.
Hill, Geoffrey. *Collected Poems*. Harmondsworth: Penguin, 1985.
———. *For the Unfallen: Poems 1952–1958*. London: Andre Deutsch, 1959.
———. *Geoffrey Hill: Collected Critical Writings*. Edited by Kenneth Haynes. Oxford: Oxford University Press, 2008.
———. *Tenebrae*. London: Andre Deutsch, 1978.
Hilton, Boyd. *The Age of Atonement: The Influence of Evangelicalism on Economic and Social Thought, 1795–1865*. Oxford: Clarendon, 1988.
Hogan, Trevor. "Modernity as Revolution: Thomas Carlyle and the Absent Centre of British Social Theory." Unpublished PhD diss. La Trobe University, Bundoora, Victoria, Australia (1995). http://arrow.latrobe.edu.au:8080/vital/access/manager/Repository/latrobe:37668.

Hopkins, Gerard Manley. *Poems of Gerard Manley Hopkins*. 4th ed. Edited by W. H. Gardner and N. H. Mackenzie. London: Oxford University Press, 1967.

Housman, A. E. *A Shropshire Lad*. London: K. Paul, Trench, Treubner, 1896.

Howard, Thomas Albert, and Mark Noll, eds. *Protestantism after 500 Years*. Oxford: Oxford University Press, 2016.

Howarth, R. G., ed. *Minor Poets of the Seventeenth Century*. London: Dent, 1931.

Hughes, Ted. *Birthday Letters*. London: Faber, 1988.

———. *Crow: From the Life and Songs of the Crow*. London: Faber, 1970.

Hughes, Ted, and Peter Keene. *River*. London: Faber, 1983.

Hulme, T. E. *Speculations: Essays on Humanism and the Philosophy of Art*. Edited by Herbert Read. New York: Harcourt Brace, 1924.

Jacobs, Alan. "Auden and the Limits of Poetry." www.firstthings.com/article/2001/08/auden-and-the-limits-of-poetry-10.

Jarvis, Simon. *Night Office*. London: Enitharmon, 2014.

———. *Wordsworth's Philosophic Song*. Cambridge: Cambridge University Press, 2007.

Jennings, Elizabeth. *Every Changing Shape*. Manchester, Carcanet, 1996.

Jones, David. *The Anathemata*. London: Faber, 1990.

———. *In Parenthesis*. London: Faber, 1963.

Jones, Emrys, ed. *The New Oxford Book of Sixteenth-Century Verse*. Oxford: Oxford University Press, 1991.

Keats, John. *Selected Poems*. Edited by John Barnard. London: Penguin, 1963.

Kenny, Anthony. *Arthur Hugh Clough: A Poet's Life*. London: Bloomsbury, 2006.

Kipling, Rudyard. *The Works of Rudyard Kipling*. Ware: Wordsworth Editions, 1994.

Koestler, Arthur, et al. *The God that Failed*. Reprint of 1949 original. New York: Columbia University Press, 2001.

Kozuka, Takashi, and J. R. Mulryne, eds. *Shakespeare, Marlowe, Jonson: New Directions in Biography*. Farnham, UK: Ashgate, 2006.

Larkin, Philip. *Collected Poems*. Edited by Anthony Thwaite. London: Faber, 1988.

———, ed. *The Oxford Book of Twentieth-Century Verse*. Oxford: Oxford University Press, 1973.

Larsen, Timothy. *Crisis of Doubt: Honest Faith in Nineteenth-Century England*. Oxford: Oxford University Press, 2008.

Lash, Nicholas. *Theology on Dover Beach*. London: DLT, 1979.

Leighton, Angela. "God and A. E. Housman." Address at Trinity College Chapel. trinitycollegechapel.com/media/filestore/sermons/LeightonHousman181009.pdf.

Levertov, Denise. *The Stream and the Sapphire: Selected Poems on Religious Themes*. New York: New Directions, 1997.

Loewenstein, David, and Paul Stevens, eds. *Early Modern Nationalism and Milton's England*. Toronto: University of Toronto Press, 2008.

Louth, Charlie, and Patrick McGuiness, eds. *A C. H. Sisson Reader*. Manchester: Carcanet, 2014.

Lyons, Sarah. *Algernon Swinburne and Walter Pater: Victorian Aestheticism, Doubt and Secularisation*. London: Legenda, 2015.

MacIntyre, Alasdair. *Ethics in the Conflicts of Modernity: An Essay on Desire, Practical Reasoning, and Narrative*. Cambridge: Cambridge University Press, 2016.

Mackenzie, Victoria. "Review of Drysalter by Michael Symmons Roberts." *New Welsh Review* 102 (2013). www.newwelshreview.com/article.php?id=708.

Manning, Bernard L. *The Hymns of Wesley and Watts*. London: Epworth, 1942.

Martin, David, ed. *Anarchy and Culture: The Problem of the Contemporary University*. London: Routledge, 1969.

———. *Christian Language and its Mutations: Essays in Sociological Understanding*. Aldershot: Ashgate, 2002.

———, ed. *Crisis for Cranmer and King James*. Poetry Nation Review 13:6 (1979).

———. *Pacifism: A Sociological and Historical Study*. London: Routledge, 1965.

———. *Religion and Power: No Logos without Mythos*. Farnham, UK: Ashgate, 2014.

———. *The Religious and the Secular: Studies in Secularization*. London: Routledge, 1969.

———. *Ruin and Restoration: On Violence, Liturgy and Reconciliation*. London: Routledge, 2016.

———. *A Sociology of English Religion*. New York: Basic, 1967.

Martin, Jessica. *John Milton: How to Believe*. Guardian Shorts. Guardian, 2012.

———. *Walton's Lives: Conformist Commemorations and the Rise of Biography*. Oxford: Oxford University Press, 2001.

Martz, Louis. *The Poetry of Meditation: A Study of English Religious Literature of the Seventeenth Century*. New Haven: Yale University Press, 1954.

Masurel-Murray, Claire. "Conversions to Catholicism among Fin-de-Siècle Writers: A Spiritual and Cultural Genealogy." *Cahiers Victoriens et Édouardiens* 76 (2012) 105–25.

McLeod, Hugh. "La Religion et l'Essor du Sport en Grande Bretagne." *Revue d'Histoire du XIXe Siècle* 28 (2004) 133–48.

Miller, Joseph Hillis. *The Disappearance of God: Five Nineteenth-Century Writers*. Urbana, IL: University of Illinois Press, 1963.

Morris, Brian, ed. *Ritual Murder: Essays on Liturgical Reform*. Manchester: Carcanet, 1981.

Morris, David B. *The Religious Sublime: Christian Poetry and Critical Tradition in 18th-Century England*. Lexington: University of Kentucky Press, 1972.

Muldoon, Paul. *Selected Poems 1968–2014*. London: Faber, 2014.

Nicholson, D. H. S., and A. H. E. Lee, eds. *The Oxford Book of English Mystical Verse*. Oxford: Oxford University Press, 1917.

Nicholson, Norman. *Collected Poems*. London: Faber, 2009.

Niebuhr, Reinhold. *An Interpretation of Christian Ethics*. New York: Harper, 1935.

O'Donoghue, Bernard. "Language and the Transcendent in Modern Irish Poetry." www.theway.org.uk/Back/s081ODonoghue.pdf.

Owen, Wilfred. *The War Poems of Wilfred Owen*. Edited by Jon Stallworthy. London: Chatto and Windus, 1994.

Plath, Sylvia. *The Colossus*. London: Faber, 2008.

Pope, Alexander. *An Essay on Man*. Princeton: Princeton University Press, 2016.

Popper, Karl. *The Poverty of Historicism*. London: Routledge, 1957.

Prickett, Stephen. *Romanticism and Religion: The Tradition of Coleridge and Wordsworth in the Victorian Church*. Cambridge: Cambridge University Press, 1976.

———. *Words and the Word: Language, Poetics and Biblical Interpretation*. Cambridge: Cambridge University Press, 1976.

Punter, David, ed. *A New Companion to the Gothic*. Oxford: Wiley-Blackwell, 2012.

Quiller-Couch, Arthur, ed. *The Oxford Book of English Verse 1250–1900*. Oxford: Clarendon, 1919.

Rahim, Sameer. "Interview with Seamus Heaney." *Telegraph.* https://www.telegraph.co.uk/culture/books/5132022/Interview-with-Seamus-Heaney.html.

Rattenbury, John Ernest. *Wesley's Legacy to the World: Six Studies in the Permanent Values of the Evangelical Revival.* London: Camelot, 1928.

Rieff, Philip. *The Triumph of the Therapeutic: Uses of Faith after Freud.* New York: Harper & Row, 1965.

Riesman, David, et al. *The Lonely Crowd: A Study of the Changing American Character.* New Haven: Yale University Press, 1950.

Robinson, Marilynne. *Absence of Mind: The Dispelling of Inwardness from the Modern Myth of the Self.* New Haven: Yale University Press, 2010.

Rossetti, Christina. *The Complete Poems.* Harmondsworth: Penguin Books, 2001.

Sassoon, Siegfried. *The Complete Memoirs of George Sherston.* London: Reprint Society, 1937.

———. *Memoirs of a Fox-Hunting Man.* London: Faber and Gwyer, 1928.

———. *The War Poems of Siegfried Sassoon.* London: Faber, 1983.

Sawday, Jonathan. "A Kinder Isle? Sources for Andrew Marvell's 'Bermudas,'" *Times Literary Supplement* no. 5937 (Jan 2017).

Schama, Simon. *The Embarrassment of Riches: An Interpretation of Dutch Culture in the Golden Age.* New York: Knopf, 1987.

Schmidt, Michael, ed. *The Great Modern Poets: The Best Poetry of Our Times.* London: Quercus, 2006.

———, ed. *The Harvill Book of Twentieth-Century Poetry in English.* London: Harvill, 1999.

Seligman, Adam B., and Robert P. Weller. *How Things Count as the Same: Memory, Mimesis and Metaphor.* Oxford: Oxford University Press, 2018.

Seymour-Smith, Martin, ed. *The English Sermon: An Anthology.* Vol. 1, *1550–1650.* Manchester: Carcanet, 1976.

Sharpe, Eric J., and Arvind Sharma, eds. *The Sum of Our Choices: Essays in Honour of Eric J. Sharpe.* Atlanta: Scholars, 1996.

Shell, Alison. *Catholicism, Controversy and the English Literary Imagination, 1558–1660.* Cambridge: Cambridge University Press, 1999.

———. *Oral Culture and Catholicism in Early Modern England.* Cambridge: Cambridge University Press, 2007.

Shelley, Percy Bysshe. *The Selected Poetry and Prose of Percy Bysshe Shelley.* Ware: Wordsworth Editions, 1994.

Sisson, Charles H. *The Avoidance of Literature: Collected Essays.* Edited by Michael Schmidt. Manchester: Carcanet, 1978.

———. *Christopher Homm: A Novel.* Manchester: Carcanet, 1995.

———, ed. *The English Sermon: An Anthology.* Vol. 2, *1650–1750.* Manchester: Carcanet, 1976.

———. *In the Trojan Ditch: Collected Poems and Selected Translations.* Manchester: Carcanet, 1974.

Sitwell, Edith. *Collected Poems.* London: Duckworth Overlook, 2009.

Smith, Anthony, and Matthew Riley. *Nation and Classical Music: Handel to Copland.* Music in Society and Culture. Suffolk: Boydell and Brewer, 2016.

Smith, Christian. *Moral, Believing Animals: Human Personhood and Culture.* Oxford: Oxford University Press, 2003.

Smith, Mark A. *Secular Faith: How Culture Has Trumped Religion in American Politics.* Chicago: Chicago University Press, 2015.
Smith, Stevie. *All the Poems: Stevie Smith.* Edited by William May. New York: New Directions, 2016.
———. *Stevie Smith: Selected Poems.* Edited by James MacGibbon. Harmondsworth: Penguin, 1978.
Spaide, Christopher. "The Improbable Life and Prescient Poetry of Basil Bunting." *The New Yorker*, Aug. 2, 2016.
Spurr, Barry. *'Anglo-Catholic in Religion': T. S. Eliot and Christianity.* Cambridge: Lutterworth, 2010.
Stallworthy, Jon, ed. *The New Oxford Book of War Poetry.* Oxford; Oxford University Press, 2014.
Stannard, Julian. "Charles Tomlinson at Brook Cottage." *Poetry Review* 71 (1981), 71–78. www.slope.org/slope26/2/maa/tomlinson1.pdf.
Symmons Roberts, Michael. *Corpus.* London: Jonathan Cape, 2004.
———. *Drysalter.* London: Jonathan Cape, 2013.
Talmon, J. L. *Political Messianism: The Romantic Phase.* New York: Praeger, 1960.
Taylor, Charles. *A Secular Age.* Cambridge, MA: Harvard University Press, 2007.
———. *Sources of the Self: The Making of the Modern Identity.* Cambridge, MA: Harvard University Press, 1989.
Tennyson, Alfred Lord. *Poems, Including In Memoriam.* London: Macmillan, 1899.
Thomas, Dylan. *Twenty-Five Poems.* London: Dent, 1936.
Thomas, Edward. *The Annotated Collected Poems.* Edited by Edna Longley. Northumberland: Bloodaxe, 2008.
Thomas, R. S. *Collected Poems, 1945–1990.* London: Dent, 1993.
Thompson, Edward P. *The Making of the English Working Class.* London: Gollancz, 1963.
Uglow, Jenny. *In These Times: Living in Britain through Napoleon's Wars, 1793–1815.* London: Faber, 2014.
———. *The Pinecone. The Story of Sarah Losh—Forgotten Romantic Heroine—Antiquarian, Architect, and Visionary.* London: Faber, 2012.
Walcott, Derek. "The Art of Poetry No. 37." Interview conducted by Edward Hirsch. *The Paris Review* 101 (1986).
Walsham, Alexandra. *Providence in Early Modern England.* Oxford: Oxford University Press, 2001.
Weightman, John. *The Concept of the Avant-Garde: Explorations in Modernism.* London: Alcove, 1973.
Wilde, Oscar. *De Profundis.* London: Unicorn, 1905.
Willey, Basil. *Nineteenth-Century Studies: Coleridge to Matthew Arnold.* New York: Columbia University Press, 1949.
Williams, Merryn. *Thomas Hardy and Rural England.* London: Palgrave Macmillan, 1972.
Wilson, A. N. *God's Funeral: The Decline of Faith in Western Civilization.* London: John Murray, 1999.
Woodhead, Linda, ed. *Reinventing Christianity: Nineteenth-Century Contexts.* Aldershot: Ashgate, 2001.
Wordsworth, William. *The Collected Poems of William Wordsworth.* Ware: Wordsworth Editions, 1995.

———. *Selected Poems*. London: Penguin, 1996.
Yeats, W. B., *Collected Poems of W. B. Yeats*. London: Macmillan, 1973.
———, ed. *The Oxford Book of Modern Verse, 1892–1935*. Oxford: Oxford University Press, 1936.

Index

Absence of Mind (Robinson), 159
Absolute Music and the Construction of Meaning (Chua), 8–9
abstraction(s), 3, 44, 62, 110, 151, 178–79
"Abt Vogler" (Browning), 56–57, 162–63
"Action Française" movement, 138
Addison, Joseph, 35–37
"Adonais" (Shelley), 50
aesthetic(s)
    and biblical poetry, 46
    and hymnody, 167
    and Romanticism, 52
    and secularization, 110, 162
    and self-abnegation, 70
    in Swinburne, 74–75
affections, 57, 140, 169
Age of Reason. *See* eighteenth century
agnostic tourist poems, 74–75
"Akbar's Dream" (Tennyson), 67–68
Alexander, Cecil Frances, 86
Algernon Swinburne and Walter Pater: Victorian Aestheticism, Doubt and Secularisation (Lyons), 74
alienation, 69, 74–75, 77, 102, 111, 180
Allott, Kenneth, 71
American-influenced hymnody, 171–73
American poetry, and Tomlinson, 123
Amis, Kingsley, 129
The Anathemata (Jones), 98
"The Ancient Mariner" (Coleridge), 151–52

Andrewes, Lancelot, 31, 111
Anglican Church
    atmospherics, 15, 78, 122
    and Auden, 112–14
    and Catholic poets, 28–29
    high church tradition, 80
    and Housman, 80
    hymnody, 39, 167–72, 175–76
    and Pitter, 133
    rejection of, 50
    and Smart, 38–39
    and Smith, 134
    and Tennyson, 67
'Anglo-Catholic in Religion': T. S. Eliot and Christianity (Spurr), 111–12
Anglo-Saxon language, 21
animal poems, 104–5
"Anthem for Doomed Youth" (Owen), 153–54
anthropomorphism, and Swinburne, 76
anti-Catholic rhetoric, in Swinburne, 74–75
antinomianism, 5, 20, 164
anti-war radicalism, of Levertov, 143–44
architecture, in Williams, 55–56
Areopagitica (Milton), 26, 150
Arnold, Matthew, 12, 68–73, 74, 161
Ashby, Cliff, 101–2
"Ash Wednesday, 1984" (Duffy), 135
"Ash Wednesday" (Eliot), 9, 111–12
Askew, Ann, 26
Atalanta in Calydon (Swinburne), 74
"At a Solemn Musick" (Milton), 32–33

atheism, 75–76, 80–81, 135, 145
Athelstan, 21
atomic bomb, 99, 105
Auden, W. H., 9, 108–9, 112–17
Auden and Christianity (Kirsch), 114
"Auguries of Innocence" (Blake), 44
Aurora Leigh (Browning), 62–63

"Babylon" (Graves), 97
"Bagpipe Music" (MacNeice), 117
The Baptistry (Williams), 55–56
bardic tradition, in Hughes, 131
Barnes, William, 78
beauty, 51–52, 65, 74, 86–87, 105
Beckwith, Sarah, 28
"Before a Crucifix" (Swinburne), 74–75, 76
"Before Life and After" (Hardy), 78
belief
    and Christianity, 17
    in eighteenth century, 16
    in Empson, 54
    in Newman, 66
    religious attitude, 138
    and secularization, 2, 11, 148
    in Smith, 134–35
    and unbelief in Browning, 58–59
Belloc, Hilaire, 87
Beowulf (Chaucer), 22
"Bermudas" (Marvell), 34
Betjeman, John, 122–23
"A Better Resurrection" (Rossetti), 64
Bible
    aesthetics, 46, 95
    in Arnold, 69–71
    biblical criticism, 2, 7, 54, 56, 58, 60, 87, 148, 161–62
    biblical poetry, 45–46
    in Browning, 62
    collective and communal response in poetry, 157
    in Fenton, 106
    in Kipling, 85
    in Lawrence, 88
    as literature, 46, 110, 144
    Methodist hymnody, 169
    in Nicholson, 121
    non-biblical poetry, 29
    in Owen, 95
    and psalm-singing, 173
    in Roberts, 146
    and secularization, 28, 159
    in Smart, 39
    and sublimity, 38
    and Wordsworth, 118–19
Birthday Letters (Hughes), 132
"A Birthday" (Rossetti), 64
"Bishop Blougram's Apology" (Browning), 58–59
Blair, Kirstie, 55–56, 67–68
Blake, William, 20, 43–46, 150, 164
The Bludy Serk (Henryson), 25
"The Boar's Head in Hand Bear I" (poem), 23
Book of Common Prayer, 55–56, 137
Bowring, John, 179
Boyse, Samuel, 36
the Break, 3, 13, 18, 54, 57, 138, 148, 158, 160, 164
"Break of Day in the Trenches" (Rosenberg), 96
Bridges, Robert, 19, 53, 86–87, 170, 175–76
Briggflatts (Bunting), 100–101
"Bright Star" (Keats), 153–54
Broad Church Christianity, 66–68
Brooke, Rupert, 92, 150–51
Brooks, Cleanth, 39, 110, 124
Brown, George Mackay, 119
Browne, Thomas, 31
Browning, Elizabeth Barrett, 60–63
Browning, Robert, 56–59, 162–63
brutality, of knightly honor code, 1–2, 21–22
Bunting, Basil, 100–101
Burke, Edmund, 37–38
Butler, Marilyn, 42, 45, 47
Butterworth, George, 82
Byron, 50
"By the North Sea" (Swinburne), 75–76

A C. H. Sisson Reader (McGuiness and Louth), 138
Cambridge Platonists, 31
Campbell, Roy, 103–4

Index

Carew, Thomas, 30
"Cargoes" (Masefield), 86
Carlyle, Thomas, 77
carols, 22–24, 171–72, 175–77
"Carrion Comfort" (Hopkins), 65
cathedral tradition, 175
Catholicism
    in Auden, 112–14
    in Belloc, 87
    in Browning, 58
    in Chesterson, 87
    in Eliot, 111–12
    in Hopkins, 64–65
    imagery in Keats, 154
    imagery in Owen, 154
    marginality of Catholic poets, 28–29
    and priesthood in Jennings, 133
    recontextualization, 164–65
    seventeenth century, 26
    shift towards, 52–53
    sixteenth century, 25–26
    in Swinburne, 74–75
Catholicism, Controversy and the English Literary Imagination, 1558–1660 (Shell), 28–29
Caudwell, Christopher, 103
Causley, Charles, 121
Cecil, David, 20, 27, 30
Celtic melodies, 176–77
Chadwick, Owen, 12
chastity, 27, 33
Chaucer, Geoffrey, 25
Chesterton, G. K., 87–88
A Child of the War (Macbeth), 104
Children in Exile (Fenton), 106
"The Children's Song" (Kipling), 85
"The Choirmaster's Burial" (Hardy), 79
choral traditions, 166–73, 175–77
Christ
    and the Brownings, 62
    in Chaucer, 22
    Christology, 178–80
    in Hopkins, 66
    in Housman, 81
    and incarnation theology in Auden, 115
    in Milton, 32
    psalm-based hymnody, 173
    in Rossetti, 64
    in Smith, 134
    in Swinburne, 76
    in Wilde, 76–77
Christianity
    Auden's return to, 112–13
    Axial Revolution, 13
    and biblical poetry, 45–46
    the Break, 3, 13, 18, 54, 57, 138, 148, 158, 160, 164
    and Brown, 119
    and changes in English education, 173–74
    condition of in England, 177–78
    as distinct from religion, 3–4
    in eighteenth century, 17–18
    and essentialism, 11–12
    and exile narrative in Judaism, 5–6
    feminization of, 53
    identification with, 54
    and the liturgy, 54
    and lived experience, 44
    and Marxism, 92, 148–49
    muscular, 53
    and negative reciprocity, 4–5
    and pagan codes of honor, 1–2, 13, 21–22, 161
    and paganism, 13, 21–23
    Platonic element in, 19
    and politics of war, 91–92
    popular culture, 173
    represented in divine poems of John Donne, 31
    resilience of in modernity, 2
    and Sassoon, 94
    and secularization, 2, 18, 20
    and Yeats, 124–25
Christian poetry
    and agnostic tourist poems, 74–75
    and Coleridge, 49
    in the eighteenth century, 16
    and Macbeth, 104–5
    and Metaphysicals, 15–16
    and misapprehension in Houseman, 81
    vs. religious poetry, 19

Christianity *(continued)*
   in the seventeenth century, 15–16
   shift to Catholicism, 52–53
   in sixteenth century, 14–15, 25–28
   themes of in Masefield, 86
   and Wordsworth, 48–49
The Christian Year (Keble), 19, 55
"A Christmas Carol" (Coleridge), 49
"Christmas Day" (Browning), 60
"Christmas Eve" (Browning), 163
Christology, 178–80
Christopher Homm (Sisson), 139
Chua, Daniel, 6, 8–9, 162
"Church Going" (Larkin), 74, 130
Church of England, 51, 53
Clare, John, 47
Clemo, Jack, 119–20
"Cleon" (Browning), 60
"Clifton Chapel" (Newbolt), 84
Clough, Arthur, 73, 74–75
Coleridge, Samuel Taylor, 45–49, 150, 151
Collected Poems, 1950–1970 (Davie), 140
collective poetry, 52, 157
The Colossus (Plath), 132
Commonwealth, 32
"The Complaint: Night Thoughts on Life, Death and Immortality" (Young), 37
comprehension, 43
Comus (Milton), 33
conceptualization in poetry, 151
confessional poetry, 110, 123, 132
congregational hymns, 40, 175–76
conscientious objectors, 100–102, 126
consecutive rationality, 49–50
Corcoran, Neil, 80
"Counter-Attack" (Sassoon), 94
counterculture, 100–101
Coverdale, Miles, 26
Cowper, William, 41–42, 179
Crashaw, Richard, 28–29, 32
creole, 22–23
The Crisis of the European Mind: 1680–1715 (Hazard), 147, 163–64
criticism
   biblical, 2, 7, 54, 56, 58, 60, 87, 148, 161–62
   Eliot's, 108–10
   hymnody, 174
Crosby, Fanny, 172
"Crossing the Bar" (Tennyson), 68
Crow (Hughes), 131
crusaders, 1–2
culture/cultural
   and Betjeman, 122
   the Break, 158
   and Christianity, 2–3, 18
   counterculture, 100–101
   encounters, 90
   and English poetry, 19–20
   in Heaney, 125–26
   hymnody, 167
   modernity, 160
   musical, 172
   paganism, 22
   popular, 173
   presence, 167
   provincial, 124
   of sin, 97
   substitute for religion, 69–71
   in Thomas, 121–22
   and tradition in Eliot, 109–10
   village, 78–80, 92
cyclical time, 119, 124

Davie, Donald, 20, 26–27, 40, 47–48, 54, 100, 123, 140–41, 151, 155–56
Dawkins, Richard, 159
Day-Lewis, C., 115–17
Dearmer, Percy, 176–77
death, in hymns, 180–81
"A Death in the Desert" (Browning), 58
decadence, 52–53
"Defence of Poetry" (Shelley), 47
Deity: a Poem (Boyse), 36
demythologizing Christianity, 71
Dennis, John, 36
denominational colleges, 173–74
De Profundis (Wilde), 76–77
"Devotional Incitements" (Wordsworth), 49

"Didymus" (MacNeice), 117
Dieleman, Karen, 60–61, 164–65
disenchantment, in Arnold, 71
Dissent, 55–56, 60, 66–67, 137, 140–41
distributivism, 87
divine/divinity
    and Arnold, 72
    in Auden, 114–15
    and beauty, 52, 65, 86
    of Christ, 134
    direct experience of, 167
    and language, 37, 122
    natural religion, 46
    in the ordinary, 144–45
    poems of Donne, 31
    poetry as vehicle of, 37–38, 47
    providence, 35, 178
    in Rossetti, 64
    and secularization, 28
Donne, John, 30–31
doubt
    in Arnold, 68–71
    in Clough, 73
    and faith, 11–12
    and faith in Browning, 58–59
    and faith in Rossetti, 63–64
    and faith in Tennyson, 68
    in Housman, 80
    in Sassoon, 139
    and secularization, 12, 54–55, 78–79
    in Smith, 134
    in Swinburne, 74
"Dover Beach" (Arnold), 69, 72
"Drake's Drum" (Newbolt), 84
"The Dream of Gerontius" (Newman), 66, 165
"The Dream of the Rood" (Chaucer), 22
Dryden, John, 56–57
Drysalter (Roberts), 146
Duffy, Carol Ann, 135–36
Duffy, Eamon, 25
Dunbar, William, 25
The Dyer's Hand and Other Essays (Auden), 109
Dykes, John, 174–75

The Dynasts (Hardy), 77–78

Early Modern Nationalism and Milton's England (Lowenstein and Stevens), 150
"Easter Day, Naples—1849" (Clough), 74–75
"Easter Day—Naples 1849" (Clough), 73
"Easter Eve" (Browning), 60
"Easter Hymn" (Houseman), 81
"Ecclesiastical Sonnets" (Wordsworth), 56
ecology in poetic imagination, 120
"Edmonton, thy cemetery . . ." (Smith), 135
"Egocentric" (Smith), 134
eighteenth century
    Christianity, 17–18
    and Christian poetry, 16
    English poetry, 19, 151
    Methodist hymnody, 168, 173
    the Movement, 129, 131, 133, 140
    public reception of poetry, 154
    and religious poetry, 16–17, 34–42
    revolution, 162–64
    and secularization, 10–11, 158
Elgar, Edward, 165
Eliot, T. S., 9, 52, 54, 108–12, 163
elite perceptions, 17
Empson, William, 54
English education, 173–74
The English Hymnal (Dearmer and Williams), 176
English poetry
    abstraction *vs.* particularity, 151
    bardic tradition, 131
    Christ in, 76–77
    classical reference in, 35
    early Romantics, 43–50
    importance of, 18–19
    inclusion under, 20
    Latinate injection, 22
    and music, 96
    nationalism in, 149–51
    and the pagan, 22–23
    relation of music to religion, 56–57

English poetry *(continued)*
   and secularization, 1, 12, 158
   shift in Christianity, 25–26
epiclesis, 41
erotic poetry, 30–31. *See also* tears poetry
eschatology, 66, 125, 149, 162, 181–82
esoteric tradition, 131–32
An Essay on Man (Pope), 35
Essays Ancient and Modern (Eliot), 109
ethno-symbolism, 149
Evangelicalism, 16, 40–41, 55, 63, 86, 166, 168–69, 171
"The Everlasting Gospel" (Blake), 43–44
"The Everlasting Mercy" (Masefield), 86
"Every Changing Shape" (Jennings), 133
exile narrative, 5–6

The Faber Book of Religious Verse (Gardner), 19
Façade (Sitwell), 99
The Faerie Queene (Spenser), 27
faith
   in Arnold, 71–72
   and Auden, 112–14
   in Browning, 62
   Catholicism, 52–53
   and Christianity, 81
   comprehension, 43–44
   conceptualization in poetry, 151
   and doubt, 11–12, 58–59, 63–64, 68
   Evangelicalism, 171
   in Hopkins, 65
   inwardness, 60
   in Jennings, 133
   in Kipling, 85–86
   and literature, 109–10
   loss of, 87
   in Motion, 145
   Pauline doctrine, 169
   and place, 118–28
   and poetry, 155
   and reason, 36–37, 58

Reformation, 161
religious imagery, 153–54
and the revolutionary period, 55
in Rossetti, 63–64
and secularization, 11–12
in Smith, 134–35
and social concern, 60–61
in Tennyson, 67–68
and Tractarianism, 55–57
and unbelief in Browning, 58–59
vocabulary, 159–60
Farjeon, Eleanor, 176
Faulkner, William, 124
"Fears in Solitude" (Coleridge), 150
feminism, 164–65, 179
feminist theology, 97
feminization of Christianity, 53
Fenton, James, 104, 105–7
First Things (Jacobs), 113
First World War, 87, 91, 93–95, 116, 151, 154
Flecker, James Elroy, 88–89
folk poetry, 23–24
folk song tradition, 177
Ford, Mark, 78, 80
Forewords and Afterwords (Auden), 114
Form and Faith in Victorian Poetry and Religion (Blair), 55–56
"The Forsaken Merman" (Arnold), 69
"For the Time Being: a Christmas Oratorio" (Auden), 113
For the Unfallen (Hill), 142
Four Quartets (Eliot), 112
fragmentary spirituality, 49–50
funerals and hymns, 174, 181

"The Garden" (Marvell), 34
Gardner, Helen, 19
Gardner, W. H., 108
Gasgoyne, David, 132
gay movement, 101
"Genesis" (Hill), 142
Georgian poets, 92
German hymns, 41
"German Requiem" (Fenton), 106
"Gerontion" (Eliot), 163
Ghoostly psalmes (Coverdale), 26

"Goblin Market" (Rossetti), 64
"The God of Love" (Macbeth), 104–5
"God's Funeral" (Hardy), 78–79
"God the Eater" (Smith), 134
"Gold Coast Customs" (Sitwell), 99
Gothic, 38, 55–56
graphic representation in poetry, 40
Graves, Robert von Ranke, 94, 96–97
Great Awakening, 173
Gunn, Thom, 131
Gurney, Ivor, 96
"The Gyres" (Yeats), 125

haeccitas doctrine, 65
Handel, George Frideric, 169
Hardy, Thomas, 74, 77–80, 155, 163
Harris, Daniel A., 65–66
Harrison, Tony, 104, 105
The Harvill Book of Twentieth Century Poetry in English (Schmidt), 156–57
Hassan . . . on the golden journey to Samarkand (Flecker), 89
Hazard, Paul, 147, 163–64
Hazlitt, William, 47
Heaney, Seamus, 125–26
Hebrew poetry, 38, 45
Hebrew Scriptures, 4, 6, 28, 38, 47, 60, 71, 163, 179–80
hell doctrine, 178, 180–81
"Henry Purcell" (Hopkins), 64
Henryson, Robert, 25
Herbert, George, 29, 31–32, 144–45
Herbert, Mary, 26
The Hidden God: Studies in Hemingway, Faulkner, Yeats, Eliot, and Warren (Brooks), 124
high church Anglicanism, 80
Hill, Geoffrey, 9, 96, 141–43, 151
Hobbes, Thomas, 34
Hogan, Trevor, 77
"Home at Grasmere" (Wordsworth), 119
honor, pagan codes of, 1–2, 13, 21–22, 161
Hopkins, Gerard Manley, 64–66
"Horae Canonicae" (Auden), 9, 114
"Horation Ode" (Marvell), 34

Houseman, A. E., 80–82
Housman, Laurence, 100
Howarth, Peter, 80–81
Hughes, Ted, 131–32
Hulme, T. E., 99–100, 156
humanism
  in Blake, 44
  classical, 1
  humanist atheism, 80–81
  Renaissance, 13, 14–15, 17, 25
  in Wilde, 77
"Humanitad" (Wilde), 77
"Hymn before Action" (Kipling), 85
Hymns and Spiritual Songs (Watts), 41
hymns/hymnody, 166–82
  abstraction in, 178–79
  of Alexander, 86
  and choral traditions, 166–73, 175–77
  congregational, 40, 175–76
  of Cowper, 41–42
  death in, 180–81
  eschatology, 181
  Evangelical, 40–41, 86
  and funerals, 174, 181
  German, 41
  missionary, 181–82
  modern, 175–76
  nationalistic, 181–82
  plainsong, 172–73, 175, 176
  reformation of, 87, 170–71, 173, 175–76
  in Roberts, 146
  as sacred, 178
  in Smart, 39
  in Thomson, 37
  of Watts, 41
  of Wesley, 40–41
The Hymns of Wesley and Watts (Manning), 40–41
"Hymn to Proserpine" (Swinburne), 76

"If" (Kipling), 53
Illusion and Reality (Caudwell), 103
imagination
  and the aesthetic, 52
  and belief, 66

imagination *(continued)*
   and Christianity, 44
   and Coleridge, 46–48
   and ecology, 120–21
   and esoteric tradition in Hughes, 131
   and Graves, 97
   and hymnody, 39–40
   and the Reformation, 28–29
   social imaginary, 60
   and sublimity, 36–38
   and Wordsworth, 44, 46–48, 58
immanence, in Hopkins, 64–66
Immanent Will, 77–80
Immortality Ode, 48–49
"The Impercipient" (Hardy), 74, 79
incarnation, 32, 44, 49, 61, 111, 115, 125, 175, 177
influence of poetry, 154
In Memoriam (Tennyson), 67
"In Memoriam" (Tennyson), 67–68
In Parenthesis (Jones), 98, 153
"In Praise of the Present" (Roberts), 146
"Insensibility" (Owen), 95
"Inside of King's College Chapel" (Wordsworth), 49
Inspirations Unbidden: The "Terrible Sonnets" (Harris), 65–66
"In Tenebris II" (Hardy), 163
internet technology, 154
In the Trojan Ditch (Sisson), 139
inwardness, 29, 53–54, 60, 77, 144, 159, 160
Ireland, John, 86
Isherwood, Christopher, 115–16

Jacobs, Alan, 113
Jennens, Charles, 39
Jennings, Elizabeth, 133
Jerusalem (Blake), 45
"Jerusalem" (Blake), 150
"Jerusalem" (Fenton), 106–7
Jewish hymns, 179–80
Johnson, Bonnie Lander, 27
Johnson, Samuel, 30, 35–36, 40
Jones, David, 3, 54, 97–98, 153, 164
Jones, Emrys, 14
"The Journey of the Magi" (Eliot), 111
"Jubilate Agno" (Smart), 38–39
Judaism, 3–6

"Karshish" (Browning), 60
Kavanagh, Pat, 126
Keats, John, 49–50, 153–54
Keble, John, 19, 55
Kipling, Rudyard, 53, 84–86, 150, 170
Kirkup, James, 101
Kirsch, Arthur, 114
Kozuka, Takashi, 28

"The Lake Isle of Innisfree" (Yeats), 123–24
"L'Allegro and Il Penseroso" (Milton), 32–33
"Lament for the Great Music" (MacDiarmid), 102
language
   Anglo-Saxon, 21
   and Auden, 115
   divinity, 37, 122
   Latin, 22
   naming of places, 118–19
   and sublimity, 38
   and symbolism, 47
   and Thomas, 121–22
The Language and Literature of Chastity (Johnson), 27
"Language and the Transcendent in Modern Irish Poetry" (O'Donoghue), 130–31
Larkin, Philip, 74, 129–30
Lash, Nicholas, 69
"The Last Signal" (Hardy), 78
"The Latest Decalogue" (Clough), 73
Latin, 22
"Latter Day Psalms" (Ashby), 101–2
law paradox in Christianity, 59, 163
Lawrence, D. H., 88
Leavis, F. R., 69
Lee, A. H. E., 19
Leighton, Angela, 80
Letter Concerning Toleration (Locke), 34
A Letter Concerning Toleration (Locke), 26

Levertov, Denise, 143–44
Leviathan (Hobbes), 34
"Little Gidding" (Eliot), 151
liturgy
    the Break, 54, 158–59
    Catholicism, 25–26
    and Christ, 178
    in Jones, 98
    and modernity, 8–9
    and monasticism, 162
    and poetry, 152–53
    and Tractarians, 175
Lives (Walton), 31
Locke, John, 26, 34
Logue, Christopher, 101
The Lonely Crowd (Riesman), 160
Longfellow, 1–2
Louth, Charles, 138
love poetry, 30, 34, 63, 106
"The Love that Dares to Speak its Name" (Kirkup), 101
Lowenstein, David, 150
Löwith, Karl, 18
Lowth, Robert, 38, 45–46
Lutheran tradition, 168–69
Lycidas (Milton), 26
"Lycidas" (Milton), 33
Lydgate, John, 25
"The Lyke-Wake Dirge" (poem), 23
Lyons, Sara, 74–76
Lyrical Ballads (Wordsworth), 47–48
lyricism, in Swinburne, 74
lyric poetry, 145

macaronic poetry, 22–23
Macbeth, George, 104–5
MacDiarmid, Hugh, 102, 152
Mackenzie, Victoria, 146
MacMillan, James, 145
MacNiece, Louis, 115–17
Magnus (Brown), 119
male comradeship, in Houseman, 82
Manning, Bernard L., 40–41
The Man with Night Sweats (Gunn), 131
Mapping Mythologies: Countercurrents in Eighteenth Century Poetry and Cultural History (Butler), 42

Martin, Jessica, 33
Marvell, Andrew, 33–34
Marxism, 92, 102–4, 112, 114, 148–49, 163
Masefield, John, 53, 86
"Master Hugues of Saxe-Gotha" (Browning), 57
Masurel-Murray, Claire, 53
material world, 146, 151
Matthew Arnold: A Selection of his Poems (Allott), 71
Maurice, F. D., 178
McDiarmid, Hugh, 163
McGuiness, Patrick, 138
"Memoriam" (Thomas), 93
The Memory of War (Fenton), 106
Mendelson, Edward, 114
metanoia, 162
metaphor, 6, 64–65, 135, 152–53, 182
Metaphysicals, 15–16, 30
meter, Hulme on, 156–57
Methodism, 40–41, 46–47, 166–73, 175
Methodist Hymnbook of 1933, 168–71
metrical psalmody, 169, 172–73
Meynell, Alice, 52
Middle Ages, 23
Midlane, Albert, 171
military imagery, 32
Milton, John, 15–16, 26, 31–33, 36, 56–57, 150, 181
Mishra, Vijay, 38
missionary hymns, 181–82
modern hymnody, 175–76
modernism, 93, 94, 110, 138, 155
modernist poets. *See* Bunting, Basil; Eliot, T. S.; Sitwell, Edith
modernity
    and Christianity in Donne, 31
    and the Church of England, 53
    and culture in Arnold, 70–71
    and nationalism, 149
    and religion, 8
    and resilience of Christianity, 2
    and secularization, 158
    and tradition, 110, 160
    and violence in Hill, 142

monasticism, 2, 21, 162
Monk, 174–75
Moral, Believing Animals: Human Personhood and Culture (Smith), 160–61
moralities, of Lydgate, 25
morality
  ambiguity, 4
  in Arnold, 70–72
  in Blake, 43–44
  in Clough, 73
  and Davie, 141
  in Hardy, 77
  and law paradox, 163
  moral epistles, 35
  sociological approach, 160–61
  and virtue, 27
  in war, 92–94
Moral Satires (Cowper), 42
Morris, David B., 36–40
Motion, Andrew, 144–45
The Movement, 129, 131, 133, 140
Muldoon, Paul, 130–31
Mulryne, J. R., 28
muscular Christianity, 53
music
  in Bunting, 100–101
  in Gurney, 96
  in Hardy, 79–80
  and religion, 56–57
  and religious poetry, 56–57
  in Sitwell, 99
  turn to aesthetic, 52
  See also hymns/hymnody
"My Baptismal Birthday" (Coleridge), 49
mysticism, 19
mythology, 58–59, 105, 125, 127, 135, 150

naming, in Wordsworth, 118–19
nationalism, 36, 45, 139, 149–51, 159, 163
nationalistic hymns, 181–82
nature
  in Arnold, 72
  in Blake, 46
  in Hebrew Scripture, 38
  in Hopkins, 65
  in Hughes, 131
  in Levertov, 144
  in Smart, 38–39
  in Swinburne, 75–76
  in Thomas, 93
  in Thomson, 35–37
  in Wordsworth, 48, 56
Near East, 89
"The Necessity of Atheism" (Shelley), 50
negative reciprocity, 4–5
"The Negro's Complaint" (Cowper), 42
neoclassical poetry, 40
Neoplatonism, 19, 32, 53, 87, 159
Newbolt, Henry, 53, 84–85, 150
Newman, John Henry, 66, 165
New Oxford Book (Davie), 26–27
The New Oxford Book of Christian Verse, 20
New Statesman (magazine), 126–27
New Welsh Review (journal), 146
The New Yorker (magazine), 100
New York Review of Books (magazine), 114
Nicholson, D. H. S., 19
Nicholson, Norman, 120–21
Nietzsche, Friedrich, 88
nineteenth century, 10–12, 19, 49–50, 51–53, 66, 147–48, 158–59, 174–75
Nineteenth Century Studies: Coleridge to Arnold (Willey), 70–71
"Noel: Christmas 1913" (Bridges), 87
non-biblical poetry, 29
Nonconformity, 167–68
"Non nobis Domine" (Kipling), 85
nonsense poetry, of Fenton, 106
normative scriptures, 1–2, 4, 161–62
nostalgia, 73, 74–75, 78, 88, 92, 123
"Not Waving but Drowning" (Smith), 133–34
the novel, 19, 57, 110, 154
Noyes, Alfred, 99

objective poetry, in MacDiarmid, 102
occultism, and Yeats, 123–24

"Ode on the Morning of Christ's Nativity" (Milton), 32, 56–57
"Ode to Duty" (Wordsworth), 163
"Ode to Saint Cecilia" (Dryden), 56–57
O'Donoghue, Bernard, 130–31
"The Old Vicarage, Grantchester" (Brooke), 92
Olney Hymns (Cowper), 41
On Education (Milton), 15
"Ordinary God" (Davie), 141
orientalism, 84, 89–90
"Our Father" (Davie), 156
Owen, Wilfred, 94–95, 153–54
Oxford Book of Carols (Dearmer, Shaw, and Williams), 177
Oxford Book of Christian Verse (Davie), 40, 47–48
The Oxford Book of Mystical Verse (Nicholson and Lee), 19
Oxford Movement, 16, 55

pacifism, 91–92
  poets, 100–102
paganism
  and Christianity, 13, 21–23
  codes of honor, 1–2, 13, 21–22, 161
  and secularization, 159
Paine, Tom, 46
pantheism, 50, 178
Paradise Lost (Milton), 32–33
Patore, Coventry, 52
patriotism, 84–85, 151
Pauline Christianity, 66, 169–70
"Peace" (Vaughan), 32
Pearl (unknown), 24
penitential psalms, 26–27
Pentecostalism, 41, 168
"The Pentecost Castle" (Hill), 142–43
performance poetry, 154
pessimism, in Hardy, 78
"Piano" (Lawrence), 88
"Pied Beauty" (Hopkins), 65
piety, in Arnold, 70
pilgrimage, 112, 130
Pinckney, Darryl, 106
Pitter, Ruth, 133

place
  and pilgrimage, 112
  poets of, 92–96, 118–28, 140–41
  and sentiment, 151
plainsong, 172–73, 175, 176
Plath, Sylvia, 132
Platonic element in Christianity, 19
Plowman, Max, 44–45
PNR *(Poetry Nation Review),* 101–2, 137–38
Poems and Prophecies (Blake), 44–45
Poems from the Trenches (Rosenberg), 95
"Poems on the Naming of Places" (Wordsworth), 118
poetic
  and Arnold, 71
  as distinct from poetry, 154–55
  drama, 77–78, 89
  and ecology, 120
  rhetoric, 7, 106–7
  voices, 60
poetry
  availability of, 154
  and Christianity, 7
  as distinct from the poetic, 154–55
  erotic, 30–31
  folk, 23
  love, 30, 34, 63, 106
  macaronic, 22–23
  public reception, 154
  quality *vs.* quantity, 19
  and religion, 135–36
  tears poetry, 28–29
  See also Christian poetry; English poetry; religious poetry
Poetry Foundation, 34
Poetry Nation Review (PNR), 101–2, 137–38
poets of place, 92–96, 118–28, 140–41
politics
  of Clough, 73
  in hymnody, 181–82
  satire, 103
  and secularization, 2–5, 161
  and Sisson, 138–39
  the thirties, poets in, 116–17
  and war, 91–92

"The Pomegranates of Patmos" (Harrison), 105
Pope, Alexander, 35
Popper, Karl, 8
popular culture, 173
positivism, 53, 159
The Poverty of Historicism (Popper), 8
prayer, 32, 67, 113, 125, 135, 152
"Prayer" (Duffy), 135
"A Prayer for My Son" (Yeats), 125
"Prayer" (Herbert), 32, 145
preachers, 66
The Prelude (Wordsworth), 49, 151
presence, 64–65, 67–68, 167
Prickett, Stephen, 45–47, 71
priesthood, in Jennings, 133
printed media, 40, 154
privatization, 57
Proctor, Adelaide, 60–61
prophecy, 4–5, 44–45, 152
prose, 7, 31, 93–94, 150, 154–55
Protestantism, 25–27, 29, 53–54, 84–85, 87–88, 112–13
proto-modernity, 55
providence
   divine, 35, 178
   doctrine, 33
   secularized, 7–8, 163–65
provincial culture, 124
provincial party, 42
Psalm 54, 26
Psalm 130, 26
"Psalm Fragments (Schnittke String Trio)" (Levertov), 144
Psalm 51 ("*Miserere Mei*") (Wyatt), 27
psalms, 26–27, 41, 141, 146, 155, 169, 171–73, 175
psalm-singing tradition, 172–73
public reception of poetry, 154
Puck of Pook's Hill (Kipling), 85

Quarles, Francis, 30
"Queen Mab" (Shelley), 50
"Quia Amore Langueo," 23

radicalism
   of Blake, 43–45
   and Christianity, 8, 148
   of Clough, 73
   of Levertov, 143–44
Raine, Kathleen, 132
"Rain" (Thomas), 93
rationalism, 39
rationalism, in Yeats, 124
realism, 94, 138–39
realization of Godhead, 59–60
reason, 36–37, 58
"The Reason" (Smith), 134
"Recessional" (Kipling), 85–86
recontextualization, 164–65
Redgrove, Peter, 132
Reformation, 14–15, 26, 28–29, 31, 46, 50, 147, 160–61
reformed hymnody, 87, 170–71, 173, 175–76
religion
   culture as substitute for, 69–71
   as direct personal experience, 46
   education, 174
   and Graves, 97
   and hymnody, 166
   and Larkin, 129–30
   and literature, 109–10
   and modernity, 8
   and music, 56–57, 181
   musical cultures in, 172
   and nationalism, 149–51, 159
   natural, 46
   and pacifism, 91–92
   and poetry, 7, 135–36
   privatization of, 57
   religious attitude, 138
   and Romantic poets, 49–50
   and secularization, 10–12, 147–49, 158–59, 161
   sociological perspective, 3–4, 58–59
   and sublimity, 36–38
"Religion and Literature" (Eliot), 109
Religious Imaginaries: the Liturgical and Poetic Practices of Elizabeth Barrett Browning, Christina Rossetti and Adelaide Proctor (Dieleman), 60–61
"Religious Musings" (Coleridge), 151
religious poetry

and Arnold, 68–72
and Belloc, 87–88
and the Brownings, 56–62
vs. Christian poetry, 19
and Clough, 73
and Duffy, 135
in eighteenth century, 16–17, 34–40
and Hopkins, 64–65
and imagery, 153–54
and Lawrence, 88
and Levertov, 144
and Masefield, 86
Metaphysicals, 16
in nineteenth century, 49–50
and Reformation, 28
and religious utterance, 152
and Rossetti, 63–64
Schmidt on, 156–57
in seventeenth century, 30–32
and Tennyson, 67–68
and Thomas, 127
The Religious Sublime: Christian Poetry and Critical Tradition (Morris), 36–40
relocation of sacred, 15
"Resignation" (Arnold), 72–73
"Resolution and Independence" (Wordsworth), 47–48
revelation, 47, 65, 127
revivalist tradition, 167–68, 172
revolution, 6–9, 12–13, 49, 55, 162–64
"Reynard the Fox" (Masefield), 86
Rickword, Edgell, 102–3
Rieff, Philip, 12, 160
Riesman, David, 160
Ritson, Joseph, 47
Roberts, Michael Symmons, 145–46
Robinson, Marilynne, 159
Rolle, Richard, 23–24
Romanticism
and Christianity, 18
in England, 43–50
and hymnody, 171
and music, 52
nationalism, 163
and Nature, 76
and originality, 141

and religious poetry, 49–50
and secularization, 2
and Watkins, 128
Romanticism and Religion: The Tradition of Wordsworth and Coleridge in the Victorian Church (Prickett), 71
Romanticism and Religion (Prickett), 47
Rosenberg, Isaac, 95–96
Rossetti, Christina, 52, 60–61, 63–64, 65, 164
Rumsey, David, 168–70

sacred
in the everyday, 144
hymnody as, 178
music, 168–69
narrative, 152
poetry, 31, 40
process of secularization, 39
relocation of, 15
representation of, 49
theology of incarnation, 115
The Sacrifice (Roberts), 145
"Samson Agonistes" (Milton), 33
Sartor Resartus (Carlyle), 78
Sassoon, Siegfried, 93–95, 151
satire, 25, 103
"Saul" (Browning), 59–60
Sawday, Jonathan, 34
Scannell, Vernon, 98–99
Schmidt, Michael, 156–57
"The Scholar Gypsy" (Arnold), 69
science
in Arnold, 69–70, 72
in Carlyle, 77
and Catholicism, 53
in Fenton, 106–7
in Graves, 97
secularization narratives, 2
in Thomson, 35–36
in Yeats, 124–25
Scottish Renaissance, 102
Scottish tradition of satire, 25
Scruton, Roger, 104
"Sea Fever" (Masefield), 86
The Seasons (Thomson), 35–37, 150

"The Second Coming" (Yeats), 124
Second World War, 98–99, 117, 126, 151, 155
A Secular Age (Taylor), 12
The Secularisation of the European Mind in the Nineteenth Century (Chadwick), 12
secularization
   and Arnold, 69
   and Browning, 59
   and Christianity, 18
   and Davie, 20, 141
   and Dieleman, 60
   early Romantics, 43–50
   eighteenth century, 36, 39
   and Hardy, 78–79
   and Larkin, 130
   of literature, 39, 110
   and Lyons, 74–75
   narratives, 1–5
   overview, 10–13
   and pacifism, 91–92
   paganism, 21
   and Protestant patriotism, 85–86
   public sphere, 34
   secular Providence, 164–65
   sixteenth century verse, 14–17, 28–29
   teleological assertion, 158–63
   trajectory, 147–49
   Victorian period, 54–55
self, 64–65, 144, 160, 164
self-abnegation, 70
"The Send-Off" (Owen), 95
sentimentality, Morris on, 37–38
"The Seraphim" (Browning), 61–62
sermon on the incarnation (Andrewes), 111
sermons, 31, 39–40
"The Servant-Girl at Emmaus" (Levertov), 144
seventeenth century, 10, 15–16, 26, 30–32, 35, 36, 158–59, 175
"Severn and Somme" (Gurney), 96
"Shadow" (Lawrence), 88
"The Shadow of Cain" (Sitwell), 99
Shakespeare, William, 27–28, 56–57, 149–50

Shakespeare and the Grammar of Forgiveness (Beckwith), 28
Sharp, Cecil, 177
Shaw, Geoffrey, 176–77
Shaw, Martin, 176–77
Shell, Alison, 25, 28–29, 164
Shelley, Percy Bysshe, 47, 148, 154
The Shepheardes Calendar (Spenser), 27
The Shires (Davie), 141, 151
A Shoropshire Lad (Houseman), 82
"Shrapnel" (Harrison), 105
Sidney, Philip, 37
Sidney Psalms (Herbert and Sydney), 26
Siegfried Sassoon: The War Poems (Sassoon), 94
"Simple" (Motion), 145
Sisson, Charles, 101, 138–40, 151
Sitwell, Edith, 99–100
sixteenth century, 14–15, 25–28
Skelton, John, 25
Smart, Christopher, 36, 38–39, 49, 150
Smith, Christian, 160–61
Smith, Stevie, 133–35
social imaginary, 60
social science, in Browning, 62–63
sociology, 10–11, 57, 59–60, 62, 69, 130, 161
"The Soldier" (Brooke), 92
Songs of Experience (Blake), 45
Songs of Innocence (Blake), 45
Songs of Praise (Dearmer and Williams), 176
"A Song to David" (Smart), 38
"Sonnet 30" (Shakespeare), 27
"Sonnet 146" (Shakespeare), 27–28
Southwell, Robert, 14
"The Spacious Firmament on High" (Addison), 36
Spaide, Christopher, 100
Speke, Parrot (Skelton), 25
Spender, Stephen, 115–16
Spenser, Edmund, 27
spirituality, 19, 49–50, 66, 111
Spring-Rice, Cecil, 170
Spurr, Barry, 111–12

Index

"Stanzas from La Grande Chartreuse" (Arnold), 74
"Stanzas from the Grande Chartreuse" (Arnold), 72
Stevens, Paul, 150
"Still Falls the Rain" (Sitwell), 99
The Stream and the Sapphire (Levertov), 144
Studies in a Dying Culture (Caudwell), 103
sublimity, 36–38, 46
"A Summer Night" (Auden), 115
Summoned by Bells (Betjeman), 122
"Sunlight" (Heaney), 126
Swift, Jonathan, 36
Swinburne, Algernon, 73–76
Sydney, Philip, 26
symbolism, 47, 56, 71, 99, 124, 140, 149
Symond, John Addington, 170

"The Tables Turned" (Wordsworth), 44, 48
"The Task" (Cowper), 42
Taylor, Charles, 12, 165
tears poetry, 28–29
"Temenos Academy of Integral Studies," 132
The Temple (Herbert), 32, 145
Tenebrae (Hill), 9, 142–43
Tennyson, Alfred, 66–68
Terminal Moraine (Fenton), 106
"Terrible Sonnets" (Hopkins), 65–66
"Testament of Beauty" (Bridges), 86–87
"That Morning" (Hughes), 131
"The Age of Anxiety: A Baroque Eclogue" (Auden), 113
The Cambridge Companion to Twentieth Century Poetry (Corcoran), 80
"There is No God" (Clough), 73
"The Respectable Burgher: on 'The Higher Criticism'" (Hardy), 79
The School Hymn Book of the Methodist Church, 171

"The Sea and the Mirror: A Commentary on The Tempest" (Auden), 113
the thirties, 115–17, 125, 148, 163
"The Thirty-ninth Psalm, Adapted" (Davie), 141
Thomas, Dylan, 126–27, 153
Thomas, Edward, 93
Thomas, R. S., 121–22
Thomas Hardy: Half a Londoner (Ford), 80
Thomas Hardy and Rural England (Williams), 79–80
Thompson, E. P., 165
Thompson, Francis, 52
Thomson, James, 35–37, 150, 163–64
"The Three Doctrines of the 1933 Methodist Hymnbook" (Rumsey), 168–69
"Thyrsis" (Arnold), 69
time, 119, 124
The Times Literary Supplement (newspaper), 34
"A Toccata of Galuppi's" (Browning), 57
Tomlinson, Charles, 123
To Scorch or to Freeze: Poems about the Sacred (Davie), 141
totalitarianism, 124, 142, 151
Tractarianism, 55–57, 62, 63, 175
tradition, and Eliot, 109–10
"Tradition and the Individual Talent" (Eliot), 109
Traherne, Thomas, 30–31
Trinitarian orthodoxy, 178–79
Tristram of Lyonesse (Swinburne), 76
The Triumph of the Therapeutic (Rieff), 12, 160
twentieth century
    the Break, 3, 18, 54, 57, 138, 148, 158, 160, 164
    and Causley, 121
    horrors of, 115
    and Hughes, 131
    and hymnody, 167–68, 173
    muscular Christianity, 53
    and mysticism, 19
    poets, 83–90, 137–46

twentieth century *(continued)*
    and Schmidt, 156–57
    and war, 91
Twenty-five Poems (Thomas), 127

unbelief, 58–59
"Undenomination" (Betjeman), 122
Under Briggflatts: A History of Poetry in Great Britain, 1960–1988 (Davie), 54, 100
Unitarianism, 150, 178–79
universalism, 6, 180
"Up-Hill" (Rossetti), 64
"The Usk" (Sisson), 139

"Vacillation" (Yeats), 125
The Vanity of Human Wishes (Johnson), 35
Vaughan, Henry, 29, 32
"Vexilla Regis" (Jones), 98
"V" (Harrison), 105
Victorian period, 16, 54–76, 87–88, 125, 174–76
village culture, 78–80, 92
violence, 4–5, 6, 50, 91–92, 105–7, 142, 161–62
"Vitae Lampada" (Newbolt), 84
"Vitai Lampada" (Newbolt), 53

Waley, Arthur, 89–90
"Walking Wounded" (Scannell), 99
Walsham, Alexandra, 33
Walton, Izaak, 31
war
    in Causley, 121
    and Hardy, 83
    and nationalism in English poetry, 151
    in Newbolt, 84
    poets, 91–107
    and radicalism of Levertov, 143–44
    and violence in poetry, 105–7
Warner, Sylvia Townsend, 103
"The Waste Land" (Eliot), 111

"Water" (Larkin), 130
Watkins, Vernon, 127–28
Watts, Isaac, 41, 179
The Well Wrought Urn (Brooks), 110
Wesley, Charles, 40–41, 169–70, 172
Wesley, John, 41, 169–71
Wesleyan tradition, 167–68, 172
Westbrook, Deeanne, 118–19
"What a piece of work is Man" (Sisson), 139
The White Goddess (Graves), 97
Whittier, John Greenleaf, 86, 170
Wilde, Oscar, 76–77
Willey, Basil, 70–71
Williams, Isaac, 55–56
Williams, Merryn, 79–80
Williams, Ralph Vaughan, 170–71
Williams, Rowan, 126–27
Williams, Vaughan, 176–77
Wilmer, Clive, 155
Wilson, A. N., 78–79
Wimsatt, W. K., 39
"The Windhover" (Hopkins), 66
witchcraft, in Warner, 103
With the Grain: Essays on Thomas Hardy and Modern English Poetry (Wilmer), 155
Wordsworth, William, 43–49, 56–57, 118–19, 150, 151, 163
"Wordsworth and the Sacralization of Place" (Westbrook), 118–19
working class, in Harrison, 105
"The World" (Rossetti), 64
"The Wreck of the Deutschland" (Hopkins), 65
"Wrestling Jacob" (Wesley), 40–41
Wright, Terence R., 88
Wyatt, Thomas, 14, 26–27

The Yattendon Hymnal (Bridges), 175–76
The Year of the Whale (Brown), 119
Yeats, William Butler, 123–25, 152
Young, Edward, 36–38

You may also be interested in:

Divinity in a Grain of Bread
By David Martin

A series of powerful and intelligent meditations
by Professor David Martin, spanning a wide variety of subjects,
with a foreword by Robert Runcie.

David Martin's *Divinity in a Grain of Bread* is a fresh and stimulating collection of meditations covering a wide range of topics. Part One contains meditations arranged for the Christian calendar, such as Advent and Christmas, while Part Two includes meditations on subjects such as Grace and Nature, and Harmony and Peace.

David Martin's powerful and intelligent prose will stimulate the reader into deeper thought. His mediations are of interest to clergy and lay people alike, of all denominations.

With a Foreword by Dr Robert Runcie, the former Archbishop of Canterbury.

DAVID MARTIN is an internationally known sociologist now Emeritus Professor at the London School of Economics and specialising in religion. He has taught extensively in the USA, and has been guest lecturer in many countries, including Israel, Turkey, Japan and Australia. He is honorary assistant at Guildford Cathedral and F.D. Maurice Lecturer and Visiting Professor at King's College London. He has also been Gore Lecturer at Westminster Abbey.

Print Paperback ISBN: 978 0 7188 2787 8
Published: October 1989

You may also be interested in:

Heaven in Ordinary:
Poetry and Religion in a Secular Age
By David Jasper

A personal journey through poetry and faith, exploring the themes of five English poets in relation to Christianity and the Anglican tradition in particular.

Poets, in times of great faith and times of doubt, have expressed for us their sense of both the presence and the absence of God in language that is sometimes almost sacramental in its weight of beauty, love, fear, anger or despair. The poets considered here all relate, in some way, to the traditions of Anglicanism through the centuries, reflecting both a common humanity and a wide breadth of human experience as it struggles with God. *Heaven in Ordinary* is deliberately autobiographical in approach, as it is grounded in David Jasper's own lifetime experience of reading poetry since his school years, and over four decades as a priest. The poets he so beautifully discusses have related both positively and negatively to the Christian faith and the Anglican tradition. Some are deeply religious, others are haunted by God and the divine mystery.

DAVID JASPER is both a priest, and Professor Emeritus at the University of Glasgow. He holds degrees from Cambridge, Oxford, Durham and Uppsala Universities and has taught for many years as Visiting Professor in Renmin University of China, Beijing. He is concerned with theology and the power of words, and with the poet as pastor and guide.

Paperback ISBN: 9780718895419
ePub ISBN: 9780718847760
Published: November 2018

You may also be interested in:

The Voluble Soul:
Thomas Traherne's Poetic Style and Thought
By Richard Willmott

'The world's fair beauty set my soul on fire.'

In this first study of the full range of Traherne's poetry Richard Willmott explains his 'metaphysical' poetry to all who are attracted by the beauty of his language, but puzzled by his meaning. He offers guidance both for the student of English, uncertain about Traherne's theological ideas, and the student of theology, put off by seventeenth-century poetic conventions and diction. Using a wealth of quotation, he examines Traherne's verse alongside that of a variety of his contemporaries, including Andrew Marvell, Lucy Hutchinson, Anne Bradstreet and Edward Taylor.

Central to Traherne's poetry and generous theology is his delight in the capacity of his soul to approach God through an appreciation of His infinite creation. This soul is 'voluble', not only because it can express its thoughts with fluency, but also because it can enfold within itself the infinity of God's creation, taking in everything that it perceives, considering the latest scientific speculations about the atom and astronomy, but also looking clear-sightedly at Restoration society's materialism and – in one startlingly savage satire – the corruption of the royal court.

RICHARD WILLMOTT is a retired headmaster of the Dixie Grammar School and Chairman of the Traherne Association. He read English at Cambridge, and took a further degree in Renaissance French drama at UEA. In retirement he has taught poetry classes for the WEA and helps as an education volunteer at Hereford Cathedral. His previous publications include student editions of Blake's *Songs of Innocence and of Experience* and of Ben Jonson's *Volpone and The Alchemist*, and an introduction to metaphysical poetry.

Hardback ISBN: 978 0 7188 9568 6
Paperback ISBN: 978 0 7188 9569 3
PDF ISBN: 978 0 7188 4829 3
ePub ISBN: 978 0 7188 4830 9
Published: June 2021